MORAL **GRAY ZONES**

MORAL **GRAY ZONES**

SIDE PRODUCTIONS, IDENTITY, AND
REGULATION IN AN AERONAUTIC PLANT

Michel Anteby

PRINCETON UNIVERSITY PRESS   PRINCETON AND OXFORD

Published by Princeton University Press, 41 William Street, Princeton, New Jersey 08540

In the United Kingdom: Princeton University Press, 3 Market Place, Woodstock, Oxfordshire OX20 1TW

Library of Congress Cataloging-in-Publication Data

Anteby, Michel, 1970–
Moral gray zones : side productions, identity, and regulation in an aeronautic plant / Michel Anteby.
    p.   cm.
Based on a field study of a French aeronautic plant, Pierreville (pseudonym), which manufactures airplane engines.
Includes Bibliographical references and index.
ISBN 978-0-691-13524-3 (hardcover : alk. paper)
1. Industrial relations—Moral and ethical aspects. 2. Organizational behavior—Moral and ethical aspects. 3. Homers (Manufactures). 4. Psychology, Industrial. 5. Group Identity. 6. Aircraft industry—France—Case studies. I. Title. II. Title: Moral gray zones. III. Title: Side productions, identity, and regulation in an aeronautic plant.
HD9712.A657 2008
174'.4—dc22   2007044056

British Library Cataloging-in-Publication Data is available

This book has been composed in Palatino Typeface

Printed on acid-free paper. ∞

press.princeton.edu

Printed in the United States of America

10   9   8   7   6   5   4   3   2   1

Contents _____

Figures and Table _____

Figures

Table

Preface

IT IS OFTEN EASIER to mark the end of a project than its beginning. I will therefore start with the end. Gray zones are areas in which workers and supervisors together engage in officially forbidden yet tolerated practices at work. This book discusses the drivers and outcomes of organizational gray zones, presents extensive research on the occurrence of one such gray zone in a French aeronautic plant, and deals with some fundamental questions of control, identity, and morality in organizations. I completed the field data collection for this book in 2005, when almost three years after my first encounter with the person I should call my "informant zero," I visited him to let him know I would soon return to the United States. Before we parted, he insisted on giving me a gift: I initially refused, but upon his insistence, I accepted. He handed me a key chain that represents a small jet engine fan blade. I immediately recognized it as an artifact manufactured in the aeronautic plant he worked in, most probably on company time and with company tools and materials. The way in which it was manufactured, as merely one in a large batch of key chains, and the way it was described as it was handed to me, as a reminder of my link to the plant, positioned me as a lower-level colleague in the plant's hierarchy. This, however, I understood only after completing the analysis for this book. At the time, the artifact more importantly represented, in my eyes, the concrete manifestation of an organizational gray zone.

During the time I spent working on this project, I accumulated many debts—one of the largest being to this informant. He initially helped me understand how the aeronautic plant operated and what the artifacts meant. As he taught me more about what he knew, I gathered more data on these artifacts, the social systems that supported them, and the gray organizational zones they revealed; I soon began to see patterns that he somehow did not. Most poignantly, for instance, when he retired, despite the fact that many of his colleagues received artifacts upon their departure (artifacts similar to, though oftentimes more elaborate, than the one he gave me), he received none. By then I knew that as an unskilled worker who had risen in the hierarchy, the probability of him receiving such an artifact was low. Still, I felt disappointed for him, because not receiving an artifact signaled his true position in the plant. Given that we are relatives, I also felt slightly embarrassed.

In conducting research for this book, I learned something our family never clearly articulated, namely, my informant zero's low social standing at the plant. When I quizzed him three years earlier about his knowledge of side productions in manufacturing settings, I never imagined such productions existed in his plant. I was betting on his knowledge of the industry, not any specific job-related knowledge. But when I asked about side productions, he started opening his kitchen drawers, pulling out knives and metal trays, cigarette lighters and wall ornaments—all of which, he told me, were manufactured in his plant. That day I knew I had found the field setting for my study of gray zones around the manufacture and exchange of these artifacts.

My first thanks go to all the plant members and retirees, especially my informant zero, who generously spent time sharing with me their lives, hopes, and fears with respect to their work in this aeronautic plant. They taught me more than I can ever thank them for. Without an early endorsement by the factory Labor Council, an elected employee body in France headed by the Confédération Française Démocratique du Travail (CFDT) labor union, I would never have begun this project in that plant. I owe an enormous debt to the late RM, who was one of the first retirees I met, and who encouraged me to pursue this topic. (Not wishing to compromise his and other plant members' and retirees' anonymity, I use only initials.) His kind words gave me the courage to start what was for me, at that time, a fairly exotic journey. On this journey JLP, MDS, and SC provided expert guidance at crucial moments; their insight frequently helped me connect the dots. And more than anybody else, I want to thank GS for making the plant such a welcoming place.

My second thanks go to those colleagues who inspired me and mentored me throughout the project. Amy Wrzesniewski took an early interest in the research and, through her constant support, guided me through its completion. I am also deeply grateful to Florence Weber for her insight into French factory life and to Erhard Friedberg, Joe Porac, Calvin Morrill, Bill Starbuck, and Irène Théry, who helped me advance in this journey. The idea for this project emerged in a sociology of culture seminar led by Priscilla Pankhurst Ferguson at Columbia University in the spring of 2001. As other seminar participants shared their interest in mostly high-brow cultural fields (such as art galleries, architecture, and dance), I felt an urge to examine less highly regarded fields, or what I thought of at that time as factory art. A year-long seminar led by Harrison White, also at Columbia, provided a stimulating forum for developing this project. I greatly appreciate the input of all its members. Finally, I cannot thank enough Viviana Zelizer, whose select interventions positioned her, in my eyes, as a critical yet encouraging guardian angel throughout this project. This book is also the result of discussions with numerous colleagues, many of whom offered new angles of approach. My colleagues in the organizational behavior area at the Harvard Business School, specifically Tom DeLong, Robin Ely, Linda Hill, Rakesh Khurana, Jay Lorsch, Nitin Nohria, Leslie Perlow, and Mike Tuschman, provided me with both the advice and the support I needed to complete this book. I would also like to acknowledge those who provided more "surgical" yet very helpful comments and references: Etienne and Marie de Banville, Steve Barley, Roger Dunbar, Mitch Duneier, Roberto Fernandez, Pierre François, Noëlle Gérôme, Yanina Golburt, Doug Guthrie, Jean-Pierre Hassoun, Robert Kosmann, Don Kulick, Daniel Mercadier, Frances Milliken, Virág Molnár, Christine Musselin, Gwenaële Rot, Bambi Schieffelin, John Van Maanen, Diane Vaughan, Loïc Wacquant, Katia Weidenfeld, Paul Willis, Martha Zuber, and Ezra Zuckerman. I am also grateful to Mikell Hyman, a colleague in all but name, who provided first-rate research assistance.

My third thanks go to the institutions that helped shape this book, supported the research for it, or provided me with opportunities to present parts of this project. At Princeton University Press, Tim Sullivan, Sara Lerner, and their colleagues provided expert guidance to see this book to completion. Karen Verde also skillfully copyedited the manuscript. The research was funded through the combination of a dissertation fellowship, a dean's fellowship, and the Donald and Valerie Ruth Honerkamp fellowship at New York University. In addition, the hospitality of the Centre de Sociologie des Organisations (CNRS and Institut d'Études Politiques de Paris) greatly facilitated this project. The Harvard Business School also provided generous support for the completion of this project, specifically in the form of Marissa Mathieson's and Leah Taylor's editorial assistance and Amie Evans's friendly daily help. Sections of this book benefited from the feedback from participants in the Academy of Management annual meeting, the American Sociological Association annual meeting, the Centre de Sociologie des Organisations research seminar, the École Normale Supérieure research seminar, the European Group for Organization Studies annual meeting, the May Meaning Meeting, the joint Massachusetts Institute of Technology–Harvard University economic sociology seminar, New York University's brown bag seminar, Princeton University's economic sociology workshop, and the University of California, Davis annual conference on qualitative research. Some of the material in chapter 2 first appeared in my article "Factory 'homers': Understanding a highly elusive, marginal, and illegal practice" (*Sociologie du Travail* 48, no. S1 (2006): e22–e38), and some passages from chapter 10 initially appeared in my article "Identity Incentives as an engaging Form of Control: Revisiting Leniencies in an Aeronautic Plant" (*Organization Science* 19, no. 2 (2008).

My greatest thanks, though, go to Patrick, who stood by my side during the joys and the trials of this project and whose craftsmanship is a constant source of inspiration. I am also most grateful to my parents, my sister, and other family members, specifically the younger ones, for bearing the brunt of my absorption in this project.

MORAL GRAY ZONES

Introduction

The Persistence of Organizational Gray Zones

In 1997, in a steel mill in northern France, an ashtray rested heavily on a desk, its luster dimmed by time. It seemed to blend quite easily into the plant's surroundings, and yet something about it caused it to stand out. Upon noticing my gaze, the person with whom I spoke took the ashtray in his hand and began to recount his life. An hour later, when he finished, he returned the ashtray to the desk.[1] This ashtray, which he made with his own hands, was my first encounter with "homers," or as they are called in French, *perruques*. Two close observers of factory life, Michel de Certeau, who as a Jesuit priest spent time in the industrial town of Villeurbanne (France), and Miklos Haraszti, a former milling machine operator in a tractor plant in Hungary, offer the following interpretations of these terms. *La perruque*, according to de Certeau, "is the worker's own work disguised as work for his employer. It differs from pilfering in that nothing of material value is stolen. It differs from absenteeism in that the worker is officially on the job. *La perruque* may be as simple a matter as a secretary writing a love letter on 'company time' or as complex as a cabinetmaker 'borrowing' a lathe to make a piece of furniture for his living room."[2] "A homer," Haraszti explains, "is an object made for his own purpose or pleasure by a worker using his factory's machines and materials. It is not an object made for sale as an additional income source. The word does not appear in most dictionaries, such as the Oxford or Webster's, but appears to be most widely used in England and America of a number of variants."[3]

The focus of this book, which centers on interactions around artifacts produced for personal use by plant employees, on company time, and with company materials or tools, might at first seem anecdotal. Artifacts such as these are found on coffee tables and in garages and attics, are easily mistaken for trinkets, and do not hold up very well to intergenerational transmissions. They seem merely part of an industrial folklore that will become slowly extinguished with the arrival of new generations. In context, however, artifacts are an inherent part of social systems and can offer fruitful insight into social meanings and processes, especially when, as will be shown, these artifacts are fairly prevalent in those systems.[4] In that regard, delicate glass flowers and sturdy steel ashtrays (two fairly typical homers) are perhaps not merely anecdotal. Both Haraszti and de Certeau caution us against dismissing these artifacts too quickly: "Connoisseurs of folklore may look on homers as a native, decorative art," remarks Haraszti. "As yet, they are not able to see further than that."[5] De Certeau makes a similar point when he observes that institutional custodians of knowledge oftentimes extract the products [homers] in order to "set off a display of technical gadgets and thus arrange them, inert, on the margins of a system that remains itself intact."[6]

This book goes beyond a study of homers as folklore.[7] It explores, in the context of a particular plant, the gray zone in organizations that surrounds the manufacture and exchange of homers. Primo Levi, in the context of the Nazi concentration camps, referred to a gray zone as a "zone poorly defined, where the two camps of masters and servants both diverge and converge"—a zone, he added, that "possesses an incredibly complicated internal structure and contains within itself enough to confuse our need to judge."[8] In the less contentious context of work settings, gray zones are areas in which workers and their supervisors together engage in practices that are officially forbidden, yet tolerated by the organization. Examples of gray zones outside factory environments might include a manager in a financial firm authorizing an employee to trade at work on the side; a supervisor allowing a mail carrier to "hide" (meaning to return home or engage in non-work-related activities) once the mail has been delivered but before the end of the official workday; or a supervisor letting industrial bakery truck drivers take unaccounted loaves of bread to sell to their customers for added income. In this last example, the collusion between supervisors and workers is clear; management makes sure that there is enough extra bread available every day on the stock racks where drivers supposedly only take "their" bread. In all these cases, though, official rules are broken, and management, aware of these breaches, tolerates them.[9]

Organizational gray zones are found in many work settings, and as such, warrant our attention. Most people can easily identify gray zones in organizations for which they work: small, repeated leniencies tolerated by their bosses; informal, collective arrangements that violate company rules; or multiple infractions of official rules overtly endorsed by management.[10] How these gray zones emerge and are sustained constitute key questions that this book addresses. The persistence of gray zones in organizations is puzzling. Outsiders would be quick to point to them as occurrences of theft; the truck drivers and their supervisor in the industrial bakery just mentioned above would easily be labeled thieves. Yet management with knowledge of these practices seems oddly unconcerned. The reasons for such apparent leniency confuse "our need to judge." Consider, for instance, the practice mail carriers have developed to "hide." When a carrier with more than fifteen years of seniority (who was most likely hiding the entire time with the consent of his supervisors) was convicted of a minor offense (stealing lunchmeat) while hiding, he was immediately discharged for "improper conduct" because he hid.[11] The surprise lies as much in the harshness of the sentence as in the length of time such hiding was most likely tolerated. Setting aside for a second the offense itself, what did the mail carrier have in mind when he was hiding? Or, to draw another parallel, what do factory members believe they are engaging in when they make homers? Moreover, why does management tolerate these behaviors? How can the collusion be explained?

Answers to these questions mainly revolve around a close examination of the identity dynamics that occur in gray zones. Gray zones constitute ideal settings in which to explore the ways participants see themselves, since participants, rather than organizations, are mainly the ones defining the rules of gray zones. At the onset, few guidelines are given once participants decide to navigate gray zones; if anything, the participants in gray zone activities seem left to their own devices. Although the material and monetary rewards are obviously tempting, the choices made around such engagements also influence the self-images participants build for themselves. For instance, the industrial bakery truck driver who decides, with his supervisor's approval, to sell the "unaccounted for" loaves of bread, appears to do so after reflecting not only on the potential material gains, but also on the implications the decision might have on how he views himself and is viewed by others. The call one makes regarding whether or not to participate—and how to participate—in some ways is a window into one's enacted identity. Numerous identities might surface in gray zones. Some of these identities are individual (the driver Jim's identities), others occupational (the bakery drivers' identity across organizations), and perhaps some even organizational (the Wellbreads bakery's identity, the pseudonym for this bakery) or national (a British identity, since Wellbreads is located in the United Kingdom). Each of these identities is of interest; however, the focus of this book is the occupational identities of gray zone participants since they specify and help explain many of the gray zone practices presented and analyzed here. More generally, other identities might explain other gray zones; but many gray zones are likely to contain similar identity pursuits.

A study of these identity dynamics in gray zones also uncovers other dynamics, namely the delicate balance between freedom and constraint in organizations. This balance fluctuates between individuals' aspirations to express themselves and find respect at work with the managerial imperative to achieve certain goals. As such, the study of gray zones also raises questions of control within a given work group, and more broadly in organizations. While the physicality of delivering bread to customers each day or adjusting a bolt to an engine in a factory might seem sufficiently constraining to direct behaviors, repeated gray zone practices guide behaviors in perhaps more subtle but equally efficient ways than any moving conveyer belt, task description, or official rule can achieve. Similar to research on street corner societies or games at work, this book provides evidence of the significance and the regulating qualities of complex, perhaps even seemingly objectionable, informal practices for given communities.[12] Unlike past research, it shows the identity mechanisms by which such practices—here, gray zone activities—gain relevance in the eyes of participants and why, as a result, the practices are here to stay.

Homer-Making at Pierreville

This book answers the question of the persistence of gray zones through a study of the making and exchange of homers in a French aeronautic plant, labeled Pierreville (a pseudonym).[13] It explores how the occupational identity of a subgroup of plant members (craftsmen) in the plant plays into the processes supporting the gray zone of homer-making, and how management relies on this interplay to exert its control over these craftsmen. The book is divided into three parts: part 1 describes the motivations and the setting for the field research supporting the book; part 2 presents the main findings from the analyses of the field data; and part 3 discusses the implications of these findings.

The relevance of social systems, specifically those involving gray zone practices, to the understanding of human behaviors provides the theoretical impetus for this book (chapter 1: "Revisiting Social Systems in Organizations"). This leads to the examination of the fairly common, albeit rarely documented, gray zone of homer-making, or the manufacture of artifacts for personal use on company time and with company materials or tools (chapter 2: "The Side Production of Homers in Factories"). Once familiar with homers, readers can enter the Pierreville aeronautic plant, the empirical setting for the study, where aside from homers, airplane engines generate most of the production (chapter 3: "The Pierreville Plant: Setting and Status Divides"). The plant provides the stage for an in-depth study of homer-making and, more broadly, the social regulations at work unearthed in the process. Given that data collection and analyses are closely intertwined, and before continuing the roadmap to the book's content, an explanation of the methodology employed helps to appreciate the book's findings and implications.

An Overview of the Methodology

The strategy adopted in this book, to begin by observing the small (in this case, these homers) in order to illuminate the large (the social regulations in the plant), is inspired by Walter Benjamin's technique of enlargement that "brings the rigid in motion . . . drawn as it is to everything that has slipped through the conventional conceptual net or to things which have been esteemed too trivial by the prevailing spirit for it to have left any traces other than those of hasty judgment."[14] This book seeks to uncover the social dynamics that govern activity in gray zones and beyond through an examination of apparently insignificant organizational artifacts at the Pierreville plant. A combination of interview, observation, survey, and archival data are mobilized in this examination. The interviews were conducted with retirees of the plant; the observations occurred mostly at the plant Labor Council, situated just outside the plant gates; the surveys were administered to a sample of retirees; and the analyzed archives include corporate and union documents relating to the plant.[15] An overview of these four data sources follows. (For more details, see appendix A, "Data and Methods.")

After discovering via my informant zero that homers were manufactured at Pierreville, I initially sought official company endorsement of the study. Unsurprisingly, the company refused to endorse it, the official reason being that "the priorities of the plant could not accommodate the request." Though a bit disappointing, their refusal provided me with the freedom to pursue this study by other means. Having disclosed my intentions in good faith to management, I now felt I could approach any plant member without the fear of being reported. Specifically, I approached the retiree group of the plant's Labor Council since retirees are not as prone to corporate sanctions. I shared my interest in homers with them, and asked if I could interview them and if they knew other retirees I could meet. This snowball sampling technique yielded a first set of thirty interviews and allowed for entry into the Pierreville community. Many retirees expressed interest in documenting the social history of the plant and saw select homers as unique craft pieces highlighting the plant's past, so they decided to endorse the project. Their endorsement provided me with access to the contact database of all plant retirees registered at the Labor Council.[16] Direct mail solicitation of a random sample of plant retirees yielded another forty interviews. A total of seventy interviews with retirees, spanning all hierarchical levels, who worked in the plant, mainly from the 1970s to the late 1990s, therefore constitute the first source of data.

Given the methodological biases of the study—positing that interactions sustain social identities—it is only fair to describe my own relationship to these retirees. (Appendix B, "Position in the Field," further clarifies the relationship.) I never worked in the plant before or during this research project, and I had only driven by it a few times before I embarked on the study. Thus, this study began as an outsider's perspective on a given social system. Many small actions made my initial disconnection salient: minor decisions, such as selecting the "wrong" drink from a menu when visiting retirees at their home or referring to workshops by name rather than number (the former favored by management and headquarters, the latter by lower-level plant members). At the same time, that a relative of mine worked at Pierreville and that the plant had a significant population of technicians and engineers (closer in training to mine) allowed me to find ways to connect with the retirees. Though I never became an insider, by the end of the project, when I walked by groups of retirees to whom I had grown attached, they often shouted out in my direction, smiles on their faces, "Here is the homer-maker!" suggesting that despite my social oddness at Pierreville, the Pierreville members made a place for me.

One could often find groups of retirees in the Labor Council building at Pierreville, dropping off insurance claims or attending a retiree's bridge or photography club meeting, and sometimes at the factory museum attached to the plant, where they reconditioned old engines later displayed in aeronautic museums. The observations I conducted there constitute a second important set of data. Once a week for nearly a year, either between formal interviews or simply to "catch up" with retirees, I spent time in these places.

I obtained a third data source from a survey I conducted on retirement homers, which I administered to a random sample of retirees. Restricting the focus of the survey to retirement homers was a condition of the Labor Council's endorsement of the survey. The survey tested potential variations along occupational lines in patterns of receiving retirement homers and solicited interviews. A total of 184 surveys were analyzed. Whereas receiving a retirement homer is different than participating in the manufacture of a homer or in interactions dealing with more generic homers, the survey provided an additional entry point into the community of homer-makers, since homer recipients are often homer-makers as well.

Finally, I also used the factory archives, which contain both corporate and union documents, to identify evolutions in occupational dynamics at Pierreville that might yield insight into homer activities.

These archives provided data on employment trends, detailed cases of homer events gone wrong, and, more broadly, allowed me to better comprehend the Pierreville community. They added to, and often completed for me, a picture of the social system in which the retirees worked. Through an analysis of the combined data, the findings presented here gradually emerged.

Outline of the Findings

Part 2 of the book presents the main empirical findings of the research and shows how actions that take place in gray zones might look like theft, but also encompass—from the perspective of the participants—moral pursuits.[17] It starts with the act of giving homers to colleagues upon their retirement or departure. Chapter 4 ("Retirement Homers: An Entry into the Community") offers an analysis of retirement homers, but also reveals the occupational dynamics at play in their reception. Survey data indicate that craftsmen—a highly technically trained group of plant members that includes blacksmiths, fitters, and welders—are central to the receiving patterns of such homers. As such, their unique position in the plant and their occupational identity are further analyzed throughout this book. Whereas each subgroup of craftsmen (for instance, fitters who fit and assemble parts made from metal) might be considered a distinct occupational group in its own right, craftsmen sufficiently identify with each other to form an occupational group of their own. However, in this exploration of retirement homers, other homers—homers distinct from retirement gifts—surface and ultimately expand the still mostly amorphous boundaries of the homer gray zone.

Chapter 5 ("Homers Gone Wrong: Delimiting the Gray Zone") specifies the boundaries of this gray zone by examining homer interactions that do not seem to fit agreed-upon internal expectations. It clarifies the boundary between homers and theft. Refusals to engage in homer work, denunciations of homer-makers, and suspicions of theft around homer activities provide the data to examine the distinctions plant members draw between homer-makers and thieves. By contrast, specific instances of homers gone wrong inform our understanding of tolerated homers. The criteria used at Pierreville to make this distinction involve an assessment of the degree of recycling and transformation of company material: the appropriation of new material, taken directly out of storage, pointed to theft. The transformation of scrap material, instead, suggested homers. Suspicions of profiteering also evoked theft rather than homer-making. But attenuating circumstances were also noted: in the event that skill development could be made evident, the suspicion of theft was less likely. Skill development was deemed a legitimate pursuit. Thus, the morality of homer-making begins to become salient in this chapter. At Pierreville, homer-makers or "builders" are not to be confused with thieves.

But even within the more accepted nontheft boundaries of the practice, clear distinctions between meanings (and implicitly, moralities) of homer activities were made. The analysis of homer events narrated in the interview data unveils these distinctions. In chapter 6 ("Shades of Homer Meanings: Occupational Variations"), beneath the facade of surface uniformity, we see the coexistence of multiple meanings of homer interactions: "respect and recognition," "collegiality," "regular work," and "exchanges." Participants understand homer interactions framed as collegiality as generic signs of belonging to the broader Pierreville community, but they do not acknowledge participants' specific professionalism or skills. By contrast, when targeted individual acknowledgment does occur, the homer interactions are framed as signs of respect and recognition. Other homer interactions, framed as regular work, are hardly distinguishable in meaning from the official tasks Pierreville members are charged with carrying out; the main difference is that the product (the homer) is generally received by a plant member—often a supervisor—not an external customer. A final consideration of homer interactions highlights yet another meaning: interactions framed as exchanges focus on material trades that often involve money or bartering of services. Distinguishing among the various meanings of interactions that lead to homers illuminates the complex nature of these gray zones and the multiple "currencies" in which members of the gray zones trade: both hard and soft, material and symbolic.

Homer interactions in which craftsmen produce an artifact for their own or another craftsman's use are associated most frequently with respect and recognition, which suggests occupational identity dynamics within gray zones. These meanings are not randomly distributed across homer activities; the occupational background of the participant, as well as the occupational background of the recipient, are shown to specify the meaning of these interactions. Whether a craftsman engages in homer interactions with another craftsman, a supervisor, or an office worker shifts the meaning. Analyses of various "missteps" reinforce this finding that occupational background partly conditions the meanings of these interactions. For instance, when a participant attempts to frame an interaction in a manner that deviates from the norm and in a way other than what is recommended by the occupational backgrounds of the participants, the interactions are strongly resisted. An example of such a misstep might involve an office worker asking a craftsman for a homer for his office boss, trying to frame it as an act of respect and recognition, even though the craftsman thinks of it as an exchange. (See chapter 6 for other examples of such missteps.)

Despite their already fairly high standing in the plant, craftsmen seem quite keen to gain additional respect and recognition. Such acknowledgment is particularly sought after when other, more official forms of respect and recognition evanesce. Craftsmen find their positions increasingly challenged at Pierreville. They are slowly being marginalized in the plant industrial process as computer-assisted design takes hold and new recruits are able to more efficiently achieve the same results on a computer as craftsmen once did in the workshop. As a declining occupational group, the craftsmen's need for recognition is increasing. Chapter 7 ("The Rise and Fall of Craftsmanship") presents an analysis of this occupational decline that reveals the increasingly shifting context in which gray zone homer-making occurs and might be of particular interest to readers attracted by history. Whereas attractive work options for craftsmen are dwindling, homer-making allows for the maintenance, and sometimes even the fashioning, of more desired self-images. These images take root in the occupational identity of craftsmen, who value skilled manual labor and autonomy in the accomplishment of their tasks.

The trades around homers, which create the ability to enact occupational identities, are, in part, what sustains this gray zone. These trades, the organizational control that emerges around homer-making, and the ensuing situated moralities (i.e., moralities that make sense and exist only within given social boundaries) are further examined in chapter 8 ("Trading in Identy Incentives"). Homer activities are shown to be a regulating mechanism that accommodates both craftsmen's desires to enact their occupational identity and management's desire for control. By allowing craftsmen to find respect and recognition in these gray zones, supervisors who tolerate homer-making engage in trades with their workers. Supervisors and managers who ignore homer-making in whole or in part are, de facto, allocating hidden identity incentives to those involved in the activities. What management gains from participating in these gray zones, in terms of added control, might be as large or even larger than what workers gain in terms of occupational identity. Thus, the morality of gray zones might have more to do with the fairness of the exchange than with the theft of company time and materials. From within the organization, the multiple moralities of homer practices are clear. The craftsmen's quest for respect and recognition, though perhaps self-centered, is viewed as a moral one. Management's tolerance of homer-making can reasonably be construed as a moral endeavor as well, inasmuch as it furthers organizational goals.[18] Gray zones might, therefore, be best understood as venues that accommodate both identity pursuits and quests for control.

Implications and Conclusions

Homer activity is a strategic venue in which the intersection of gray zones and identity enactments can be analyzed. Owing to its concreteness, it is not easily hidden, but many organizations harbor their own, often less visible gray zones. (And many gray zones exhibit similar dynamics to those found around homers.) Gray zones are defined as areas at work in which workers and their supervisors together engage in practices that are officially forbidden, yet tolerated by the organization.

The third and last part of the book draws broader lessons on gray zone activities from the study of homer-making at Pierreville. It starts, in chapter 9 ("Organizational Gray Zones as Identity Distillers"), by reviewing some gray zones other than those associated with homer-making—analyzing, for instance, gray zones in restaurants, hospitals, and on docks—and extends the argument beyond Pierreville. This chapter offers examples in which similar occupational identity struggles emerge. Also, because the complicity of coworkers and bystanders is required—even if this complicity means turning a blind eye—their attention is more focused in gray zones than in other work settings. Thus, gray zones emerge as potentially sought-after venues for identity enactment before peers and other coworkers. Moreover, frictions around the appropriate enactment of occupational identities among members of distinct occupational groups, and between members of a given occupation, play out in these examples of gray zones.[19] Given that identities result from moments of friction (either with proponents of alternate ways to enact these identities or members of distinct identity groups), gray zones prove quite appealing to their maintenance. Thus, gray zones might be more moral than initially thought to be the case. With respect to homer-making and other examples of gray zones, this text suggests restraint from too hastily judging such instances as mere theft. Rather, it conceptualizes gray zones as likely venues for organizational and identity dynamics to converge.

The goal of this book is not to acquit or convict gray-zone participants or enablers; rather, the hope is to explain how many gray zones sustain themselves, and why their disappearance is unlikely. The conclusion and last chapter of the book (chapter 10, "Identities, Control, and Moralities") details the main implications of this study on homer interactions at Pierreville, for both organizations and the individuals who work in these settings. The implications also provide some answers to the sustainability of gray zones in organizations. The three main implications encompass: (1) a novel understanding of gray zones as conducive to identity pursuits; (2) a complementary reading of gray zones as a form of identity incentives control; and (3) the use, outside official work, of morality as an occupational boundary.

The first implication of this study is to understand gray zones as conducive to identity pursuits. Though the collusion between management and workers in these gray zones has long been documented, the mechanisms by which gray zones operate have mostly been assumed. Previous literature addressing gray zones primarily focused on the relaxation of an organizational constraint, not on the pursuit of identities.[20] These accounts viewed gray zones as (at least initially) disabling organizational rules rather than enabling individual pursuits. At best, they were depicted as generating positive attitudes toward an employing organization.[21] The previously overlooked, potentially generative aspect of gray zones for participants—identity pursuits—is here made evident.

The second implication of this text is to extend the repertoire of available forms of organizational control by suggesting identity incentives as a potent, alternate form of control. The give and take between management and workers in these gray zones constitutes a form of control, allowing for the expression and fashioning of desired identities in exchange for sustained efforts on official work or compliance with other managerial requests. Gray zones illustrate a form of organizational control, labeled here "identity incentives control," that relies on the select positive arousal of identity feelings to induce actions or efforts. These findings help balance the idea that engagement in the labor process, including gray zones, unilaterally manufactures consent.[22] They show that through this process of engagement, workers also actively build identities—specifically occupational ones—that carry value in their eyes.

Third, and last, this study makes evident the ways in which workers rely on moral boundaries, outside of official work, to sustain their occupational identities. Whereas occupations are most often defined in terms of the tasks in which members engage, or by the formal requirements (such as education or credentials) necessary to belong in the occupation, moral boundaries also define occupations. The craftsmen at Pierreville were not craftsmen only because of what they did or how they were trained, but also because they knew when not to cross the line. At Pierreville, crossing the line meant producing homers that were deemed wrong. The direct appropriation of new company material with no actual transformation constituted a breach of morality from the craftsmen's perspective, but the deployment of skill to craft a unique artifact from scrap material was deemed legitimate; thus, the question of appropriate enactment is constant within gray zone practices. Gray zones provide key venues for testing these moral boundaries and, by extension, sustaining participants' occupational identities. Moral boundaries outside of official work, in that sense, also define occupations.

Overall, *Moral Gray Zones* suggests a reappraisal of which workplace practices might be considered moral or immoral. Despite their theftlike appearances, gray zone practices might be viewed as potential moral endeavors. This is not to say that all gray zone activities are legitimate pursuits; the broader costs and benefits of the practices need to be weighed. For instance, the practice of corporate accountants colluding with supervisors to "cook the books," despite company rules banning such behavior, would not find much sympathy from outside observers. In this last example, the potential fulfillment of participants' occupational identities pales in comparison to the social costs incurred by the larger, extra-organizational community. However, the ways in which occupational dynamics illuminate the moralities of this and other gray zones provide insight into how they may attract participants. Accountants might long for the kind of "respect" they could potentially gain when developing complex book-cooking schemes, as opposed to that gained through routine work. Understanding the occupational dynamics of gray zones might allow for a more balanced assessment of the moralities of gray zones, though this assessment in no way precludes condemnation.

Far from being, as Michel de Certeau feared, "inert [objects] on the margins of a system that remains itself intact," the artifacts resulting from the gray zone practice of homer-making provide insight into Pierreville's social system and regulations.[23] These artifacts highlight tensions and resolutions, hopes and constraints, choices and compromises. The reading of gray zones as identity pursuits, the focus on identity incentives as a form of control, and the moralities of occupations together show that the associations and disassociations among individuals are crucial elements of the workplace environment. Taken together, these findings help explain the sustainability of gray zone practices. Members of organizations exhibit multiple levels of agency and create structure, which carries important implications for themselves as individuals and for their organizations. Next to the family, the work setting is probably one of the main loci of contemporary Western society. The experiences of work might therefore also inform our grasp of broader social dynamics outside of work. The decisions individuals make and the costs they are willing to incur (in terms of partial surrender of control) to enact desired identities might translate into other realms of society.[24] I trust and hope that readers will find other insights in this book. If this occurs, I will, of course, turn a blind eye, and consider any unearthed, added wisdoms to be the readers' own homers.

Part One

THE MOTIVATIONS AND THE SETTING

1

Revisiting Social Systems in Organizations

UNDERSTANDING human behaviors requires paying close attention to their settings, specifically the social systems that both result from and inform these behaviors. Small groups capture many elements of social systems in organizations. Though other, broader settings, such as demographic and economic environments, add to the understanding of human behaviors, small groups, and the interactions they afford, provide a strong basis for an inquiry into these behaviors. George Homans defined the social system (or at least its manifestation) as "the activities, interactions, and sentiments of the group members, together with the mutual relations of these elements with one another during the time the group is active."[1] This definition emphasizes both interdependencies and sentiments. In doing so, it appends earlier definitions of social systems, which focused primarily on only one manifestation: members' interdependence.[2] Whereas earlier organizational scholarship emerged from in-depth observations of given organizations and the social systems they harbored, the majority of contemporary organizational research has mostly neglected that level of analysis, focusing instead on higher, meta-organizational levels of analysis.[3] But social systems remain crucial to the study of human behaviors and have long been a focus of sociological research. As Norbert Elias noted, "The question of knowing how and in which manner humans create links among each other and form together specific dynamic groups is one of the most important problems in sociology, if not the most important one."[4]

This view of organizations as social systems gained visibility with the research of William Dickson and Fritz Roethlisberger in their study of the Hawthorne plant belonging to the Western Electric Company.[5] Upon entering the Hawthorne plant, their initial idea was merely to study the effects of lighting on workers' productivity. Instead, they found themselves mapping out in great detail the entire social system they encountered.[6] Throughout their study, they documented interdependencies both inside and outside the plant, as well as members' sentiments about the interdependencies.[7] What they initially considered rather nebulous and subjective elements of social life suddenly gained legitimacy and visibility.

Unpacking Social Systems in Organizations

Organizations, understood as social systems, are the building blocks of modern society and condition important social, psychological, and economic outcomes.[8] An organization might harbor one or more social systems, depending on its size and complexity. But Peter Blau more broadly reminds us that the social relations that form these systems are pervasive: "To speak of social life is to speak of the association between people—their associating in work and in play, in love and in war, to trade or to worship, to help or to hinder. It is in the social relations men establish that their interests find expression and their desires become realized."[9] Thus, paying attention to the interdependencies among members within a given organizational setting, and understanding the experiences members derive from these engagements, is crucial.

The formal and informal interdependencies individuals take part in at work, as well as the sentiments attached to these interdependencies, combine to form the main manifestation of work social systems. Work social systems sometimes extend well beyond the work setting and spill over into family or community contexts. Formal interdependencies are those that are officially spelled out, most often in relation to the tasks being accomplished. For instance, before an automobile is shipped out from a manufacturing plant to a dealership, the dealer often formally requests the automobile; this is an example of a formal interdependency. (Many of these are increasingly computer-mediated.) These formal interdependencies traditionally have been an important locus of research on organizational control: whether one department or another has jurisdiction over specific tasks, how the budget is controlled, or the extent to which an individual needs to report to another constitute the fabric of these interdependencies. Many historical studies of organizations, including those conducted in the Hawthorne works, analyze shifts in formal interdependencies as a means of labor performance.[10] The creation of formal teams in manufacturing settings, for instance, illustrates this concern. Regardless of the successes or failures of such teams, their adoption or modification of any formal rule that applies to their functioning testifies to the belief in the efficacy of formal interdependencies in modifying the regulation (and possibly the performance) of organizations.[11]

Yet, informal interdependencies in these settings are perhaps as important as formal ones. Informal interdependencies are often less visible; nevertheless, they help sustain organizations. Ever since Melville Dalton noticed the importance of "informal organizations," these informal interdependencies have been shown to be important levers of managerial agency, sometimes even conditioning key outcomes (such as the rate of innovation).[12] Consider, for example, informal groups within organizations, unofficial interactions between maintenance and machine workers, or even snack-time gatherings (such as Donald Roy's classic account of "banana time," during which employees stop working to share food).[13] What might appear simply folkloric constitutes an integral part of these work social systems. Even informal encounters in the copy room are not as trivial as they appear; variations in settings of copy rooms are shown to condition ways in which employees come together.[14] The practice of "making-out," a collective game workers play to defeat boredom and get work done by turning attempts to fulfill daily quotas into games, best exemplifies these informal interdependencies.[15] Research on organizational culture helps elucidate the role these interdependencies play in sustaining the collective.[16] Informal interdependencies might cement a collective more strongly than formal ones.

Once we acknowledge the complexity of social systems, we must further attend not only to those interactions that are formal and informal, but also to those that are informal and clandestine. Social systems are not always easy to see. The adjective *clandestine* refers to that which is "secret, private, concealed . . . usually in a bad sense, implying craft or deception," and when applied to social interactions, depicts those that are not openly discussed.[17] The clandestine nature of social interactions only relates to the disclosure of these interactions, and mentions nothing of the legality of the interactions. Whereas clandestine interactions may result from illegal activities, such interactions are not limited to illegal activities; they may also emerge in organizations with apparently perfectly legal objectives.

Clandestine interactions within social systems were first documented in organizations with explicitly illegal purposes, such as gangs and organized crime. The classic work on Italian street-corner societies and the descriptions of the illegal activities that occurred on sidewalks constitutes one such example.[18] Other literature on the sociology of gangs or the Mafia also provides insight into members' surreptitious interactions.[19] Clandestine interactions are expected in illegal contexts; however, the following examples illustrate the presence of clandestine interactions within work environments with apparently legal objectives, as well.

A review of one study that addresses corporate interlocks at the level of board directors raises this issue. It touches upon the selective disclosure of social interactions.[20] The board members in this study say their power is "limited" and their interlocks with members of other boards are of "limited significance" for the organizations involved. The author comments that participants might be conveying norms and that audiences should, perhaps, not take their replies at face value. By merely questioning the subjects in this study, the researcher finds himself a member of a social system, even simply as a bystander. Corporate interlock interactions appear to be partly downplayed, if not concealed, by participants, perhaps because the meanings attributed to these interactions by the researcher or other outsiders (in the eyes of the directors) might carry potentially negative connotations. The limited significance the directors attribute to their interactions is a way in which they communicate about themselves to others. Another study of the social rituals coworkers sometimes share (such as weddings, parties, and sports competitions) makes a similar point about the selective disclosure of social interactions.[21] Unlike the previous setting, however, this study observes concealment among coworkers, as opposed to between members of a work community and outsiders. The rituals depicted bring together subsets of coworkers. What is noteworthy is that participants disclose the occurrence of these rituals to other coworkers, in proprietary ways, regardless of who physically participated. Picture colleagues playing soccer together on a company team. Participation in a soccer game might or might not be revealed to another coworker who is not part of the team. Selective disclosure within a given community (and not only vis-à-vis an external observer) is therefore also a possibility. Finally, a study of the configuration of three price-fixing conspiracies in the U.S. heavy electrical equipment industry offers yet another example of clandestine interactions in organizations with apparently legal objectives.[22] The authors rely on the transcribed court testimonies of prosecuted executives to describe a type of "white-collar crime."[23] They identify close to eighty individuals from thirteen companies who participated directly in the conspiracies. In secret, these individuals would conduct price-fixing meetings and engage in conversations about coordinating replies to calls for proposals. This last study suggests the existence of clandestine informal interactions within environments that appear to have legal objectives. Before the conspiracy was discovered and the parties were prosecuted, it occurred in a legal environment (the heavy electrical industry) for many years. The prevalence of similar clandestine interactions in other work settings with apparently legal objectives cannot be discounted.

These studies show that members of social systems may deliberately conceal certain social interactions from others. The clandestine quality of an informal interdependency can vary in degree from merely not being openly discussed (but acknowledged if uncovered) to being intentionally hidden (and denied if uncovered). Moreover, these studies demonstrate that clandestine informal interdependencies are not confined to gangs, organized crime, or settings that are fundamentally illegal, but also occur in regular work environments. For these reasons, an exclusive focus on openly disclosed interactions within social systems introduces a selection bias. The study of clandestine informal interdependencies among participants should not be neglected. When such interdependencies involve workers and their supervisors who together engage in practices officially forbidden yet tolerated by an organization, the resulting practice can best be described as a gray zone.

Whereas the early organizational research, with its focus on social systems, offered powerful lenses through which to analyze gray zone activities, contemporary research, focusing on more meta-organizational levels of analysis, has partly passed over such opportunities. For instance, the Hawthorne analysis, published in 1939, though often cited, is only rarely echoed in contemporary research designs. Mark Granovetter and Richard Swedberg remark that this "mid-century industrial sociology"—positing that "a work organization is a complex, interdependent social system"—offers lessons that have "still scarcely been absorbed by the [contemporary] sociology and economics of the firm."[24]

Losing Sight of Social Systems

The roots of this gradual neglect of analysis at the organizational social system level are numerous. A first explanation probably lies in the normative undertones some readers associated with the historical proponents of these approaches. The Human Relations movement, positing humankind as eminently social and cooperative, was the main source of inspiration for early social system approaches to studying organizations.[25] Critics of the Human Relations movement, and by association social system approaches, pointed to the ideological biases of this scholarship, evidenced, in their eyes, by the absence of conflict and power relations in these readings of organizations. They saw these social system developments as the emergence of "a new vocabulary of human motives" that offered "new justifications for management authority and worker obedience."[26] In other words, the idealized view of organizations as cooperative could only be promoted at the expense of labor. (George Homans and many leaders of the Human Relations movement strongly disagreed with this assertion.) What is more, by focusing on the micro level of analysis, social system approaches might miss larger social trends (including the inequities often experienced by workers).

Adding to this normative unease, three important practical considerations also contributed to the gradual neglect of these approaches: the

first is large U.S. institutions' attempts to rationalize the study of business scholarship; the second is the broader spread of the discipline of
economics within the social sciences; and the third is the rise in information technology use in social sciences. With the hope of trans-
forming what some viewed as a fairly nonscientific field into a more
legitimate, positivistic endeavor, in the late 1950s the Ford and Carne-
gie foundations decided to reshape scholarship emanating from business schools. Both foundations issued influential reports calling for a
stronger alignment of business school scholarship with the norms of
the science community. Moreover, the Ford Foundation started direct-
ing large grants to various business schools in the United States under
the condition that the institutions follow certain guidelines.[27] Though
historically, ground-level social system observations were crucial to the
development of the field of organizational research, these foundations
seemed to posit that such observations paled in comparison to large-
scale, standardized investigations (more akin to clinical scientific trials
than to cultural anthropology fieldwork). Although not all organizational research originated from business schools, these actions still
shaped part of the research agenda, most notably by discrediting some
past research methodologies. In a parallel move, economists began
gaining ground in the social science discipline, including in organizational research.[28] The increased presence of economists shifted the burden of proof and scientific legitimacy to metrics that economists were
most familiar with: codified, ideally large datasets. Additionally, information technology became increasingly available to social science researchers and facilitated the manipulation of large datasets.[29] This combination encouraged the development of a certain type of scholarship
fairly distant from the initial social systems approach. By 1966, when
William Dickson and Fritz Roethlisberger published their follow-up
study at the Hawthorne plant, few paid much attention to it.[30] The era
of social system studies, which gained momentum mid-century, by
then had waned.

   In this context, meta-organizational levels of analysis thrived. A review of the first twenty-five years (1956—1980) of scholarship in one
of the leading journals in the field states: "The early articles were all
almost qualitative, but the notion of a science gradually developed. By
1969, most articles were systematic analyses of organizations and by
1973 most studies utilized linear statistics of some sort."[31] Among the
four research traditions that dominate contemporary organizational
sociology, three traditions focus on meta-organization levels of analysis (institutionalism, resource-dependency approaches, and organizational ecology) and only one (network analysis)—as will be detailed in
the next section—indirectly deals with social systems in organiza-

tions.[32] The development of organizational ecology best exemplifies this shift. It focuses almost exclusively on the study of collections of populations of organizations that produce similar goods or services (such as microbreweries or newspapers), and the dynamics of their emergence and death.[33] Organizational ecology produced stimulating findings that explain the rate of foundings and failures of organizations based on the material and cultural features of their environments; however, it also indirectly eclipsed the more in-depth studies of given organizations and social systems.[34] A recent project aimed at coding 156 published ethnographies, which cover more than 200 organizations, highlights the strain such new approaches impose on more social system–oriented research.[35] The idea that a statistical analysis of ethnographies might yield novel and significant results is attractive, but slightly off-putting. Much of these ethnographies lend themselves fairly easily to coding (e.g., the mode of compensation in a given setting can be fixed or variable), but the richness of these ethnographies lies in their ability to cover entire systems; connecting individuals and practices, interdependencies and sentiments, groups and spaces. Current standards of organizational research seem to favor codification of discrete data points, instead of richer, but admittedly also looser, depictions of organizations.

This is not to say that exceptions cannot be found: current scholarship has produced a steady stream of in-depth studies of work social systems. Within the sociology community, studies in the tradition of symbolic interactionism or those that rely on participant observations continue to investigate given social systems.[36] Contemporary studies of aerospace engineers, corporate executives, kitchen cooks, and taxi drivers illustrate this tradition.[37] In Europe, for instance, this tradition is quite lively: in the French automotive industry, for example, studies of workers at the Renault and Peugeot plants provide a detailed and thorough view of these social systems.[38] Moreover, numerous organizational scholars, many of whom drew inspiration from Edgar Schein, have conducted detailed analyses of banks, consulting firms, engineering laboratories, police departments, and radiology departments.[39] In addition, cultural anthropologists with an interest in corporate settings such as Malaysian and French factories have also sustained the tradition of in-depth analyses of social systems.[40] Yet, these studies are rare when compared with the organizational scholarship generated via meta-organizational-level lenses of analysis. The majority of organizational scholarship has slowly drifted away from detailed studies of work social systems.[41]

A Partial Rehabilitation of Social Systems via Network Research

One of the four dominant and growing areas of sociological organizational research, social network analysis, partly refocused scholars' attention toward social systems. Though this trend is quite noticeable, it
is also somewhat deceiving since the social system sustained or created
through these social networks and the experiences and sentiments individuals derive from them receive little attention from this community of scholars. The refocus on social systems (or at least on social
interactions) was mostly as a means to an end: examining the concrete
outcomes of such social networks, instead of seeking to know the social system itself.

In recent years, our knowledge of social networks, and presumably
of the social systems that give rise to them, has burgeoned. Whether
at the intra- or inter-organizational level, empirical research on social
networks—in multiple settings and involving various participants—
has greatly contributed to the practical understanding of the concrete
impact they have. The pervasiveness of networks came as a surprise
in a contemporary global society that often imagined itself an aggrega-
tion of individual market participants. It was indeed once commonly
accepted that "modern" Western societies relied more heavily on atom-
istic market mechanisms, whereas traditional societies functioned with
more interdependent social mechanisms.[42] Social network perspectives
and market approaches were typically considered at odds. However,
after scholars began to explore the social organization of the market,
the conventional individualistic view of markets began to be challenged.[43] Mark Granovetter argued, convincingly, that economic transactions are embedded in social structures, thus reopening the "great
divide" that confined sociologists and economists to the study of, respectively, values and value.[44] Consequently, many research efforts focused on the impact of social ties (and implicitly of social systems) on
various behaviors previously considered off-limits to sociologists. The
business of determining financial lending rates, the performance of
Broadway musicals, and the actions of corporate boards of directors
all became fruitful grounds for investigation.[45] In addition, during the
same time period, literature on social capital, which shares an interest
with network literature in social ties, gained currency in examining
trust, collective action, and economic development.[46] Social capital pre-
supposes the existence of social systems since it is always "embodied
in the relations among persons."[47] Social capital is, like other forms of
capital, "productive, making possible the achievement of certain ends
that in its absence would not be possible." But "unlike other forms of

capital, social capital inheres in the structure of the relations between actors and among actors."[48]

Despite the heavy reliance on the premise of one crucial element of social systems in network research and social capital literature, the study of entire social systems and the variations in participants' experiences and sentiments of such systems have attracted less attention in both of these approaches. This relative neglect can first be traced to methodological issues; measuring experiences and sentiments of interdependence is no simple task. Methodological network measurement often favors assumptions of homogeneity in social ties: a hypothesis that social system views of organizations would challenge, since participants' experiences of these interdependencies might vary. Some network studies, however, try to distinguish among experiences of social ties by asking respondents questions such as "Who would you go to for work advice versus for going to lunch with?" in order to separate typologies of ties.[49] Other studies rely on typologies of members of a given social network to deduct differences in network ties (for instance, kinship versus coworker ties).[50] Such approaches implicitly acknowledge the potential diversity of experiences and sentiments that are associated with interactions. But they often rely on ex-ante typologies to capture this potential diversity. Also, in spite of these attempts to address this diversity, a simultaneous focus on the concrete outcomes of these ties often trumps any concerns related to these differences.

This fairly exclusive focus in network research on the concrete outcomes (rather than more ego-centered "subjective" outcomes) is a second reason for the neglect of social systems within network research. As long as the concrete outcomes of the networks are similar (such as finding a job or obtaining a bank loan), variations in experiences have mostly been left unexplored. This reflects the "highly instrumental view of networks" that Joel Podolny and James Baron identify when they discuss job mobility patterns. They trace this view to Ronald Burt's more structuralist take on networks.[51] Indeed, from a concrete outcome perspective, why dig deeper into the experience of interactions within social systems? If the explanatory power of the typologies of social ties (advice versus friendship, for instance) is enough to accurately explain concrete behavioral outcomes, digging deeper seems unnecessary. This position assumes, however, that concrete outcomes are the most interesting elements of social systems. Yet, participants also experience more "subjective" outcomes as they navigate social systems. When focusing on more inward-looking outcomes, specifically from the participants' perspectives, analyses of social systems regain relevance.

Identity Dynamics within Social Systems

Literature on social identity offers the most compelling theoretical reason to pay attention to social systems and to the potential variations in members' experiences of those systems. Research building on social constructionism and symbolic interactionism assumes social identities to be conceptually grounded in interactions with others.[52] People rely on the feedback and confirmation others provide them in order to understand and sustain their senses of self. This perspective rests on the idea that individuals both project their identities onto and derive their identities from social interactions.[53] Thus, in this view, identity refers to a dynamic social process by which meanings develop and are maintained through social interactions. For instance, chess players rely on tournaments or interactions with other players to sustain their identities as competent players.[54] The chess tournament community, conceived as a social system, enables and frames players' identities. In this theoretical approach, the work identities and, by extension, the occupational identities of an organization's members are inherently built in social interactions within social systems.[55]

Such a focus on the identities of participants is also suggested in network research by Podolny and Baron. In their study of labor mobility within a high-tech engineering and manufacturing corporation, they distinguish social ties that convey resources (i.e., task advice or strategic information) from ties that convey organizational identities (i.e., social support or what they label "buy-in" ties).[56] In doing so, they recognize that participants' perceived identities might relate to the interactions in which they engage. They add that such ties are "often valued for their own sake."[57] Thus, some social network research has begun to acknowledge the role that social ties, and the occurrence of such ties within broader social settings, can play in conveying or reinforcing identities. (Some early network research also refers to participants' "roles" and suggests this idea.)[58] Whereas it might be assumed that only individuals facing hardship (such as minority female employees working at the above-cited high-tech firm) seek to enact given identities before their coworkers, this is rarely the case. More settled employees such as mainstream, tenured faculty at colleges and universities also often seek to enact their identities. Their interactions within a network of colleagues about endorsing or blocking the appointment of a junior faculty member are a key test of their identity (as respected academics).[59] Harrison White has perhaps pushed this line of reasoning the furthest by suggesting that social networks *are* identities.[60] This justifies looking deeper at social systems within organizations, specifically with respect to sentiments that might relate to identity. In other words, people might "find themselves" in organizations.[61]

Social systems are therefore only partially rehabilitated via mainstream network research pursuits. They appear necessary to explain concrete outcomes, but do not seem of interest beyond that function. (With the important exception of White's conception of networks.) Also, social ties are only one manifestation of social systems. Moreover, the variations in experiences of social ties remain largely unexplored.[62] Several calls have been made to shift the focus of network scholarship toward a more fine-grained analysis of what occurs within these networks. Arthur Stinchcombe, for instance, when discussing corporate board-of-director ties, writes, "We need to know what flows across these links."[63] And Gerald Salancik summed it up best, perhaps, by saying, "There is danger in network analysis of not seeing the trees in the forest. Interactions, the building blocks of networks, are too easily taken for granted."[64]

This book addresses some of the main concerns just described—namely, the limited contemporary research on variations in participants' experiences within and sentiments regarding social networks (or what could be referred to as interactions within social systems), particularly with regard to the participants' social identities. It answers calls to populate organizational research with individuals whose interactions suffuse meaning.[65] In doing so, the aim is to avoid the normative undertone toward cooperation that critics saw in earlier social system approaches to organizations. With the goal in mind of revisiting social systems, and paying particular attention to potential identity implications of these systems, a proper understanding of what gray zones entail can be attempted.

Social systems are the building blocks of organizations, but they have yet to attract the contemporary detailed scholarly attention they deserve. The social identity dynamics that permeate social systems theoretically justify such attention since members might rely on interactions within social systems to sustain their identities. The experiences and sentiments participants derive from the interactions within these systems are crucial to the understanding of human behaviors. They provide the much-needed context to explain what we observe. In revisiting the social system level of analysis in organizations, both the formal and informal interdependencies warrant consideration. Moreover, within informal interdependencies, even in organizations with apparently legal objectives, clandestine informal interdependencies should not be discounted. Whereas many such clandestine interdependencies within social systems exist, the practice of homer-making described in the next chapter constitutes an ideal research setting in which to revisit social systems. The clandestine practice of homer-making also represents a window into a gray zone—one that is, in fact, fairly common in many manufacturing settings.

2

The Side Production of Homers in Factories

> A measurer is the thing you use to measure fuel and
> because measurers are not made in steel but in bronze . . .
> they make nice objects. . . . You only need to polish them
> and to put them on a base, you insert a light bulb inside,
> and there you have a small reading lamp, a bedside lamp
> . . . it adds some charm. . . . I'm not sure there is anything
> interesting in [my telling you about] that . . . you can write
> it down if you wish, but all the rest are anecdotes, right?[1]

THE PERSON referring to the bedside lamp, which was manufactured
at his workplace, is a retiree from the Pierreville aeronautic plant,
where he worked in a testing workshop. He is reluctant to talk about
the lamp because, he says, "these things are oftentimes confidential,"
but decides that enough time has elapsed since he made it, so he can
now talk. His lamp is an example of a homer. Homer-making is a
worker's use of company materials or tools in his or her workplace,
during work hours, to manufacture or transform artifacts that are not
part of the official production of the organization. The origins of the
French word for homers, *perruque*, remain unclear, but more generally,
perruque in French denotes a wig. The purpose of a wig is to conceal
and hide. Thus, the probable association between homers and wigs exists in their similar deception, since homer activities are meant to look
like official work, when in fact they are not. As a result, both the practice and the artifacts are difficult to document, yet homer-making, especially in mechanical engineering industries, is a long-standing tradition. The legal, artistic, ethnographic, and autobiographical "traces" of
homer-making presented in this chapter highlight the prevalence of
this phenomenon.

Defining the Practice of Homer-Making

In 1870s manufacturing settings, the French term *perruque* primarily
referred to "the diverting of material belonging to the state and placed
under the supervision of the person who is culpable of this act," but

during the same period, the term also surfaced in private work environments.[2] For instance, Denis Poulot, an ex-foreman in a Parisian mechanical workshop, quotes one of his employees on homers: "The boss believes that he is not paying for the tools we are using, but three-quarters of them are made as homers in this firm. They end up costing him more than if he gave them to us." To make a homer, Poulot adds, is "to make work for oneself."[3] The association between homer-making and "work for oneself" persists to this day. A recent historical overview of homers in France also employs this definition of homers: "a job, an artifact made for oneself, during work hours, with materials and tools of the organization."[4]

Initially, homers were often tools necessary for the job or artifacts necessary for everyday life that shops did not sell. In that sense, the term "for oneself" has a historical explanation. The notion of homers as work outside of official production, done "for one's own benefit," seems, however, more accurate nowadays.[5] This more contemporary definition of homers reflects the fact that they can also be made for someone other than the homer-maker.[6] Examples of homers as gifts, specifically those given upon retirement, remind us that ultimately homers are not always made for oneself.[7] Furthermore, in the French publishing world, a homer (*perruque*) refers to written work that an employee produces at his desk at his organization, but for another publishing outlet.

Thus, there are multiple conceptualizations of a homer. What these definitions share, though, is the notion of diverting company time and company tools and/or materials.[8] Some associate the practice with fraud, but because the morality of homer-making is itself open for discussion, a more suitable definition of the phenomenon refrains from judgment. The definition offered by Robert Kosmann is, in that regard, more precise: "The use of materials and tools by a worker in the workspace, during work hours, to manufacture or transform artifacts outside of the [official] production of the organization."[9] This is the definition I will use to discuss homers in manufacturing settings.

The word *perruque* is most commonly used in French factories to describe the resulting artifacts; however, there are many French equivalents for the word: *bricoles*, *pinailles*, *bousilles*, and *pindilles* also denote homers.[10] In the United States, the practice is known as "homer-making," performing "government jobs," or creating "cumshaws," and in Great Britain, it is known as "pilfering." The term "homer" probably carries connotations about the fact that the artifact is brought home and that its maker can also be sent home (fired). Miklos Haraszti first put the term "homer" in writing in 1978.[11] Blacksmiths in the United States still understand the term today.[12] As early as 1954, Alvin

Gouldner finds the term "government jobs" in gypsum mines, and in 1959, Melville Dalton confirms its use in at least three factories.[13] Bruce Nickerson further notes its occurrence in 1974 in U.S. manufacturing plants.[14] The term "government jobs" continued to be popular in the 1980s among, for instance, workers in Bendix Corporation plants (manufacturing brakes) and in General Electric's Aircraft Engines Division.[15] The term "government jobs" ironically indicates that working for the "government" might equate to working for oneself. In the U.S. Navy, another term, "cumshaw," similarly describes the result of appropriation of navy materials for personal use.[16] The same term also describes a present or gratuity, and by extension, a baksheesh in Chinese ports in which visiting navy ships historically docked. Maintenance workshops aboard ships provided the most fruitful setting for the carpenters who often worked there to manufacture cumshaws. Last, in Great Britain, Jason Ditton and Gerald Mars documented diverse instances of pilfering across different settings from the 1970s to the 1980s.[17] Ditton observed the pilfering ways of truck drivers at an industrial bakery who made extra money by selling loaves on the side that they were able to procure for themselves. Homers, however, mostly involve more a transformation of materials than a simple pilfering of them.

Since the diversion of time, materials, or tools from an employer for personal use is generally forbidden by internal corporate codes of conduct, few employees are willing to openly discuss homer activities. Secondary data sources (legal, artistic, ethnographic, and autobiographical) nonetheless offer historical evidence of homer-making. Though the work settings in which these traces appear vary, mechanical engineering industries (such as automotive and aeronautic plants), where craftsmanship is often highly valued, seem overrepresented in these accounts.

Legal Traces of Homers

Contemporary legal cases of homer-makers caught in the act in both France and North America suggest recent occurrences of homer-making. The North American jurisdictions, which rely on a corpus of easily searchable and indexed past proceedings, better lend themselves to research than French labor courts, but illustrative cases of homer-makers surface in both geographies. The following cases were not resolved internally and are probably exceptions (since homer activities are essentially, as will be shown later, an intra-organizational affair); nonetheless, they expose such contemporary activities.

Prosecutors use homers as evidence of misconduct—evidence that oftentimes leads to the firing of the accused employee. Some items brought as evidence in court might appear fairly inconsequential, such as "a personal memorandum" typed "during company time" that was presented in a California appeals case.[18] But other times the homers seem fairly consequential, as they involve more company material or time: they can be rather utilitarian (a bumper guard for a car in a Manitoba arbitration) or akin to craft (a medicine cabinet in another case in Ontario). They all are manufactured on company time with company material or tools.[19] A search for the terms "theft of company time" in the Westlaw legal databases of six random North American jurisdictions (British Columbia, California, Indiana, Manitoba, Ontario, and Texas) post-1990 yielded these examples. The search only returned eight cases, which might appear few, but it could also suggest a low incidence of external prosecution of homer-makers. However, these few examples do point to current occurrences of homer-making. The industries from which they arose range from a chemical plant to wood and steel mills. Invariably the court finds the employee guilty, though it sometimes grants leniency depending upon the employee's ignorance of the gravity of the offense.

In the cases just discussed, suspects often defended themselves by claiming that others engaged in similar activities, and that homer activities were fairly routine. One defendant claimed that his foreman "had his own personal business . . . and at one point he welded an exhaust fan or cover for a bathroom for him."[20] The mediator of an Ontario arbitration also highlights the prevalence of homer-making when he remarks that building a medicine cabinet is an "abuse of the government jobs."[21] This suggests that homers that are less visible or consume less materials and/or time might be more easily tolerated. To stress the relative normalcy of certain homer-making activities, another defendant accused of manufacturing a gasket for his car testified that other employees did similar things in the past, and that no one was asked to refrain from doing so.[22]

In France, the testimony of fired homer-makers (one of which was fired after the discovery of a homer at his home) suggests a similar legal equation between homers and theft.[23] A ruling by a French labor court indicates that homer-makers are fired on grounds of use of company material, noncompliance with internal codes of conduct, and furthering of personal instead of company interests.[24] A search in an indexed database of partially archived French legal cases using the key words "theft of material" and "employer" produced several cases of prosecuted homer-makers.[25] Bringing suit against a suspected homer-maker in these cases did not require proof of intended fraudulent behavior; the mere theft of material was usually enough to have the worker dismissed. For instance, a case against a worker who "recycled" metal scraps did not need to demonstrate intent to defraud his employer.[26] He was found guilty of recycling material that did not belong to him. Of greater interest, however, is the case of a worker who set aside fifty kilograms of zinc for personal use under orders from his boss. The French Court of Appeals that reviewed his case wrote that even though his behavior begot consequent and serious grounds for dismissal, he should not be punished because he acted under orders.[27]

What these legal proceedings and mediation cases provide is, first, evidence of the contemporary occurrence of homer-making. They also showcase a certain legal view of homer-making, found in both North America and France, that usually associates homers with theft. In legal settings, the morality of homer-making is regarded as highly dubious. Evidence of the practice almost certainly yields penalization unless important attenuating circumstances become salient (such as complete ignorance of the liability involved or, as in the French case, unless the worker can prove that he acted under orders).

Artistic Traces of Homers

Artistic venues provide a second intriguing arena to identify homers. These "folkloric" artifacts are sometimes pieces of interest to industrial museum curators and collectors. Exhibits of homers at French industrial museums in Le Creusot or in the Basse-Loire region provide such evidence.[28] Sometimes it is difficult to determine whether the artifacts were made at work or outside of the workplace. (The exhibit at the museum in Le Creusot seems more focused, in that regard, on productions done outside the plant.) Yet, this difference is crucial in distinguishing homers from work done on the side but outside of the workplace, mostly as a hobby at home.[29] The case of the artist Pincemain clarified this distinction. Pincemain, a former welder, made a move from the factory world to the artistic world.[30] His initial creations were homers, but the pieces he produced after leaving the plant, though similar in appearance to his initial creations, could not be called such since they were not made in the workplace. More generally, a move into the official art world also signals the end of a certain homer-making trademark. Work "done for oneself" (the most narrow definition of homers) does not fit well into a network of commercial art. If homers are described as "free, creative, and precisely not directed toward profit" as Michel de Certeau suggests, the value the art world bestows upon the artifacts becomes suspicious.[31] A "homer" specifically produced for the commercial art world is probably not viewed in the factory as a legitimate homer. A French photography exhibit included a picture of artifacts seen during a labor strike. One of these photographs was an obvious representation of a homer. It was labeled "the head of a [miniature] rocket manufactured in the LIP quartz watch corporation."[32] Given that the rocket head was not made to be sold and was only later photographed as art, its integrity as a homer probably remains. Nonetheless, the entry of homers into the world of art in some ways challenges the archetypical view of these artifacts.[33]

It comes as no surprise, then, that homers that find their way into museums are most often displayed for their historical rather than their artistic characteristics. Homers are generally set in their broader historical contexts (even though elements surrounding the production of homers are often hard to historically document). For the most part, homers are not intended or described as art.[34] A notable exhibit should be highlighted, though. In 1984, the Labor Council of a French Snecma aeronautic plant organized an exhibit of approximately one hundred homers that belonged to employees.[35] The artifacts represented a subset of homers, namely retirement homers. The terms "craft," "imagination," "know-how," and "masterpiece" (with its ancient journeyman connotations) appeared in the booklet that accompanied the exhibit, but the words "art" and "artistic" were notably absent. This rare exhibit only confirms the rule that homers are not conceived as artistic productions, yet they sometimes find their way into museums or more traditional artistic venues. To fully appreciate their meanings, we must now examine more contextual accounts of homers in workshops or work communities.

Autobiographical and Ethnographic Traces of Homers

Slightly more common, autobiographical and ethnographic traces of homer-making provide insight into the artifacts' existences and meanings. The autobiographical tradition is open to managers and workers alike. Both foremen and managers write about homers, offering a managerial perspective. In one case, after working in a Parisian mechanical shop, a foreman writes about the homer activities he witnessed.[36] In another instance, a manager draws from his knowledge of large North American corporations to describe the practice.[37] But homer accounts are also offered by workers. Miklos Haraszti is probably the most prolific such writer.[38] He offers a long list of homers ranging from a key chain to an ashtray, necklace charms, television antennas, daggers, and bath mats that he saw produced in the Hungarian tractor factory where he worked. A French automotive employee also testifies about homers he saw, such as children's dolls made from foam cut-outs.[39] Another French worker describes wooden vases, firearms, and kitchen cabinets manufactured at the Renault automotive company where he once worked.[40] A retiree of a French airline company adds to the list, discussing the metal suitcases, lamps, and motorcycle parts he saw manufactured by coworkers, who he describes as "great" homer-makers.[41] Finally, an additional "informant," who went from apprentice to engineer before turning to academia, describes the artifacts he saw produced in the United States, the more common ones being "knives made from files, involving grinding, cutting, tempering, and hafting."[42]

Other studies extend these limited autobiographical testimonies. The settings for the accounts generally reflect the physical trajectory of the artifacts: usually first workshops, occasionally retirement ceremonies, and finally homes. A first series of ethnographic data reveals homers inside factory workers' homes. In these accounts, homers often almost go unnoticed. However, the examples of "small tiled tables," "flower pot holders," and "nicely twisted metal shreds," apparently mounted on a base, hint of homer-making.[43] Similarly, descriptions of artifacts at the homes and in the gardens of retirees in the Lot-et-Garonne region of France evoke homers. Though many of the artifacts were made at home, it appears that others came from a nearby metallurgic factory.[44] Another study provides a fairly exhaustive overview of homers produced in France, mainly since the 1950s.[45] This study covers an impressive variety of homers (from a kitchen spoon to elaborate sculptures) and hints at the multiplicity of homer productions. Each account still extracts the artifact from its context, presenting it by itself next to the community in which it was created, which is left mostly unspecified. A last ethnographic account brings us closer to contextualizing homers within a social system. The account focuses on ceramic pots found in homes and antique shops in Le Creusot. The author of the study incidentally notes that many employees also produce homers at work, suggesting that some of the ceramics might be produced in nearby factories.[46] Together, these accounts suggest fairly widespread homer activity across many settings.

The study of homers given as gifts upon retirement is advantageous in that the defining homer characteristics of the objects (i.e., made at work on company time with company materials or tools) are easier to identify and confirm. Recipients who receive them and coworkers who manufacture them attest more openly to the homer quality of the gifts since the special occasion of a retirement partly absolves the "culprits," allowing participants to speak more openly about the gifts' origins. These gifts are also known as "retirement homers" or "behavior homers" (*perruques de conduite*), suggesting that they are a type of reward for good behavior at work. Detailed research documents such gifts and their symbolic meanings in the aeronautic industry. The artifacts often evoke occupations and hobbies, as a "small metal toolbox of a black-smith," a sailboat, or a bicycle do.[47] The previously mentioned retire-ment homer exhibit at Snecma included multiple such artifacts and re-vealed the diversity of occupations and hobbies represented by homers.[48] But in order to capture the manufacturing process of homers, work-based accounts of homer activities are essential.

Case studies of corporations allow for an integrated view of homer-making in the work environment. Alvin Gouldner first introduced the term "government jobs" when he discussed leniencies in the gypsum mine he was studying.[49] If an employee needed a table fixed or some-thing welded, for instance, he would bring the object to the mine where raw materials and tools were available to employees. But Gouldner's account is probably slightly deceiving since it creates the impression that all employees benefited from this leniency. Stéphane Beaud and Michel Pialoux in some ways fill this gap with their discussion of the trial of a worker who, in 1990, was dismissed for exiting a French auto-motive factory with a tool. Though the trial does not revolve around homer-making per se, the authors note that during the hearings, a num-ber of the dismissed worker's colleagues shouted the names of execu-tives they had done [homer] "work" for, thus framing the dismissal in the context of homer-making. The authors also write that skilled work-ers could engage in homer-making because they had a higher degree of work autonomy than other workers.[50] The following example, in a very different setting, seems to confirm the apparently more frequent (and perhaps exclusive) involvement of highly skilled workers in homer-making. It focuses on blacksmiths who work for the Paris sub-way system.[51] The blacksmiths—considered highly skilled workers in this environment—seem able to engage in homer work and do not ap-pear to be worried about management. Another study of French ship-building yards also seems to strengthen the association between higher skill and homer-making. Homers are shown to be not equally available to all participants and in every occasion.[52] Finally, the workplaces of automotive engineers and technicians, who are also highly skilled and sometimes develop their pet projects as homer projects, provide an-other setting in which homers can be found.[53] Distant bosses officially "killed" these engineers' pet projects, but the homers progressed, thanks to the tacit approval of their local direct supervisors.

All of these traces of homers (legal, artistic, autobiographical, and ethnographic) reflect the existence of homer-making, specifically in mechanical engineering industries and among a population of fairly or highly skilled workers. Although they do not provide any estimation of the frequency of such practices, the traces testify to the prevalence of this type of gray zone in manufacturing settings.[54] Similar to the key chain described in the preface, they constitute proof of a practice few are willing to openly admit engaging in.

Estimating the Frequency of Homer-Making

Two different data sources—one historical, the other contemporary—help reveal the frequency with which homer-making might occur. The first source is a historical collection of workshop codes of conduct, and the second is a survey the French National Statistics Institute conducted in 1986 and 1987.

The Bibliothèque Nationale de France has a set of 354 workshop codes of conduct dating from 1798 to 1936. The library acquired them by legal deposit from French printers.[55] The collection includes codes of conduct from that period of most industries and from most regions. Focusing on workshop codes of conduct can provide "negative" evidence of homer-making. In other words, if homer-making was systematically forbidden, it can be inferred, by default, that homer-making probably systematically occurred.[56] A random sampling of the collection (10%, or thirty-five codes of conduct) indicates that 84 percent of relevant workshop codes refer to the removal of materials, tools, or objects from the workshop, and 25 percent specifically discuss work done for one's own benefit. In this sample of analyzed codes, removing objects, materials, or tools from the workplace is always forbidden (except with an "exit slip"). In a soda factory, for instance, these rules cover removing work-related objects; in a print shop, removing paper (regardless of its condition); and in a steel mill, taking waste materials. These same codes of conduct typically also allow for extensive employee searches upon exiting the factory. Several codes explicitly forbid personal work on the premises. Exceptions are made for some steelworkers and piece-rate laborers to manufacture or repair their work tools when "the firm provides all the materials." But, in general, codes forbid workers to manufacture anything inside the shop that is for their own use, "even during lunch hours"; "to bring work from home" into the shop; or to engage in work "other than the usual" without express supervisory consent. The last rule hints at the possibility for supervisors to commission homers. But the codes suggest that the practice needs to be policed; not all supervisors can order homers. For instance, one code forbids supervisors to commission work unless a nominally referred-to shop foreman authorizes it.

Within the subset of codes of conduct that make no mention of removing objects, tools, or materials from the workshop or engaging in
personal work (fourteen of the thirty-five codes, or 40%), five of the
codes regulate workshops where employees are exclusively on piece-
rate salaries (essentially textile mills). Piece-rate remunerations automatically regulate work done for one's own benefit since the negative
financial consequences discourage the practice; the absence of references to homers in piece-rate environments, therefore, makes sense
and is expected. Another five codes of conduct out of these fourteen
cover unusual work environments (such as that of luggage porters on
a wholesale market, a job clearinghouse, etc.). Thus, only four codes
of conduct in potential homer-making environments (a shipyard, a
printing shop, a shoe manufacturer, and that of roof tilers) fail to mention anything about removing objects, tools, or materials, or work done
for one's own benefit. This first historical source suggests, by default,
the prevalence of diverting time, tools, or materials since 84 percent of
relevant workshop codes of conduct in this sample refer to such practices and 25 percent of these relevant codes specifically penalize work
done for one's own benefit at work.

A second, more contemporary source on the relative frequency of
homer-making is a survey that the French National Statistics Institute
conducted in 1986 and 1987 on leisure at work.[57] The survey indicates
that 28 percent of male factory workers (the highest percentage among
the various social groups surveyed) reported that on the job they frequently or occasionally manufacture "something" or perform a task
not associated with their responsibilities as employees. Moreover, 40
percent of the surveyed male factory workers described the "something" as an "object." In other social categories, such as executive
males, in 62 percent of the cases where something unassociated with
their responsibilities as employees was being done, that "something"
was deemed, instead, to be "office work." The same male factory
workers also indicated that they sometimes bring home scraps, materials, and office furniture (48% of respondents). Unfortunately, the responses do not provide details about these salvaged items. The Institute conducted the survey with a representative sample of 446
individuals, thirty to forty-nine years of age, spanning all occupations.
Thus, this second data source points to a fairly high frequency of
homer activity among male factory workers.

With these two data sources in mind, we can conclude that homer-
making has probably almost always been considered illegal by workshop codes-of-conduct standards, and yet remains, even today, a
relatively frequent practice. It is important to note that traditional homer-
making could be in decline for many different reasons: the relative

decrease in the number of members in the workers' occupational group, the increased automation of tasks, a de-skilling of some factory workers, and the more accurate tracking of scrap materials as quality norms are becoming more widespread. Moreover, the greater availability outside the factory of low-priced, traditionally manufactured functional homers also renders homer-making less financially worthwhile. Nevertheless, the vivacity of homer-making—documented through the survey conducted by the French National Statistics Institute—persists.[58]

Homer-Making: A French Phenomenon?

Evidently homer-making exists outside of France. Historically, former Eastern Bloc countries (such as Hungary) and the People's Republic of China provided fruitful grounds for homer activities, where items were often procured to barter in exchange for basic necessities (blurring in these cases the line between homers and theft). And technical experts in the former Soviet Union, for instance, were sometimes found guilty of using enterprise work time and materials for personal ends.[59] The linguistic terms used to describe the practice both in the United States and in the United Kingdom point to the fact that homer-making is not limited to France and former Eastern Bloc countries, either. It is possible, however, that the practice manifests itself differently depending on the cultural context. For instance, studies have shown that the French are less work-oriented than Americans: on a work-orientation scale, on average, the French score significantly lower.[60] In addition, French workers build on centuries of contention against the State and capitalist enterprises that might render homer-making (as a means of rebellion) more tolerated in France than in other countries.[61] Thus, France might provide more fertile ground than the United States in which to study homers. While this hypothesis might be true, data collected in the United States for the U.S. Department of Justice suggests that homer-making might be fairly widespread there, as well.

It is difficult to quantify all homer activities, particularly when they are conflated with theft. (This distinction will be further discussed in chapter 5.) Yet some surveys on "theft" might help indirectly uncover the extent of the phenomenon in the United States. In an anonymous survey of 1,497 electronic manufacturing sector employees in three geographic areas (Minneapolis-Saint Paul, Cleveland, and Dallas-Fort Worth), 14.3 percent of respondents reported that they took raw materials used in production from their employer, 8.7 percent reported that they took company tools or equipment, and 1.8 percent reported that they took precious metals (such as platinum or gold).[62] There is no official account of what these individuals did with the company property they took or where they used it (at home or at work). But it is possible that they used the company tools and materials to create artifacts. And such transformation—if it necessitated certain tools located in company workshops—could have occurred at work, on or off company time.

It is possible that tolerance levels for homer-making (or other gray-zone practices) vary across countries, but this is not to say that homer-making does not occur in most countries. Furthermore, if the tolerance level is higher in a given country, that does not automatically mean the occurrence of a particular practice will be more frequent. It could simply mean that open discussions of a practice are more or less common in certain contexts—but the frequency of the practice remains unchanged. Bruce Nickerson, who worked for more than a decade in various capacities (as an apprentice, mechanical inspector, piecework machinist, draftsman, technical writer, and process-control engineer) in plants in Massachusetts and the Midwest, reports that he found homer-making ("government jobs") in every plant he worked in. He calls the practice "traditional."[63] Although there may very well be a French specificity to disclosure around homer-making, nothing precludes the prevalence of similar practices, perhaps in varying degrees, in other countries. Whether the actual frequency of the practice or its mere disclosure is what varies between France and other countries remains unclear.

The Elusiveness and Attractiveness of Homers

Homers are clearly illegal artifacts; yet, even accounting for this characteristic, their visibility is fairly low. Why is that? Other work practices that appear to be as illegal as homers, such as "goldbricking," or engaging in quota restriction, are more visible.[64] This low visibility might reflect the fact that many individuals appear to be involved in homer activities, including supervisors and executives. Homers are unquestionably illegal, but more important, they remain elusive probably because they highlight a real complicity at the workplace between employees and management. This complicity does not easily fit in a labor union narrative (historically constructed as "we" against "them"), nor does it fit well in a managerial one (construed as officially upholding company rules).

Notions of resistance have long dominated labor union discourse. Homers represent a potential form of "resistance" but, more generally, a form of complicity—or in more pejorative terms, a form of collusion. Isaac Joseph sums up well the reluctance some trade union members exhibit toward the practice:

> One should not be surprised if the dissenter has taken over from the activist and homer-making replaced class struggles. The weakness and limits of homers are known upfront: homers only play on salvaging and on bits and pieces, homers only operate by diverting flows, they assume an intimate understanding of the system of supervision, an over-adaptation to methods of control. The geography of freedom that homers allow us to explore is pathetic, as pathetic as all small acts of resistance—escapes, retreats, silence, jokes, wit—that are not inscribed in a logic of contradiction.[65]

Joseph adds that homer practices are "already lost battles" since they are so intimately "integrated" into the system. A union representative from the metallurgic branch of the French Confédération Générale du Travail (CGT) union does not exactly echo the position, but he very consciously discusses his reluctance to address the topic. "If I were to talk about homers, I would say up front, and would insist, that there is not an official position of the CGT on homers. This means there are exchanges on the subject; it's part of the labor movement . . . the CGT does not have a position on it, and in practice, we leave it up to every one to decide for him or herself, and come up with his or her own position." This clearly illustrates the union's "nonposition" (or relative silence) on the topic of homers.[66] The fact that in practice, foremen and even managers might also be part of the homer community seems difficult to reconcile with the idea of a distinct workers' community.

On the corporate side, talking about homers amounts to destroying them. Because homer-making is an illegal practice, the employer cannot officially acknowledge it (unless workshop codes of conduct are rewritten). To openly discuss homers is to admit to a shared complicity and to management's carelessness, or by default, to pigeonhole the practice as an individual deviant behavior. Etienne de Banville writes about an attorney (representing employers) who was sent to "the exhibit halls of an industrial museum where a homer exhibit was in the making." Photographic evidence was gathered, oral commentaries recorded, but no legal action was initiated. The employers understood the dilemma: it is hard to talk about homers without incriminating managers and executives, so homers are best dealt with by not talking about them at all. Thus, the general rule is to simply remain silent.

The only voice that remains is that of the individual participants who produce, facilitate, and sometimes benefit from homers. This single voice is hard pressed to resonate in traditional institutional settings. The voice does not exactly fit the workers' culture imagined by some labor activists. Nor does it fit in a managerial discourse since homers apparently contradict management's function. And if this voice ever ends up in court, it is often limited to a defendant trying to convince a judge that he (and more rarely she) is not a deviant isolate.

———————

Factory homers probably seem difficult to grasp because of their surface illegality, but in practice, the difficulty likely exists because they elude traditional institutional settings, present in the factory, that might acknowledge their existence. Neither management nor labor unions feel comfortable talking about homers. However, the history of the practice is documented, and its frequency can be estimated both indirectly (via the workshop codes of conduct) and directly (the French survey on leisure at work). Perhaps of greater importance is the fact that homer activities constitute ideal settings in which to study organizational gray zones. Homer activities are widespread enough to allow for data collection, and they are sufficiently at odds with official organizational rules to be labeled gray zones.

The next chapter will provide the setting for such a study through its depiction of the French aeronautic plant that forms the empirical context for this book. Documenting traces of homers in the plant proved initially difficult. Thus, breaking the silence surrounding homer-making and finding the individuals willing to discuss homer-making were integral parts of my fieldwork.[67] As this overview of homer-making suggests, not all plant members had equal access to homer-making: highly skilled workers often seemed most involved. The next chapter therefore not only describes the plant, but also pays particular attention to the most highly skilled, and respected, members at the Pierreville plant.

3

The Pierreville Plant: Setting and Status Divides

THE PIERREVILLE AERONAUTIC PLANT, part of the AeroDyn Corporation, stands beside an often vacant airstrip. It is slightly removed from the nearby highway, and is surrounded by fields of beets. Slowly but steadily, it produces airplane engines. The regular sound of what seems to be planes taking off and landing disturbs an otherwise peaceful setting. Upon hearing the engines roar, a newcomer to Pierreville might look up at the sky in vain, not realizing that the true origin of the noise is the testing that takes place in nearby workshops where meticulous routines ensure the proper live testing of the engines on the ground. The rare planes that can be seen overhead are only there for maintenance. The noise provides an awkward sense of comfort—it suggests that plant testing operations are proceeding as expected. Since the Pierreville plant is gated, it is hard to get a feel from the outside for the size of the facility. Pierreville spans 200 acres. Large parking lots and numerous company buses only allude to the volume of activity that occurs inside. In the center of a roundabout that every vehicle drives through to enter the plant stands a jetlike airplane, reminding plant members and visitors what Pierreville is about.

In order to explore the dynamics of gray zones, I conducted an in-depth study of homer practices at Pierreville that focused on the ex-post recollection of work from the early 1970s to the late 1990s. (For details, see appendix A, "Data and Methods.") Pierreville's internal code of conduct explicitly forbade the use of company materials and tools for purposes other than official work. The first article of the Pierreville code of conduct stipulated that management should immediately be notified of the deterioration, loss, or theft of company tools or materials; potential sanctions for not doing so included termination. Moreover, two additional articles stated that the use of company machines and automated tools was conditional upon management's approval. Without ever mentioning homers, most behaviors leading to the manufacture of homers (such as the one shown in fig. 3. 1) were explicitly forbidden.

Fig. 3.1.
A homer lamp
in a Pierreville
retiree's home.
Photo by author.

A Plant Representative of the French High-Technology Industry

The Pierreville plant has numerous characteristics that distinguish it from other manufacturing plants, such as its historical links to the military and its geographical isolation. But the demographics of its workforce are representative of those found in other French high-technology industries. The Pierreville workforce is predominantly male (approximately 85% in 2000, down from almost 90% in 1990), fairly technically skilled (often as a result of internal training), and middle-aged (average age of forty-three years, generally with older supervisors and younger executives and engineers).

Very few non-French citizens work in the plant by comparison to other plants that belong to broader French manufacturing industries, which often rely heavily on immigrants and second-generation immigrant workers. In 2005, just 50 of the 3,934 employees were non-French citizens, and half of those 50 came from other European countries. In that sense, Pierreville represents a higher class of French industry, which encompasses the basic chemical, glass, shipbuilding, automotive, and mechanical engineering industries.[1] In addition, Pierreville belongs to a state-owned organization; it is therefore not representative of French industry as a whole and could not be compared to other industries such as the textile industry (usually with a younger female workforce) or construction (with a larger predominance of immigrants).

Pierreville's main products are engines—mostly airplane engines. The AeroDyn organization was created after World War II and, by 2000, operated in several countries and employed approximately 40,000 individuals (one-quarter of whom lived outside France). In 2000, the company generated a multibillion-euro business. Historically, military buyers comprised the majority of AeroDyn's customer base, but through the years, civilian airlines and airplane manufacturers added to the company's clientele and gradually became AeroDyn's main focus. Throughout the period of study, approximately 4,000 people constituted the Pierreville plant's workforce.

In 1948, near a small airport on the outskirts of Paris, a set of nearly empty metal "barracks" were erected in a field, and Pierreville was born. Early on, preceding a wave of urbanization, people working there nicknamed the plant "a factory in the fields" (fig. 3.2). Over time, Pierreville slowly shifted its focus from in-flight engine testing to become AeroDyn's primary facility for research and development (starting mainly in 1963). By 1980, Pierreville also became the center for AeroDyn's engine assembly operations, which were once conducted at various AeroDyn sites throughout the country. Today, the plant consists of successive relocations of entire workshops and employees from various sites to the initial Pierreville plant.

By 2000, Pierreville's activities included engine assembly, testing, and repair; purchasing; maintenance; and research and development. In comparison to other manufacturing plants, two peculiarities stand out: first, the previously mentioned roar of engines being testing and, second, the large size of many of the workshops. Pierreville's testing

Fig. 3.2. The surrounding fields at Pierreville, with the plant in the distance. Photo by author.

chambers sit inside the plant but at its periphery, where finished engines are test run prior to their delivery to customers. The considerable size of many of the engines dictates not only the size of the workshops in which they are assembled and tested, but also the organization of their assembly. In the assembly workshops, teams of ten to fifteen workers are responsible for the final assembly of engines. The engines occupy most of the physical space. They are fixed to the ground (no conveyer belt), and workers learn to navigate around them. An elaborate performance takes place around these semifinished engines. The manner in which the workers attend to the engines can be likened to the way in which the staff of a maternity ward showers care and attention upon a roomful of newborn infants.

The overall composition of the factory workforce, as indicated, is predominantly male, middle-aged, and French. A closer examination of the shift in composition of the workforce highlights the increasing presence of "white-collar" populations in the plant. In 1977, workers (as defined by their legal employment category) accounted for nearly 30 percent of the workforce. By 2001, however, their percentage had dropped to just 15 percent.[2] By contrast, the percentage of technicians rose from 36 percent to 45 percent and executives and engineers, from 18 percent to 30 percent of the workforce. Moreover, autonomous work groups have slowly been introduced since the early 1980s, thereby contributing to the decline in supervisors as a percentage of the total workforce (down to 4% of the workforce in 2001 from 9% in 1977). Thus, Pierreville epitomizes the accelerated modernization of the French high-technology industry that sees itself more oriented toward research and development than toward manufacturing. In recent years, an increased reliance on subcontractors and on assembly in countries with comparatively lower wages further facilitated this change.

Pierreville also experienced more direct workforce adjustments, including pre-retirements and retirements, layoffs, and geographical transfers between AeroDyn sites that reflected changing corporate policies and the broader industry context. During the period from 1981 to 1984, an average of 3.42 percent of the Pierreville workforce retired or pre-retired each year (with a peak departure of 247 individuals in 1982), mainly to allow younger workers to be recruited and trained. This percentage is high in comparison with the average of 0.26 percent retirements and pre-retirements from 1977 to 2001 (excluding these four years). The ensuing periods from 1987 to 1988 and 1993 to 1999 coincided with mass layoffs in response to a declining demand for airplane engines. In each year during these two periods, AeroDyn terminated an average of 3.89 percent of the Pierreville workforce. Finally, in the 1990s, when AeroDyn redrafted the industrial configuration of its facilities, geographic transfers also contributed to changes in the workforce. In 1992, AeroDyn built a new unit near the Pierreville plant, the main purpose of which was to provide after-sale assistance to existing customers. The unit is just a few minutes away from Pierreville, and in 1992, several hundred employees were transferred there. In 1995, the experimental workshop at Pierreville (which housed several hundred Pierreville workers charged mainly with developing new engine prototypes) was transferred to AeroDyn's Terre-Neuve factory, thirty kilometers away (18.6 miles). All of these measures contributed to a combined sense of relative stability (e.g., overall workforce size) and change (e.g., arrival of new teams, mass departures) at Pierreville.

These changes in the Pierreville workforce were also reflected in the evolving political representation of the plant membership. French labor laws require the election of labor representatives to lead the factory Labor Council, and until 1979, Pierreville employees regularly favored members of the Confédération Générale du Travail (CGT) union, close to the French communist party. Starting in the early 1980s and to date, the less radical Confédération Française des Travailleurs Chrétiens—Confédération Française Démocratique du Travail (CFTC-CFDT)

gained the majority in the elections. This success is linked to the gradual arrival of more white-collar workers, which commenced after 1963
when AeroDyn focused its research teams at Pierreville, and to the experimental workshop's move in 1995.

Finally, another distinct characteristic of Pierreville is its factory museum, which stands just outside the factory gates. The museum was
started in 1985 as a joint venture of an association of retired factory
members (including the former director of the site) and AeroDyn. The
fairly large building that houses the museum belongs to AeroDyn, but
the retiree association manages the museum, which is a regular venue
for corporate events. The museum collection includes almost all of the
motors ever produced by AeroDyn, as well as panels that depict the
company's major developments and milestones, and past presidents,
test pilots, and other central figures in AeroDyn's history. In this same
building, a small workshop allows retirees to restore old engines for
exhibition. The museum proved an important resource for me while
writing this book. The plant retirees met once a week in its workshop—
a place I became well acquainted with during my regular visits. When
questions arose from interviews and discussions I conducted with
other retirees, I could always go to the museum and find a retiree who
could offer some clarification.

Assembling Engines at Pierreville

It is important to understand the nature of the activity conducted at
the plant, because it plays a large part in who Pierreville's retirees are.
By 2000, Pierreville members were assembling nearly one hundred airplane engines each month for aircraft manufacturers, commercial airlines, and military air forces. In addition to assembling engines, they
designed new engines and improved existing ones. The first component of engine construction requires steel parts, which were manufactured in an AeroDyn steel mill an hour away. Before arriving at
Pierreville, these parts were further shaped in another AeroDyn plant
(Terre-Neuve). The mill sent pieces to Terre-Neuve, located a half hour
from Pierreville, where they were assembled into semifinished elements. In addition to AeroDyn's own semifinished elements, the
Pierreville plant also received other semifinished elements from subcontractors or partner manufacturers. Upon delivery to the Pierreville
plant, workers assembled these many elements into engines, which
they then tested and delivered to customers. At any given moment at
Pierreville, either in the assembly or testing workshops, groups of men,

occasionally joined by a rare woman, bustled around silent or roaring engines, ensuring their correct manufacture and delivery.

The assembly workshops housed fairly autonomous teams of workers, where each team was responsible for the final assembly of an engine. In the late 1980s, AeroDyn began experimenting with self-managed or "autonomous" assembly teams. The company gradually applied this concept to the majority of its assembly teams. The main assembly workshops were divided into two different sectors (civilian and military) and evenly dispersed throughout the plant. There were very few women on these teams; in 2000, they accounted for only 5 of the 735 assembly workers. Workers spent as much energy if not more on the quality control and testing of the assembled engine elements as they did on the actual assembly. Most plant members were highly mindful of the extent to which hundreds of individuals—individuals who each day boarded airplanes equipped with AeroDyn engines—depended on the quality and precision of their work. Working on engines involves both heavy tasks, such as welding metallic components, and very delicate ones, such as wiring electrical elements to the outside of an engine. Welders focused on the former, whereas electricians executed the latter. Fitters tried to ensure that assembled elements were within the accepted official product specifications before they went to the "controllers" for quality inspection. Once AeroDyn implemented the concept of the autonomous team, self-control increasingly replaced ex-post control, thereby reducing (but not eliminating) the controller's role.

In addition to the main assembly workshops at Pierreville were a dozen testing workshops. Testing workshops were smaller buildings, that usually accommodated only a limited number of engines at a time. The testing phase involved analyzing engine reactions under conditions of extreme use to assess their reliability. Plant members who worked in these workshops had to install each engine on a fixed base, measure certain parameters during the tests (which were extremely loud), and inspect the engines after testing was complete. Both the testing teams and the engineers and technicians who worked in other areas of the plant analyzed the resulting data. Test procedures were constantly improved to expedite the tests. This entire process—from receiving parts and materials to delivering finished engines to clients—constituted the "mass assembly"—and most visible part—of the plant.

Designing and Developing Engines at Pierreville

An entirely different world, that of engine design and development, coexisted with the world of mass assembly. For the most part, the design and development work took place in Pierreville's technical department, broken down by engine part (propulsion, blades, body, etc.) and/or technical specialty (acoustics, aerodynamics, etc.). In 2000, the department employed more than 2,500 engineers, technicians, and workers. These individuals focused on any specific problems, from noise reduction to combustion, that the project management teams encountered in the development of new engines. In large part, they addressed the technological challenges posed by the physical constraints of flying. This often involved the development of new materials which had to be lightweight, yet resilient enough to resist high temperatures. The technical department consisted primarily of offices equipped with the latest computer technology used to create drawings and run models to visualize the impact of suggested modifications. The department encouraged communication and sometimes collaboration with external research laboratories or other manufacturers to insure they remained at the forefront of scientific discovery.

Computer modeling of engine tests was advantageous since, unlike the actual physical testing of an engine, computer models allowed the plant to run tests without incurring damage to the engines. For instance, one common danger during airplane takeoff and landing is accidental intake of flying birds into the engine. Historically, testing occurred in the workshops using actual dead birds. The resulting destruction often precluded any subsequent use of the tested engines. Modeling these tests on the computer, however, preserves the integrity of the engines, which are very costly. Although the birds posed just one of many problems the technical department faced, it illustrates the type of work this department engages in: constant back and forth between workshop and office, an increasing reliance on technology, and extremely high levels of specialization among department members. This example also suggests the gradual ways in which white-collar staff could replace blue-collar workers.

Until its move in 1995 to Terre-Neuve, the Pierreville experimental workshop worked alongside the technical department. Communication between the experimental workshop and the engineers and technicians occurred daily, thus facilitating the circulation of homer artifacts between these occupational groups. The workshop's primary task was to build prototypes of new engines and ensure that engineers' calculations executed well in practice. Part of AeroDyn's founding mission, in the wake of World War II, was to achieve independence for France in aeronautic technological capability. Many of the plant members who worked in the experimental workshop worked with engineers and technicians to attain this goal, which contributed to a feeling that they were indirectly participating in a valued collective mission.

The experimental workshop was more oriented toward craft than toward large-scale mass assembly, and subgroups of craftsmen occupied different parts of the workshop. The main subgroups were blacksmiths, welders, fitters, and electricians. (Pierreville did not keep records of membership by subgroup.) Blacksmiths shaped bars, rods, and pieces of metal by hand or with tools to produce or repair metal parts. They hammered, punched, and cut pieces of metal to size, and then shaped them on an anvil or another surface. Blacksmiths were, by far, the noisiest inhabitants of the experimental workshop. They took pride in being able to engage in multiple tasks, including some that fell under the jurisdiction of other craftsmen subgroups, such as welding. Welders constructed metal products by joining parts manually or by machine. The robustness of the engine depended on the welder's agility, so their work was also highly valued at Pierreville. In a similar manner, fitters assembled parts made from metal and other materials into engine parts. Most of the craftsmen in the experimental workshop, including fitters, also produced tools that were used to manufacture new engines, thereby broadening the variety of work they could engage in. Finally, electricians installed electrical wiring systems, essential to the operation and controls, in and around the engines. In French, the term *habiller*, used by the electricians, literally means "to put on clothes," which is just what they did—"dress" the engines. On occasion, when it was necessary to conduct a more detailed examination of a work in progress, engineers could be found interspersed among craftsmen in the experimental workshop. Many craftsmen considered themselves akin to independent contractors: working project by project, with their own tools, and fully responsible for their outcomes. With only one exception, a position involving bathing parts in chemicals (in order to modify their properties), most positions in the experimental workshop were considered fairly desirable, and few workers were eager to move.

The divide between mass assembly and research and development work did not undermine the communal sentiment expressed by many at Pierreville. They felt as if they were part of "a large family." For many plant members, this feeling extended beyond the physical workplace since they also interacted with each other outside the plant. A survey of Pierreville employees conducted in 1991 found that 20 percent lived within a zero- to ten-kilometer radius (0 to 6.21 miles) of the factory, 38 percent within ten to twenty kilometers (6.21 to 12.43 miles), 19 percent within twenty to thirty kilometers (12.43 to 18.64 miles), and only 23 percent lived more than thirty kilometers (18.64 miles) away.[3] Anecdotal evidence suggests that many Pierreville members engaged in hobbies or sports with one another outside work. Geographical

proximity coupled with extended tenure at the plant facilitated frater-
nization, both at work and outside of work.

French factory workers are not typically known to integrate their
work and family environments, but this does not mean Pierreville
members did not engage with colleagues in places other than their
homes.[4] Numerous social settings such as markets, shopping areas,
schools, and doctors' and dentists' offices offered venues for interaction. AeroDyn's bus service, which brought Pierreville members to and
from home and the plant, offered another venue for socializing outside
work. Finally, the Pierreville Labor Council organized numerous social
events (such as club gatherings, group outings to shows or large aeronautic events like the Paris Air Show, group holidays, and day camps
for children), which provided additional opportunities to socialize. In
spite of this "large family" feeling, distinctions between members remained clear.

Status Divides at Pierreville

Interview data highlight the status divides at Pierreville. Though the
rest of this book primarily revolves around one occupational group—
craftsmen—contextualizing their standing vis-à-vis other Pierreville
groups is central to understanding their high status and valued identity. At Pierreville, several status divides emerged. These divides operated along hierarchical, technical, and occupational lines.

In French workplaces, hierarchical status often coincides with the
legal categories of employment. Five such categories are found in manufacturing settings: workers (*ouvriers*), employees (*employés*), technicians (*techniciens*), supervisors (*maîtrise*), and executives or engineers
(*cadres*). In passing, Pierreville members frequently referred to these hierarchical distinctions, and informants proudly described their progres-
sions through the hierarchy (if any) during their careers. Workers at
Pierreville usually engaged in unskilled or skilled manual labor; employees typically occupied administrative and office jobs; technicians
normally had a few years of post-baccalaureate education; supervisors
were often ex-workers or technicians who were put in charge of a group
of ex-peers; and the last category, executives and engineers, included
employees with bachelor's degrees or higher levels of education. All of
Pierreville's trained engineers were cadres. Whereas in most French
work settings, executives and engineers are considered to have the
highest standing, in manufacturing settings, the need for highly skilled
manual labor complicates this hierarchy. Technical ability, for which
technical education serves as a proxy, also plays into status divides.

Technical education was an important factor in determining status in the plant. Workers who were hired because they did well on a professional entry exam were called "qualified" (even if they were in lower-level occupations). Qualified workers referred to themselves by profession (e.g., coppersmiths, metalworkers, welders, or fitters), whereas less skilled colleagues usually referred to their position in the workshop (e.g., operator of machine X). The certificate of professional aptitude, Certificat d'Aptitude Professionnelle (CAP) in French, which represents training that workers obtain before entering the plant, allowed me to identify the qualified workers in my survey and interviews. An incorrect assumption would lead one to believe that highly trained workers only performed highly skilled tasks. This was not always the case. Some individuals advanced to managerial positions, assumed administrative functions, or were asked, because they were needed somewhere else, to perform unskilled work (such as the assembling of mass-produced engines versus the manufacturing of new prototypes). Thus, the task a Pierreville member performed was not always fully commensurate with his or her social standing.

Instead, the occupational group to which a Pierreville member belonged was the most relevant status maker. Members of three distinct occupations were repeatedly lauded in the factory: test pilots, "great" designers or engineers, and craftsmen. But only the craftsmen constituted a strong, cohesive, high-status occupational group. Unlike the ten or so test pilots, craftsmen formed a large enough group (several hundred) to develop a strong identity. Moreover, by contrast to the engineers, craftsmen as a whole seemed to be viewed as high status, whereas only a small subset of engineers (thirty out of several hundred) were deemed "great."

Test pilots flew planes equipped with new engines to assess their safety and robustness. By 1972, however, AeroDyn had transferred all in-flight testing activities to another location. Nevertheless, the memory of these test pilots lives on. Several pilots, specifically during the early times in the 1950s and 1960s, lost their lives during these tests. As one technician noted, "These were people who risked their lives more than we did." Test pilots were few since generally only one was assigned to each new engine, and new engines could take many years to complete. (Less than ten test pilot names were cited in the seventy interviews I conducted.) Test pilots often represented the public face of Pierreville in external news coverage and internal communication. They enjoyed a high level of respect at Pierreville, and speaking against any one of them seemed almost taboo. One telling episode is that of a test pilot who accidently knocked over a toolbox that belonged to a highly skilled worker. This worker, who was fixing the pilot's plane, interpreted the gesture as a sign of disrespect and started a fight with the pilot. The worker's supervisor punished him by reassigning him to work, until his retirement, with younger engineers in a nontechnical capacity outside the main factory. His colleagues subsequently called him "The Rebel." At Pierreville, the individuals who actually flew the planes received the greatest respect and were heralded as exemplars of what the plant stood for.

A subset of the Pierreville engineers who designed engines also received a high level of respect. Those referred to as "great" designers or engineers were a well-known and popular subset of engineers who invented new processes and engine parts. Interviews suggested a total of thirty "great" designers or engineers during the period from 1970 to 2000. Designing an engine core, namely the "hot" (core) part of the engine where combustion occurs, was more prestigious than working on other parts of the engine. A retired ("nongreat") engineer who never got to work on the "hot" parts, but instead spent his career in acoustics, noted, "Working on the pollution of an engine is not the same as working on the engine per se. Noise is in some ways a byproduct—pollution—associated with what engines do. I would have preferred to work on another area, for instance, the core dynamics of the engine." Great engineers mostly worked on the core. As engine design became more integrated and involved larger teams, however, it became more difficult to identify designers or engineers as "great" ones.

The third high-status group at Pierreville was that of the craftsmen (*compagnons*, or companions, in French). Unlike the aforementioned test pilots and great engineers, there were enough craftsmen to constitute a cohesive, visible group, which resulted in their collective rather than their individual recognition. Moreover, most craftsmen could claim high status (unlike only select engineers and designers). Administrative staff sometimes referred to craftsmen as "golden hands." They often expected new supervisors to address them in the *vous* (you) form, which, in French, denotes respect, instead of the informal *tu* form. In addition, their work on experimental prototype development distinguished many craftsmen from the other workers engaged in the mass assembly of engines. A craftsman usually possessed his own tools, always received technical training (a CAP), and was identified at Pierreville by his profession (e.g., welder, blacksmith).[5] The highest concentration of craftsmen could be found in the experimental workshop, where blacksmiths, welders, fitters, and others worked. To a lesser extent, testing workshops and some maintenance workshops that were attached to the larger assembly workshops also employed craftsmen. Craftsmen constructed their occupational identity in opposition to less skilled manual labor (in this case, assembly labor). Less skilled laborers were often timed in the performance of their tasks, whereas craftsmen had less time constraints. Or as one craftsman said, "We spent the necessary time to do the job." In 1982, the transfer of several hundred assembly workers from other AeroDyn plants to Pierreville highlighted these divisions. A former union assembly worker remarked that even though he was part of the same union as other craftsmen in the experimental workshop, he often felt "separated" and found it difficult to interact with his fellow (higher status) union members. His presence, as he put it, seemed to "devalue their work."

This is to be expected if Roger's reaction to unskilled laborers, detailed here, exemplified that of other craftsmen. Roger began working for AeroDyn as a blacksmith in 1952. Prior to joining AeroDyn, he once spent a summer working as a metal cutter—a position typically held by less skilled laborers at Pierreville, not blacksmiths. "I needed some money during the holidays," he recalled, "and left because it wasn't a solution; to be a cutter is given to anybody willing to do that, right? It still is part of blacksmithing. Welding, cutting, shaping, drawing, etc., all are part of blacksmithing. Blacksmithing, you see, is a type of work that deals with all the metal aspects in the firm. A good blacksmith can [also] make a good draftsman, a good shaper, a good welder, etc."

So, while anybody could be an unskilled laborer, belonging to the craftsmen group was a desirable distinction. The promise of practicing as a craftsman drew many into employment at AeroDyn. Two craftsmen, Alain and Manuel, who began working for AeroDyn nearly thirty-five years apart (1946 and 1982, respectively), both described their motivation to work for AeroDyn as the desire to engage in rewarding work with their hands. Moreover, both saw an opportunity for professional development at AeroDyn. Alain worked in the automotive industry for four years before he started at AeroDyn. He decided to apply to AeroDyn because he had "no future" where he was working. "If one stayed in my old job 'the hands on the wheels,' as we used to say at that time, we were stuck at that level. We had no future. Since I was good at my work, I decided to look elsewhere. So I came for a test at AeroDyn, and this test that I could not pass with my former employer, I successfully passed this time." Almost sixty years later, Alain was able to recall the details of the test, especially the risk of grinding the inside of a manufactured piece too much and destroying it in the process. Once he passed the test, Alain began working as a welder for AeroDyn in the experimental workshop.

By contrast, Manuel, a fitter by trade, came to AeroDyn with more experience. He had lived overseas, he had owned a garage, and he knew how to fly planes. He was looking for a job in 1982, and learned that AeroDyn was looking for fitters. He needed work, but the prospect of working for AeroDyn frightened him. Factory work sounded constraining. So when he saw the assembly work he was supposed to do, he asked if he could move to a more interesting job in the testing workshop. AeroDyn promised they would transfer him within a year. Having owned a garage, he knew that he would enjoy technical, manual work and the opportunity to engage in difficult tasks. Manuel accepted the position. As promised, within a year, and for the next ten years he spent at Pierreville, Manuel remained in the testing workshops. The job allowed him to replicate, within the setting of the plant, his desire to be an independent entrepreneur. His only regret was that he was not able to become a test pilot; by the time he was hired, test pilots had already been relocated to another site.

The ways in which craftsmen epitomized some of the plant's aspirations are critical to understanding the emerging occupational dynamics around homers. On the rare occasions when craftsmen did not get along with their supervisors, being reassigned to menial work, even though they would maintain their salaries, was a genuine threat. Unless clear physical limitations due to age or an accident motivated a reassignment, craftsmen viewed reassignments to menial work as severe forms of punishment. Working was, of course, preferable to unemployment, but menial assembly work implied a loss of independence. This demonstrates how two key concepts, manual skills and independence, further inform status variations among Pierreville members. An overview of each will yield insight into why craftsmen were so highly regarded at Pierreville.

Manual Skills as a Status Enhancer

Plant members repeatedly stressed the value of being able to do something with their hands. Both at the individual level and the collective level, plant members attempted to convey their ability to craft something from nothing; in some instances they did so by mimicking the behaviors of those at a higher skill level than their own. Mimicking was common at the individual level, specifically when the bystander was not in a position to properly assess the manual skills of the informant. The account of a formerly unskilled laborer, Richard, provides an example of this type of behavior.

Richard started off as an unskilled laborer and was gradually promoted to a supervisory position in an engine testing workshop. Though quite skilled with his hands, he was not able to produce artifacts as delicate and elaborate as those the craftsmen often made. He did make a fairly elegant homer, though, that depicted a flying crane above a dented wheel (traditional symbols of the aeronautic industry). He proudly commented, "I did this one, as I mentioned, with my own hands. I found some scrap copper, I drew the flying crane and then I glued it together. I made it with a nail file. I spent hours on it." I later learned from craftsmen that this homer could have been made much faster with other tools, and that relative to others', his work was not very precise. Nevertheless, Richard's insistence on the time and effort he put into his artifact was a way for him to enhance his status. Although he was not a craftsman, he could emulate one in front of noncraftsmen.

At the collective level, these attempts were most visible among the quality control staff. Controllers were assigned to specific work groups to verify that engines were built correctly. Whereas controllers were subject to less geographical constraint than other workers, craftsmen mocked them because of their role as inspectors rather than producers. Like each of the craftsmen, the manager of the quality control group passed a practical technical exam upon joining AeroDyn. Over time, however, he was promoted away from the workshop and into a quality control function. Sixty years later when I met him, he could still recall what was asked of him on the day of his exam, and when he was in a position to decide who to recruit as a quality controller, he instituted a compulsory practical exam for all recruits. Though many controllers were not craftsmen, the exam he instituted was meant to mimic rituals normally associated with craftsmen. He said, "even individuals with higher degrees had to succeed on a small [practical] exam, including two or three problems in their field of concentration, either electronics or mechanics." These attempts to mimic the manual skills of craftsmen were all the more paradoxical for a function essentially geared toward assessing finished products or machinery and writing reports. Craftsmen often teased quality controllers—on whom they depended to get approval for their finished products—by calling them names such as "paper shitters" or "ink shitters." Nonetheless, controllers tried to associate with the craftsmen's rituals.

These tensions between Pierreville members highlight what was necessary to gain status in the plant. Though office work was sometimes associated with a higher "grade" level and therefore translated into higher salaries, it also carried the stigma of not producing any concrete material outcomes aside from paperwork. Workers placed great value on their ability to create with their hands. Laurent, an unskilled laborer working in an assembly workshop, recalled when some of his friends transferred from the office back to his workshop. Laurent opined that they transferred because "they were fed up; they found that offices were a bit monotonous and since they realized that assembly work was active, they came back." Ironically, Laurent's son was a notary public who performed office work exclusively. As he ambiguously put it when he described his son's profession: he earned a good living, but it was his son's own "problem" that he decided to earn it by doing office work.

Manual skills were assessed primarily in the plant environment, but they were sometimes also evaluated based on work done in other settings. For instance, work completed at home and showcased at the plant (such as additions to a motorcycle or automobile) could also serve as a status enhancer.[6] Manual skills were developed through practice; idleness, or for that matter, sitting at a desk as office employees do, was construed as impeding such development. Thus, a "respectable" retirement meant moving on to other activities. Alain's account of retirement illustrates this. A recent retiree who enjoyed gardening and riding his bicycle in the countryside, he explained, "One can keep busy without work, and I do a lot of stuff since I retired. I could not have stayed here doing nothing. I would have a hard time doing that." His wife then interjected that she was surprised that he and I were still sitting around their kitchen table. We had been sitting for almost an hour, talking over coffee.

Independence as a Status Enhancer

But manual work was not the only kind valued at Pierreville: independent work towered in importance over interdependent manual activity. In an environment in which most tasks were intertwined, the luxury of being able to work independently on a piece, with little outside input, was rare. Manuel, the former garage owner and pilot, talked about the independence he enjoyed testing airplane engines. When an engine arrived, he was solely responsible for making sure it ran smoothly. Other craftsmen echoed this ideal of independence. "We were part of AeroDyn, you see," said Roger, a blacksmith who once worked in the experimental workshop, "but really we were independent from AeroDyn," he immediately added. The tensions craftsmen felt when they interacted with quality controllers also epitomized this ideal; it was as if they needed to tease them because they felt controllers were, in a way, robbing them of their autonomy.

Jacques, a blacksmith who received a miniature replica of his workstation when he left Pierreville, described to me in great detail the manufacturing processes employed in his workshop. When he finished working on a piece, he would pass it on to quality control. The controller would take some measurements, but the blacksmiths would also measure the piece before the controller received it, because they knew that bad pieces would be rejected. They used what he referred to as "blacksmith tricks" to make sure the piece fit the expected standards. He would never share these tricks with the controllers since "it was none of their business." Ultimately, however, it was the controller's stamp of approval that went on the piece. Jacques referred to this as the controller's signature (not his own). He then added that they were in no position to "make decisions." If he noticed something wrong, he would alert his supervisors. In rare cases, engineers from the research department would come down to the workshop when pieces went wrong. "They [the engineers] had drafts, and they would make decisions, because we didn't. It was forbidden. We were supposed to follow the specs."

Even the most skilled workers felt somewhat constrained in their work autonomy. Safety concerns justified these constraints (the controller's stamp, the standards, the oversight of the engineers) and Jacques perfectly understood this. Nonetheless, the ideal of an independent worker fully in control of his or her output loomed large. In that sense, when a homer-maker said, "I made this homer myself," it evoked the values primarily associated with higher status in the plant: manual work and independence

---

Within the Pierreville plant, craftsmen constituted a high-status occupational group. Unlike the other high-status groups (the test pilots and the great engineers), the sheer size of the craftsmen group and their cohesiveness helped them build a strong collective identity. Though subdivisions among craftsmen existed (blacksmiths, for instance, enjoyed a higher status than welders), they presented a fairly united front when dealing with other social groups. Craftsmen grounded their identity in skilled manual work and independence. They relied on their prior technical training and the continued practice of their trades to position themselves as a distinct social group.

To be called a craftsman (or a compagnon) clearly indicated belonging to a distinct community. Craftsmen used this term with each other, but were also referred to in this way by other plant members. Pierreville internal communication also labeled them in this way. With these distinctions in mind—specifically the unique position craftsmen held—the next chapters offer an analysis of narratives around homer activities. Retirement homers, which mark one's departure from Pierreville, provide the entry point into this homer community. These retirement homers signaled the end of the roaring noise of tested engines. More important, they also pointed to the exit from a plant in which many spent decades working.

Part Two

THE FINDINGS

4

Retirement Homers: An Entry into the Community

THE PRACTICE of giving retirement homers, or gifts given to departing colleagues, and by extension, the gray zone practices that lead to making them, constitute the most tolerated and visible homer gray zone at Pierreville. These homers are presented in what are often semipublic ceremonies, and plant members are more willing to comment on this type of homer than on any other. Focusing first on retirement homers therefore provides a fairly nonthreatening way to ease into the homer community (spanning all levels of the plant hierarchy, including management). It also allows for the identification of the specific role the craftsmen play in this practice.

Results of a survey on retirement gifts administered to a random sample of Pierreville retirees suggest that craftsmen are very likely recipients of retirement homers. But craftsmen are not the only ones who receive these gifts, so looking at retirement homers given to other Pierreville plant members might also yield insight into occupational identity dynamics at play within organizational gray zones. This chapter focuses on retirement homer activities that occur in and across occupational lines. These activities include those among craftsmen, those between craftsmen and management, and those between craftsmen and lower status Pierreville members (such as office workers and unskilled laborers).[1] Ultimately, craftsmen remain at the center of these homer activities.

Retirement Gifts and Retirement Homers

Assessing the receiving patterns of retirement homers helps illuminate who is likely to be involved in and benefit from this gray zone. To better understand the patterns, a broad survey on retirement gifts at Pierreville (both homers and commercially purchased gifts) was sent out to Pierreville retirees. Receiving a commercially purchased gift upon departure was common at Pierreville. Most survey respondents (84%) reported receiving such gifts, including fishing rods, bicycles,

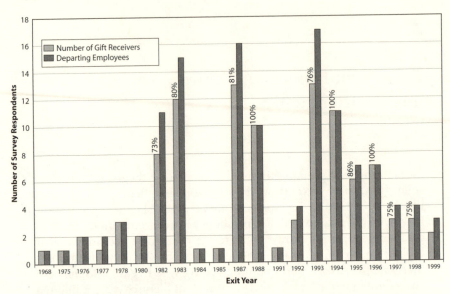

Fig. 4.1. Retirement gifts for departing employees (in percent of departures by year). Note: This figure was constructed based on survey responses (N = 124). Only the years for which respondents provided data appear in this figure. Fishing rods, bicycles, garden chairs, televisions, video players, and tools are some examples of gifts.

skis, garden chairs, radios, televisions, VCRs, and tools. Many of those who did not receive gifts (16%) left at a time when the number of departing employees was extremely high (more than 150 departures over the course of a year due to retirement, pre-retirement, and/or layoffs). Aside from these historical peaks, no other factor (such as tenure in the factory, hierarchical level, employment in the experimental workshop, or technical training) explained whether or not one received a departing gift. (Popularity might have been an important factor, but other than controlling for tenure in the factory, no ex-post measure of employee popularity was attempted.) With this caveat in mind, receiving a gift such as a television or a fishing rod (not a homer) appeared to be a fairly common practice. Figure 4.1 shows the relative frequency of receiving gifts upon departure from the factory.

Receiving a retirement homer, however, reflected a more selective process. Only 34 percent of the sampled respondents received one. Figure 4.2 shows the frequency of retirement homer reception upon departure from the plant.[2] Pierreville members used the term retirement homer as shorthand for departure homer since AeroDyn offered many employees early pre-retirement packages or negotiated layoffs. When

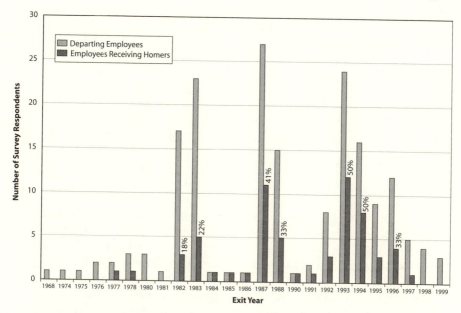

Fig. 4.2. Retirement homers for departing employees (in percent of departures by year). Note: This figure was constructed based on survey responses (N = 184). Only the years for which respondents provided data appear in this figure.

asked who received retirement homers, the standard answer was that it was "random" or "depended on one's luck." A more perceptive craftsman nonetheless specified:

> Most Pierreville members do not get a retirement homer. In some ways, it's a bit random. Let's say between 20 and 30% of us received one. There first needs to be someone who is willing to do it . . . "Do something for Paul," and then the excitement starts. It is luck, chance . . . You need to be in a network—it's a question of possibility. Someone needs to think it up in advance, find the guy in the control department to give you the scrap piece, the guy to give you the scrap blade, and find the people who will make the wooden base. Many parameters can block the system and make it halt.

Despite the prevailing sense of randomness, a closer look at the data reveals clear patterns of who received retirement homers: technical training (holding a CAP degree) was an important predictor, followed to a lesser extent by employment in the experimental workshop. (See table 4.1 for these results.) These observed patterns of receiving retirement homers at Pierreville suggest some intra-craftsmen group dynamics; craftsmen are assumed to be the main producers of homers, but they are also the main recipients—of retirement homers, at least.[3] Given that retirement homers are products of craft, the fact that highly skilled craftsmen (with a CAP) and those who practiced in the experimental workshop (more likely to work on prototype development) tended to receive retirement homers is somewhat expected. Interestingly, hierarchy did not explain whether one received a homer or not. Supervisors and executives as well as technicians were equally likely to receive them. The relative illegality of retirement homers (taking time away from "work" time) did not prevent members from giving them to those in higher levels of the hierarchy. Moreover, during the time span covered by this study, the practice did not seem to decrease. (Factory hire dates and dates of departure offerred no explanation of retirement homer reception patterns.) Informants claimed that homer-making was becoming increasingly difficult because of a dearth of available skills, accessible materials, and time, yet retirement homers were still manufactured at Pierreville for the duration of this study.

Thus, receiving patterns of retirement homers—the most tolerated homers in the plant—suggest hierarchical involvement at the highest level. Moreover, the Pierreville members who were most likely to receive retirement homers held either or both of previously identified status markers: technical education via the possession of a CAP degree and/or practicing craftsmanship in the experimental workshop. Whereas these initial findings do not indicate much about the interactions leading to the manufacture of retirement homers, they do show that craftsmen occupy a unique position in the receiving pattern. Given their strong occupational identity in the plant, it is necessary to further examine their interactions with other Pierreville members. Although homer activities frequently involved multiple plant members, most homer events from the interview data were narrated in a dyadic context. This allows for the isolation of craftsmen-only retirement homer interactions from those that involved lower-level hierarchical members (e.g., office workers or unskilled laborers) and higher-level hierarchical members (e.g., supervisors, engineers, or executives).

Retirement Homers among Craftsmen

Retirement homers given among craftsmen were often narrated with reference to the work in which the recipient engaged. Respect was commonly associated with these artifacts. In many instances, the retirement homers given to craftsmen evoked respect by depicting the recipient's occupation, the contributions the individual made to specific engine developments, or the expertise for which the recipient was

TABLE 4.1.
Factors Determining Who Receives a Retirement Homer[1]
(N = 184, Logistic Regression Results)

Variables	b
Exit Year	.022
	(.049)
Entry Year	-0.034
	(.032)
Number of Years Spent at Pierreville (Only)	-.008
	(.027)
Male	2.460*
	(.975)
Employment in the Experimental Workshop	1.109*
	(.549)
Technical Training[2]	1.424**
	(.449)
Hierarchical Level[3]	
Employees	-1.999†
	(1.143)
Technicians	-.136
	(.647)
Supervisors	.040
	(.769)
Executives/Engineers	-.403
	(.738)

[1] Receipt of a retirement homer was coded as "1" and not receiving one as "0."
[2] Technical training was coded as "1" for respondents with a Certificat d'Aptitude Professionnelle (CAP) or Brevet Professionnel (BP), and "0" for respondents who did not have those degrees. Those who held a BP usually already held a CAP. Thus, in the analysis, those with a CAP or a BP were abbreviated as holding a CAP.
[3] Comparison group is "workers" since most craftsmen were concentrated in that category.
† $p < .10$, *$p < .05$, **$p < .01$

known. A typical example of this type of artifact was given to Jacques, a blacksmith who showed me his retirement homer (a miniature reproduction of his work environment), which he proudly displayed in his home (fig. 4.3). "These were pals, the friends at my workshop who did this. We got along fairly well. This is the sand bag. The sand bag allows you to stretch metal. Here, that's the marble, for when we needed to manufacture small pieces . . . and the stool." Jacques then went on to describe every tool of his trade. By depicting his trade, in detail, his peers, his "pals," conveyed their respect for his skill: being a blacksmith in the factory was a position of honor.

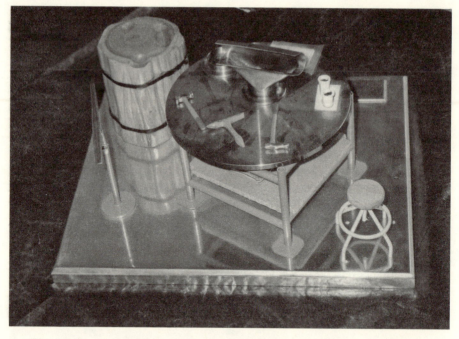

Fig. 4.3. A retirement homer gift given to a blacksmith. Photo by C. Blanchet.

In another illustrative case, a craftsman—whose job was to go to the sites of crashed planes to technically assess the damage suffered by AeroDyn engines—received a burnt aluminum compressor that was found after a crash and mounted on wood. And another craftsman, who spent most of his career working on one type of engine model, received a fully motorized miniature replica of the model upon retirement. One might reasonably assume that the amount of time and level of skill involved in the production of a retirement homer are what informed its value. Whereas this certainly contributed to the value, it also depended on how the homer was made. Craftsmen who received retirement homers often described the work and the coordinated efforts their coworkers engaged in to manufacture the artifact before talking about the artifact itself. The artifact alone rarely suggested respect; instead, the interactions that led to the manufacture of the gift were what indicated respect. Thus, how the artifact was made and who made it greatly influenced the retirement homer's underlying meaning.

The following example also illustrates the respect encapsulated in retirement homer interactions among craftsmen. Philippe, a blacksmith, built small models that were tested in wind tunnels. Throughout his career, he mainly depended on other craftsmen, often carpen-

Fig. 4.4. Wooden keel with wings. Photo by author.

ters, who complemented his skills. A few weeks before his retirement, he noticed one of his peers, a carpenter, working with a piece of wood that had been fashioned into a wing. Philippe said, "I told him, 'What you are making is beautiful' "; the carpenter agreed. It was not until weeks later, when Philippe received a wooden keel with attached wooden wings, that he realized he had seen his retirement homer in the making (fig. 4.4). In France, a keel commonly symbolizes the end of military conscription—and by extension, the end of an engagement. In this case, it was one of Philippe's closest work peers who made the wings: "It pleased me to see this, because it represented work. You know? A keel is easy to make with a wheel, but essentially it's the work on the wings. The two wings represent aviation. The keel represents a departure, but the wings represent an aeronautic worker. It was done by my coworker."

The same held true for the homer-makers. What homer-makers sought to achieve by making retirement homers was to express their respect for departing colleagues. The homer-makers were more willing to work on retirement homers for individuals they respected: "If someone asked us to do something for him, like this retirement homer," a craftsman pointed out, "we had to have esteem for him. If not, we did not do it, we grumbled. We would ask, 'Who is it for?' And then we would say, 'Hmm, we'll see. If we find time.' " Both the makers and the recipients of retirement homers were aware that the artifacts were embedded in close work communities. The individuals involved in creating the gifts and the interactions that gave rise to them were what made peer-related retirement homers so valuable. As one retirement homer-maker recalled, "This would have no meaning [for the recipient and me] if I had not made this gift myself. We do all we can here [at Pierreville]. If not, it has no meaning."

This understanding of respect around retirement homers also explains the disappointment of not receiving one, specifically when someone worked in a workshop in a skilled occupation. Reasons for not receiving a retirement homer varied from a perceived lack of respect to job mobility or periods of high numbers of retirements and layoffs. Georges, a former craftsman, commented, "I would have liked at least a blade when I left AeroDyn, but it was out of the question. Besides, we didn't celebrate my retirement—it was a discrete departure." Georges attributes this "discrete" departure (which also means without a retirement homer) to being transferred out of the workshop where he spent most of his career to an after-sales unit before retiring. He subsequently lost touch with his colleagues. Geographic mobility was often required for official promotions, but it also tended to gradually dissolve the bonds with initial coworkers. Luc, a former craftsman who was promoted in the late 1980s to work in a maintenance position overseas and in other AeroDyn plants, was also upset that he did not receive a retirement homer. "When you move, it's difficult [to receive a retirement homer]. I spent 36 years at AeroDyn. I spent time at Pierreville, in Toulouse, in Hamburg and in the United States, always working for AeroDyn. But when I retired, I felt as if I had lost it all; I only got a very small gift."

The occurrence of a large number of departures at about the same time was another reason certain people did not receive a retirement

Fig. 4.5. A common homer made from an engine blade. Photo by author.

homer. Members were less likely to receive a retirement homer during years with more than 150 departures resulting from retirement, pre-retirement, or layoffs.[4] These trends also modified the dynamics of retirement homer manufacturing. One worker recalled: "At the start of the layoffs, what happened was the large-scale development of retirement gifts. And this was also done with hierarchical tacit approval. This meant that instead of creating individual pieces in a small, personalized series, we started with ten or twenty pieces in a series that we completed for a specific date. And we used to say, okay, we know that December 31 there will be twenty departures because there was a layoff."

Though the way in which artifacts were manufactured was most important in determining their value for participants, their external appearance also mattered. Georges, the former craftsmen quoted earlier, stated that he would have liked "at least" a blade. Many craftsmen, and even workers, would prefer to receive something other than an engine blade. Engine blades (such as the one shown in fig. 4.5) made nice home decor but were relatively easy to manufacture and deemed almost generic by most craftsmen. When asked if he would appreciate an engine blade as a retirement homer, another craftsman was quick to reply: "To be honest, no. For a director, yes! But not for someone like me who saw these [blades] all his life, and who would have seen much nicer ones go through his hands. [He shakes his head to indicate his disapproval.] So, personally, it would not do much for me. These kinds of gifts are more for directors, high-ranking executives, people like that, but for me, honestly? No. I must admit that a worker is more partial to a personal artifact that is uniquely manufactured."

These examples of retirement homer interactions among craftsmen imply that although at first artifacts appeared to encapsulate meanings, it was also, and often more important, the interactions that gave rise to them that allowed craftsmen to make sense of the retirement homers they received. When a craftsman received a retirement homer from coworkers, the gift was often construed as a double form of respect: respect, on one side, expressed by the homer-makers for the recipient and, on the other, by the recipient for the homer-makers.

Retirement Homers Up the Hierarchy

When retirement homer interactions occurred up the hierarchy, the meanings of the artifacts and the interactions leading to their production were quite different from those among craftsmen. The homer interactions sometimes suggested respect, but they were mostly akin to regular work—with the particularity that the practice seemed to make the hierarchy uneasy. Retirement homer interactions "up the hierarchy" are the retirement homer interactions that occurred between craftsmen and supervisors, engineers or executives. In the official plant hierarchy, the recipients or the requesters of the retirement homers ranked above craftsmen.[5]

Although supervisors, engineers, and executives usually appreciated receiving retirement homers, they also sometimes slightly devalued or mocked their gifts, suggesting that the artifacts and, by extension, the interactions that led to their creation, should not be taken too seriously. The connection between these homers and respect was much less salient. Instead, higher-level members depicted homer-makers as "having fun." In a few instances, homer-makers intended the gifts to be funny (e.g., an airplane with chicken feet), although generally this was not the intention of most retirement homers. The subtle mockery by some members of the Pierreville hierarchy of the retirement homers they received signaled their discomfort with homer practices. Those higher in the hierarchy frequently asked craftsmen to make retirement homers for their friends, who were often at the same or a higher hierarchical level than they were. Thus, unlike homer-making among craftsmen, many higher-level recipients of retirement homers could not narrate the sequence of receiving a homer as pure respect. The commissioner of the artifact evidently respected the recipient, but the craftsmen who created the artifact acted as much, if not more, out of obligation to their boss than out of respect for the person who received the gift.

A higher-level member of the plant hierarchy who received a homer often needed to laugh about the gift.[6] The following example of an upper-level executive describing a retirement homer he received illustrates this alternate meaning of homer practices. Marc was a high-ranking executive who spent his entire career in quality control. He recalled the gift he received when he retired: "Yes, there was a homer ... a manometer with a crooked pointer, but what can I say? It wasn't anything sensational. And I also got a battered blade with a tag on it indicating that it was scrap material [laughs]. They had fun making it." Though Marc was aware of my broader interest in homers, during the two-hour exchange we shared, this was the only reference he made to them. The gifts either were peripheral to his occupation or they were embarrassing to him. Concomitant to his ambivalence around retirement homers was ambivalence around retirement ceremonies and ceremonies at Pierreville in general—fairly common among higher-level Pierreville members. This was truer for executives and engineers than for supervisors. The social ceremonies and rituals in the factory probably seemed to collide with the competitive image Pierreville wanted to project to the outside world.[7] Denis, a former high-ranking production executive, expressed his annoyance with the ceremonies: "Personally, I am a bit against these events for departures and all that. I am anti-these-kinds-of-things, celebrating birthdays, getting together to drink. . . . We are here for things other than that." Jacqueline, another executive, reinforced his point. However she took a slightly different angle with her critique. Her reluctance rested more in her ambivalence toward her coworkers than in the disruption the ceremonies can cause: "[Departure ceremonies] are among the things I like so-so. I don't really like going away parties. There is so much hypocrisy in the speeches. Among the masses, there always is a minority to whom the party means something important. One therefore has to organize a party. But, in general, all the speeches are rather hypocritical."

Each of these individuals (Marc, Denis, and Jacqueline) was in a position to veto the organization of any ceremony or party in their department. And upper management did. They justified such vetoes with legitimate health and safety concerns. (Alcohol served at a party in the proximity of a workshop could create a potentially dangerous situation.) But the executives' and engineers' reluctance to endorse any kind of unofficial ceremony at Pierreville went further. This reluctance translated into a factory-wide official ban on retirement ceremonies, and by the late 1990s, retirement ceremonies were to take place only outside the plant. Unless an understanding boss turned a blind eye to the rules and offered his office or workshop as a place to hold a party, ceremonies were held outside the factory gates. Just as retirement homers were viewed differently depending on participants' relative occupational statuses, retirement ceremonies at Pierreville also carried distinct meanings. Several retired craftsmen showed me photo albums of these ceremonies and described them in great detail, but few executives or engineers kept photographic evidence of their departure. This does not mean they did not organize parties for themselves, but the parties usually consisted of lunches at the Pierreville restaurant or, in some instances, private dinners at their homes with only a few close colleagues.

Such ambivalence toward retirement ceremonies and retirement homers also suggests ambivalence toward the practices leading to the creation of the retirement homers. Though retirement homers were openly embraced in semipublic ceremonies that often involved higher-level members of the hierarchy, this same hierarchy was probably less eager to discuss homers because they attributed a different meaning to them. Given that retirement homers were often narrated as commanded gifts (from the perspective of craftsmen), the discomfort exhibited by higher-level Pierreville members (who ordered these gifts) probably reflects reservations they had about their *own* behavior. Overall, retirement homers that involved craftsmen and the Pierreville hierarchy were narrated with less of an emphasis on respect. Whereas the examination of retirement homer practices among craftsmen (or peers) unveils the interplay between homer meanings and the craftsmen's identity, this section highlights ways in which the irruption of participants with distinct occupational backgrounds (here, the higher-level hierarchy) can change these meanings.[8] A closer look at retirement homers given down the hierarchy further informs these variations.

Retirement Homers Down the Hierarchy

At Pierreville, unskilled workers and office employees occupied a lower social position than craftsmen. Given the overwhelming focus of discussion among Pierreville members on the concrete tasks required to transform metal into airplane engines, the presence of staff in "support" functions might easily go unnoticed. However, office employees constituted 6 percent of the total Pierreville workforce in 2001 (down from 10% during the period from 1983 to 1987). Moreover, a conservative estimate provided by labor leaders puts the number of unskilled workers at half of the legal employment category of workers.[9] Thus, unskilled workers encompassed approximately 7 percent of the Pierreville workforce in 2001 (down from 14% during the period from 1977 to 1982). Therefore, in 2001, the total percentage of lower-level Pierreville members, including office employees and unskilled workers, amounted to roughly 13 percent.[10]

The most typical retirement homer that traveled down the hierarchy involved craftsmen and an unskilled worker or an office employee, and was usually quite simple: a keel with no added work, or a small scrap engine blade. These retirement homers were less associated with the recipients' specific jobs in the factory. Instead, they evoked broader Pierreville work themes (such as the "end of work" for the keel and "the conquest of space" for engine blades). Not receiving such a gift was disappointing, but at the same time, expectations for receiving one were low. Laurent, an unskilled laborer who worked in the assembly workshop, wished he had received a retirement homer. When asked what he would have wanted, he answered: "I would have liked maybe an engine blade. I often used to work on the blades. Even a small blade on a small base. I don't know . . . yeah . . . something small like that. More than anything else, I worked on blade assembly—the discs. I would have been pleased. You know?" Moreover, when they discussed retirement homers traveling down the hierarchy, craftsmen stressed the ease with which they could make them and their relative insignificance. The simplicity of the artifact was usually pointed out first, but they equally stressed their often low involvement in the activities associated with making the artifact. In some instances, the relationship between the retirement homer's maker and the recipient appeared to hardly predate the retirement homer interactions. The craftsman might engage in such work because the requester was a friend (but not always the recipient—which put the homer receiver at a distance from the craftsman) or because the recipient/requester offered something in return. Thus, interactions around retirement homers involving lower-level Pierreville members took on very different meanings than those among craftsmen.

The following account offered by Pierre, an unskilled laborer, stands in stark contrast to those offered by craftsmen regarding retirement homer interactions among peers. Pierre had access to materials and, therefore, could sometimes provide craftsmen with the materials they needed to build homers. When I met Pierre at his home, he showed me a keel that was made for his mother-in-law. He wanted to give her a gift for her retirement, so he paid a craftsman to make the keel. When

I inquired if he knew the people who made it for him, Pierre replied: "No, not at all. I didn't know them well, but we would sometimes meet for work. And in my work relations, I tried to help others out, and if I gave them something in return, then they would do it for me. I knew they would. They would do it to thank me when I provided them with material [or cash, as he had provided to have the keel made for his mother-in-law]."

The gray zone practices around retirement homers between crafts-men and lower-level Pierreville members often seemed to lack the in-tensity of those among craftsmen. Perhaps it was because participants did not work in great physical proximity. This did not indicate an ab-sence of respect in the relationship, but as Pierre's account illustrated, the interactions were narrated entirely differently—almost as imper-sonal transactions. Such transactions still required a small level of trust since homer activities could lead to termination. But the necessary trust seemed minimal. Also, lower-status recipients were much quicker to acknowledge that the homer materials were "stolen." Though recipi-ents clearly knew that most homers were made from scrap materials, they also qualified the scraps as stolen—an association craftsmen never made. Thus, gray zone retirement homer interactions down the hierar-chy often described amicable but distanced interactions that were, in some cases, akin to transactions.

This study of retirement homers and the interactions that lead to the production and exchange of the gifts points to several variations in meaning. First, the craftsmen were shown to occupy a distinct position in the retirement homer receiving pattern in the factory. Since the skills, materials, and tools required to produce retirement homers were the same for generic homers, this distinct position might also translate into other homer activities. Second, the interactions—much more so than the artifacts themselves—are what informed the meanings of these homers. An examination of only the end product of the interactions (or the concrete output of the homer activities) was not sufficient to fully understand their meanings. Third and finally, occupational varia-tions (or a lack thereof) among participants partially informed the meaning of the interactions that led to homers. Retirement homer in-teractions in which craftsmen made homers for other craftsmen were imbued with much more respect than interactions that involved other participants. When higher-level plant members received retirement homers, respect was sometimes mentioned on both sides, but the higher-level recipients also often exhibited unease. The discomfort was probably more reflective of the moral self-assessment of those who requested the homers than that of those who made them. Lower-level Pierreville members who interacted with craftsmen around retirement homers did not share that unease. However, their attention seemed more focused on the homer than on the interactions that gave rise to the artifact. Also, in these last cases, purely transactional exchanges were found. Depending on who partakes in homer activities, their meanings seem to shift. (Chapter 6, "Shades of Homer Meanings: Occupational Variations," will further link the distinction in meanings to participants' occupational identities.) But in order to better understand the meanings attributed to the most tolerated homers (retirement homers), the threshold of the homer gray zone, or cases of what I label in the next chapter "homers gone wrong," must first be examined. The next chapter demonstrates that although somewhat ambiguous, gray zones are certainly not a free-for-all.

5

Homers Gone Wrong: Delimiting the Gray Zone

> Homers are made by people who know how to craft
> artifacts. Theft is negative. These people are builders. Even
> though we used materials, we never stole anything. This is
> not theft—take note of that. It is craftsmanship. [These
> people are] builders!
> —PIERRE, *a retired Pierreville plant member*

THE OPENING QUOTE illustrates the efforts Pierreville plant members made to distinguish homer activities from theft. The contrast between "building" activities and "theft" articulates an initial morality of homer-making; it highlights agreed-upon versus unaccepted gray zone practices. Thus, by contrast, an examination of homers gone wrong helps reveal patterns of meaning for acceptable homer gray zone practices. After focusing on retirement homers—the most tolerated homer gray zone—this chapter deals with homer practices gone wrong, which are defined as those that do not seem to fit agreed-upon Pierreville norms. Previous research highlights the benefits of outliers in providing insight into the norm.[1] Outliers have this wonderful quality of providing contrast and asperities in an otherwise monotonous field. This chapter analyzes cases of homers gone wrong by examining refusals to engage in homer activities, then discussing denunciations of homer-makers, and finally, exploring homer practices framed as theft.

Refusals to Engage in Homer Activities

Refusing to engage in homer activities was rare. At the initiation stage, most homer requests bonded the requesting party to the consenting participant (usually a craftsman), and therefore often conferred power on the craftsman accepting the request. Thus, "I never refused to do anything" was a common reply among homer-makers, and a fairly logical one. In other instances, the consenting homer-maker might be returning a favor and therefore hardly be in a position to refuse. One craftsman captured the overall sentiment when he said, "If we had a moment and someone came to ask us to do work that wasn't for Aero-

Dyn—that's the way to put it—well, we would happily accept and do it." Such comments from previously active homer-makers were common. Some homer-makers were hard pressed to think of occasions they turned down a homer request and only mentioned instances in which their official work was too time-consuming. As one craftsman put it, "homer-making became off-limits when we spent *all* of our time on it."

This does not mean that craftsmen welcomed all homer requests equally. Delaying a homer's production was a popular strategy used to deal with unwanted requests, and it equated with passing a negative judgment on the requester. In some instances, craftsmen further hinted at their reluctance to do the work by asking the requesting party to pay a high price for the service. Most other homer activities did not involve monetary payments, so requesting compensation in the form of money was already a way to set a specific request apart. Nevertheless, if participants reached an agreed-upon price, the homer was manufactured and delivered, though the homer activity leading to it took on a new meaning—one akin to a transaction.

The only instance of upfront refusal that was narrated to me was the case of a blacksmith who forbade another plant member to use his tools. This other member needed specific tools to make a homer, so he asked if he could borrow them from the blacksmith. But the two had a history of bad blood between them. The blacksmith warned the person that if he continued asking for tools, he would denounce him by filing a complaint with his supervisor (on the grounds of homer-making). The person who asked to borrow the tools rode the company bus with the blacksmith each day to and from work. The bus driver often let the blacksmith get off the bus at an unofficial stop. The member who asked for the blacksmith's tools resented that favor, and he complained to management that unauthorized bus stops were being made. In retaliation, the blacksmith chose to stick to the corporate code of conduct, which prohibited any homer work. Apart from this instance, I found no other outright refusals.

However, the rules of engaging in homer activities were not uniform: time constraints, cost of materials, and availability of similar artifacts in retail stores were cited as reasons to accept, delay, or (theoretically) refuse to make a homer. A cognitive map of appropriate versus inappropriate requests emerged: "My guiding principle was that a homer shouldn't be something that required ten hours to make ... 'Here, can you help me out with this small homer?' Fifteen minutes? Sure, no problem. An hour? Why not? Because my guiding principle was that I was willing to help someone out, but only if a similar artifact couldn't be found in a shop and didn't cost too much [either in time spent or in the value of the materials]." But the occupational identity of the requesting party seemed to more accurately predict the rules of engagement and what constituted an acceptable amount of time and materials to invest. What was tolerated from some was less tolerated from others. For example, requests from supervisors and executives were hard to dismiss, and they were often honored for the simple reason that they were considered "jobs." Even if they involved large quantities of costly materials, homer-makers accommodated these requests since the hierarchy had given its explicit approval. Requests for homers from other craftsmen were usually only entertained once official work was done, and requests from lower-level plant members were assessed on a case-by-case basis and were honored, time permitting, at the homer-makers' discretion. The priority for making these homers was the lowest.

Overall, from the craftsmen's perspective, very few homer requests were dismissed outright and hardly any shame was associated with homer practices. The following account of a retired executive, Thierry, reinforces this idea of absence of shame. Thierry was upset when he accidentally discovered a storage room full of homers, but the worker who led him to the room seemed much less concerned:

> Once a director came to see me [Thierry] to tell me we needed to draft a repair plan, and we both went to the blacksmithing workshop. . . . There weren't many people there. . . . We asked a worker to move things around to find the appropriate metal sheet [for the repair]. When he did that, we saw a storage room with stools, chandeliers, homers—real homers! [Indicates their length with his hands.] The director pretended he had not seen anything. I did the same. There was no disciplinary action, but once the director left, I went back and told the worker it was a serious mistake to make these things. I scolded him a bit.

This illustration is typical of homer practices gone wrong. Within the craftsmen's community, these homers, and the gray zone practices that led to them, were considered appropriate; they often indicated respect (among participants). When dealing with a higher-level member of the plant hierarchy, though, the practices that led to the creation of the artifacts suddenly took on a different meaning: a slightly faulty one, from the perspective of the Pierreville hierarchy, but rarely enough to warrant dismissal. The sudden disclosure of homers to the supervisor's superior—as evidenced by the discovery of the homer storage room in the presence of a director—also reveals distinct interpretations of homer practices. Though nobody was denounced in this case and the worker was only slightly "scolded," such instances suggest that homer practices among plant members were tolerated as long as they were not too visible. They also point to how homers could go wrong: blatant disclosure in front of those higher in the plant hierarchy was considered off-limits.

The relative lack of refusals to engage in homer-making initially suggests that all homers were equally accepted. However, subtle tactics employed by the craftsmen, such as delaying production, or more blunt ones, such as requesting payment, point to differing views of homer requests. In addition, management's unease in some cases further suggests variations along occupational lines in interpretations of these practices. Thus, even if many homer requests were honored, not all of them were deemed acceptable; a level of morality was de facto being associated with each homer request. Direct denunciations by fellow plant members, more than refusals to engage in homer work, might further reveal which homer practices were more or less accepted at Pierreville.

Denunciations of Homer Activities

The fact that everyone who participated in homer activities either had a stake in the activities' outcomes or covered up what was happening (in the case of supervisors) often kept homer activities from being openly disclosed. In this context of shared, semipublic secrets, accusations that homer-makers were violating internal codes of conduct were usually made by Pierreville insiders. The following three cases of homer-maker denunciations illustrate examples of when insiders blow the whistle. Two of these denunciations were intentional and the last one was, it seems, more accidental.

In the first case of denunciation, a Pierreville office employee, also the wife of a Pierreville department head, saw a craftsman she knew exit a workshop and put a metal object, which she believed to be a homer, in the trunk of his car. At the time, the car was parked on the Pierreville premises. The craftsman's wife, who also worked at the Pierreville plant, explained that materials often needed to be transported between workshops. Nevertheless, the office employee suspected illegal homer activities and alerted the plant guards. That evening, upon leaving the plant, the guards stopped and searched the craftsman's car. The craftsman felt he was wrongly accused because of an earlier conflict between his wife and the denouncing office employee's husband. He interpreted the incident as an instance of indirect and misguided "vengeance."

A second denunciation involved a worker anonymously tattling on one of his coworkers for taking pieces of scrap material from the workshop. The coworker was caught at the factory gate, and he received an eight-day suspension without pay. A union leader from the workshop organized a collection to mitigate the denounced worker's monetary loss. Enough money was collected from the majority of his coworkers to cover his loss, and the money was presented to him. Whereas none of my informants knew the name of the denunciator, all agreed that it was the denunciator and not the homer-maker who was at fault. They speculated that the denunciation was motivated by reasons unrelated to the homer activity itself. The supervisor who had to discipline his direct report might have been in the awkward position of having to condemn something he did not really disapprove. The fact that the materials used were scraps pointed more to recycling (and tolerated homer activities) than theft, but at the same time, they still belonged to the company, and technically the worker's actions constituted a breach of Pierreville's internal code of conduct. Nonetheless, the denunciation still seemed overzealous, thus allowing the union leader to jokingly ask the supervisor to contribute to the funds they were raising to help their friend. (The supervisor declined.) Ultimately, the behavior deemed most inappropriate was not the worker using scrap materials to make a homer, but his denunciation.

The third denunciation was probably unintentional, but led to an internal AeroDyn audit investigation. An engineering student and intern at AeroDyn wrote a report for the director of his engineering school upon the completion of his internship. The report described his experience at Pierreville (a common requirement in the French educational system). In his report, the student wrote about what a senior craftsman told him: "At this point [in my career], I prefer to spend half my time making homers, and the other half working for my boss." Unfortunately for the student (and the craftsman), the head of Aero-Dyn was also a former classmate of the engineering school director. Surprised by this comment, the school director informed the head of AeroDyn about what he read in the report. Subsequently, the head of AeroDyn called for an internal investigation. The internal auditors recognized that homer-making often occurred in industrial settings such as AeroDyn, but they stressed that the real issue was controlling *the level* of homer activity (not forbidding it). Fifty percent of plant members' time spent on homers seemed, in their opinion, a very high estimate. They added that the term "homer work" might be used to describe work done not only in the plant, but also sometimes at home (a definition the craftsmen I met would largely disagree with). Thus, the internal auditors concluded that the student's observation "warranted no justification; either he had embellished some accounts that were shared with him, or he was led astray by a bragging craftsman." Again, the denunciator is blamed, not the homer-maker.

These three cases (the case of vengeance, the anonymous tattler, and the unintentional whistle-blower) first alert us to the widespread legitimacy of homer practices: in all three cases, the denunciators rather than the homer-makers are the ones who appear to act inappropriately. When a denunciation is made public and the facts are hard to refute—as in the tattler's case—disciplinary action is imposed, but it can also be mitigated (in the tattler's case, by the funds colleagues raised). This fundraiser, at odds with the company's official disciplinary action, points to the high legitimacy of certain homer activities. Moreover, in the case of the unintentional whistle-blower, the internal auditors not only seemed to blame him, but they also avoided negatively depicting homer practices.[2]

For the most part, vengeance, personal animosity, and poor judgment explain these three examples of denunciation. This suggests that homer activities might be pretexts for denunciation, but that the practice of homer-making itself rarely constitutes a reason for denunciation. Moreover, whereas homer activities could easily be depicted negatively, the Pierreville/AeroDyn community (including its internal auditors) resists such one-sided depictions. There appears to be a customary tolerance of engaging in homer activities as long as official work is done. However, the hierarchy seems to expect reserve with regard to the disclosure of homer activities (specifically in front of superiors). These examples help to define the "good" practice of homer-making. Tracing a clear boundary between homer activities and theft further clarifies what this customary tolerance is about, and what it does not entail.

Suspicions of Theft in Homer Practices

Despite the fact that both theft and homer activities involve company property, there were at least three ways to distinguish homer activities from theft at Pierreville. First, homers required a transformation of the plant materials rather than a simple appropriation of them. Second, homers were typically built from scrap materials, not new ones. Thus, any activity involving the removal of new materials from the plant carried suspicion of theft. Finally, when the possibility of profiting was high, homer-like activities were more likely to be perceived by plant members as theft. The following cases highlight these rules and show that it was the way in which the materials were used more than the appropriation of the materials that distinguished homer activities from theft.

In general, craftsmen rarely narrated homer activities as theft. In some instances, specifically when executives and engineers were commenting on homers, the phrases "small theft" and "small dishonesty" were used. As previously mentioned, lower-level Pierreville members also occasionally used the term "stolen" material instead of "scrap" material to qualify homers. A closer study of the plant archives helps specify when suspicions of theft were voiced, either by management or by other plant members at Pierreville. The archives highlight the accepted norms and the slippery slope that often lead to homers gone wrong: four illustrative archival cases dealing with homer activities and suspicions of theft are analyzed here.[3] These cases often suggest a negotiation between management and the accused plant member(s) on the qualification and the meanings of their homer practices. Before detailing these cases, though, the way by which AeroDyn attempted to eliminate (or at least deter) theft at Pierreville is explained.

With several thousand employees and hundreds more contract workers on-site, theft was a normal concern in the plant. The widespread use of expensive materials such as titanium, which fetched high prices on external black markets, promised large monetary rewards that were often very easy to obtain.[4] The plant's internal code of conduct condemned such practices. But because theft could not be confirmed unless someone was caught, AeroDyn implemented a policy that instituted random searches of employees exiting the plant at the end of their shifts. On average, guards performed 700 random searches per year, yet discovery rates remained fairly low (less than five cases per year). In order to complement the information gleaned from these searches, theft activity was additionally monitored by tracking the disappearance of raw materials and other company property. From 1976 to 1981, an average twenty-three cases of missing property per year were reported at Pierreville. Though some of the missing items were personal belongings, others were company tools and equipment (such as power drills, protective goggles, and motor pumps).[5] Logistically, keeping track of disappearing tools and equipment was feasible since the company gave each craftsman a booklet in which his or her tools and equipment were listed. (Craftsmen also often owned their own personal tools that were not listed in the booklet.) Supervisors kept copies of each craftsman's booklet. Checking the booklets against the inventory of tools at the plant would allow for a precise accounting of all company tools and equipment. However, in practice, it seemed this procedure was rarely used. Internal corporate documents note the low occurrence of "discoveries" of lost tools. Though no flagrant cases of purposeful collusion were observed, the internal auditors advanced the hypothesis of management's occasional "flexibility" with regard to this issue.[6] This leniency does not directly concern homer-making, but it is likely indicative of other plant practices.

Flexibility in the use of disciplinary actions also emerged when employees were caught in illegal homer acts. Disciplinary actions varied and included an oral reprimand, a report filed with the personnel office, a note in a personal file, a suspension without pay, the firing of an employee, and criminal charges. Repercussions ranged from a confidential one-on-one meeting with a supervisor to a full-fledged public hearing in court. The case of a Pierreville worker who brought tools and materials home from the stockroom illustrates the type of incident that could land a person in court on criminal charges. The worker was found guilty and fired from his job.[7] (Homer-making might have been a pretext for firing the worker, rather than the reason.) Upper management, supervisors, and human resource representatives jointly determined the severity of imposed disciplinary actions. Factory management usually asked a workshop head to "value" the corporate loss in order to determine the appropriate severity of sanction. In the case just described, the workshop head provided such a figure, but an internal audit report later deemed his evaluation flawed. According to the auditors, his figure erred on the lower side, probably to mitigate the punishment.[8] In the same manner that supervisors turned a blind eye to homer activities, they often tried to protect their team members from harsh company sanctions.

Supervisors often tried to mitigate these punishments because "recycling" property, within certain boundaries, was tolerated. Individual "recycling" initiatives outside the boundaries, however, were not tolerated. Supervisors were in the unique position of knowing how official company rules translated in their workshops and what the rules' boundaries might entail at a local level; this probably explains the added flexibility built into the disciplinary system.[9] These layered flexibilities (in the application of the plant rules and in the determination of the level of punishment) contribute to setting moral boundaries within given communities. The four cases that follow are situations in which boundaries were pushed so far that upper management (slightly removed from these local communities and practices) deemed official company intervention necessary; as such, internal audit reports relating to the events were archived. In many other instances, the boundaries of what was deemed morally acceptable were probably respected. The narratives of dubious homer activities, provided by the individuals directly involved in the cases (or by those trying to defend them), however, reveal how the meanings of homer activities can be altered.

In one of the few discoveries made as a result of the random searches, a guard caught an unskilled worker exiting the factory with "used electrical wires." The worker claimed he found the wire coil among other scraps that were left after an external contractor completed a maintenance job. Since he needed to do some home improvement, and apparently nobody needed the coil, he decided to bring it home. The goal here is not to assess the veracity of his claims; instead, it is to understand how suspicious homer activities might be normalized. First, the coil is said to belong to a contractor, not to Aero-Dyn; thus it is not company property (and AeroDyn should not have pursued him). Second, the coil is labeled a scrap, thereby legitimizing his recuperation. Finally, the worker does not profit from this recuperation, but uses it for his home. Although AeroDyn's internal auditors wrote that his statement was "not unfounded," the worker still received a five-day suspension and notification that, if caught again, he would be fired.[10] We can infer from his deposition that theft might involve (A) the appropriation of company materials; (B) preferably the appropriation of new materials, neither recycled (from scrap) nor transformed (into something different); and (C) the potential for profiting monetarily.

Whereas this first case suggests an individual awareness of the norms, the second case points to a more collective level of awareness. This time, a craftsman was at the center of the controversy. He was caught (again, one of the rare annual discoveries) exiting the factory with twelve new iron corners in the trunk of his car. He was asked on the spot not to show up for work the next day: a "conservation" measure meant to protect the company from immediate threat. A few days later, his definitive punishment—a five-day suspension—was communicated to him. That same day, twenty-eight fellow craftsmen from his workshop stopped working for one half-hour. They went on strike not because they believed the punishment was undeserved, but because they thought the immediate conservatory measure, imposed without any substantive inquiry, was too harsh. In doing so, these craftsmen also signaled that they understood that appropriating company materials (criterion A), specifically when the materials were new (criterion B), was something the company (and they) could not tolerate. However, their dispute was with what seemed to be a hasty, arbitrary response.[11] The due process of justice had not been respected and the accused party had not had sufficient opportunities to defend himself.

In the two previous cases, the theft quality of the behaviors is hard to dismiss; the next two cases are marked by greater ambiguity that blurs the distinction between theft and homer activities. This third event occurred at another AeroDyn plant, but it is relevant because it gained national press coverage and was widely discussed at Pierreville. To summarize the facts, in 1980, suspicions of "trafficking" cast iron chimney mantels grew, and the suspicions were communicated explicitly in union leaflets. During an official labor management meeting, a labor representative asked management why, despite widespread knowledge of the trafficking, no action had been taken (presumably against the supervisor who turned a blind eye to the activity). In the labor representative's words, the trafficking was "akin to theft" (*vol*, in French). During the meeting, management first reacted by claiming they were unaware of the trafficking, then by explaining that a supervisor in the suspected workshop had probably made a mistake by ordering a homer job (with no reference to what the job might entail), but that disciplinary action had been taken. Management assured the labor representative that the punishment was "in proportion to the supervisor's mistake, which had nothing to do with 'theft.'" Though the facts are still in dispute, the supervisor appeared to have brought a mantel from home to the workshop to be repaired. Management was using the same line of defense previously used by accused employees—that the materials were not AeroDyn property (criterion A). Moreover, since the contentious object involved actual work, the materials taken from the factory were not new, but transformed (criterion B). And finally, the supervisor's work was for his home, not for profit (criterion C). A new argument was introduced when management stated that the mantel was only repaired, not produced. In practice, however, repairs could entail as much work or more (trying to match the metal, the polish, etc.) than the production of a new piece. Nevertheless, management claimed that the incident did not constitute theft.[12]

Following the recorded verbal exchange at the labor management meeting, AeroDyn management initiated an internal audit investigation to assess the validity of the suspicions. The auditors concluded that chimney mantel production "requires the active participation of ten to fifteen different individuals and cannot be ignored by all the other [members of the workshop], including supervisors," so the existence of such trafficking was therefore "highly improbable." The circularity of the argument (nobody spoke so nothing occurred) appears in retrospect surprising. It is easy to conclude that the auditors seem to exhibit a bias toward protecting the plant and its members. But instead, their reports might try to explain accepted workshop norms, specifically those that make a distinction between customary homer activities and theft.

The last example of a homer event that was framed as theft involved an AeroDyn draftsman who was caught engaging in paid subcontracting work for an AeroDyn supplier while he was on the job. In response to a written request from AeroDyn to clarify the situation, the supplier who solicited the services of the draftsman explained that it was a "one-time, and now terminated relationship." It remains unclear how flawed the draftsman's judgment might have been in accepting the work since his behavior was clearly at odds with the plant rules. But the draftsman's supervisor was also admonished for not paying enough attention to his draftsman's career progression, and for not offering him more opportunities to develop a greater capacity for "critical thinking." Because the draftsman had performed the same job function for thirty years, he was not disciplined. The auditors blamed the supervisor for this abuse of the homer system.[13] Though the draftsman's behavior was clearly illegal—a full-time employee was being compensated for work he did for an entity other than AeroDyn on company time—upper management exhibited significant leniency. Had he not received compensation for the outside work, the draftsman's behavior might have been deemed entirely legitimate. It seems as if upper management (and the auditors) understood the reasons for his engaging in homer activities: hinting at either boredom on the job and/or long tenure in his job, which might explain his desire to put his long-honed skills to new use. Thus, the primary wrongdoing rested in the supervisor's failure to keep the draftsman engaged and stimulated, not in the draftsman's bad judgment in accepting monetary compensation for additional work.

This last case frames homer activities in a very positive manner—as activities that offer variety and stimulation to Pierreville members' daily work. "Useful work" was traditionally valued at Pierreville. An article published in one of the first internal company bulletins spells this out by highlighting the dangers apprentices might face. It explains that one is "the feeling of being useless," and adds that "usefulness is one of the large nobilities of work." Pictures of small artifacts made by apprentices during their training years appear alongside the article. The artifacts were often tools or items useful to the apprentices. Titled "Displeasure by the Uselessness of Work," the article might explain the unexpected leniency that upper management exhibited in the draftsman's case. Ultimately, the draftsman was engaging in useful work. Doing so, albeit in an inappropriate fashion, was recognized as a worthy pursuit.

Contrary to the widely tolerated retirement homers, these four cases of more generic homer activities force the articulation of a homer gray zone boundary. First, theft always involves only company materials, whereas homers can be made using materials from the plant, but also from elsewhere. The examples show that claiming to bring something from home for repairs (in the chimney mantel case) or to use property belonging to a contractor (the worker exiting with coil) mitigates the suspicion of theft. Second, homer activities assume a transformation of material, ideally scrap material (which evokes linkages to "manual competence" and "independence," discussed in chapter 3). Thus, new, nonrecycled materials (such as the new iron corners) and nontransformed materials (such as the coil) point to theft. Finally, profiting from homers strengthened suspicions of theft. Two of the defendants (the supervisor involved in the chimney mantel case and the worker who left with the coil) claimed that the materials were for their homes, suggesting that they would not be used to turn a monetary profit. But the case of the draftsman shows that this is not a clear-cut criterion. The draftsman clearly was profiting financially from the activity he was engaged in, yet he was not disciplined. The homer-maker fulfilled his desire to engage in stimulating work, which legitimized his homer work and, in this case, trumped the intolerance of profit.

The definition of theft at Pierreville appears fairly consistent in these four accounts: use of new company material, neither recycled nor transformed, with the potential for monetary profit. In contrast, using scrap materials to manufacture something at the plant for personal use, even during work hours, was not considered theft. Moreover, because homer-making contributed to feeling useful and fulfilled at work, leniency could sometimes be expected. The potential benefits a plant member might gain from the experience could therefore be construed as an attenuating circumstance. As the opening quote of this chapter reminds us, homer-makers are "builders." The supervisor in the mantel case might have been exonerated because he managed to combine the three homer criteria (the mantel was not company material, transformation occurred, and no profit was sought). Despite the fact that he profited from his venture, perhaps the draftsman was not disciplined because the outside activity allowed him to remain engaged in his work. And the worker who took the coils and the craftsman who took the iron corners most likely were disciplined because they exhibited signs of theft.[14]

Refusals to engage in homer activities were rare at Pierreville, and for the most part, craftsmen deemed homer activities appropriate as long as their official work was finished. As a result, most requests for homers were ultimately filled. But on a rare occasion, a homer did go wrong; denunciations indicate that not everyone considered all homers legitimate. However, denunciations usually brought more dishonor to the denunciator than to the homer-maker. In the absence of tangible material proof or when the denunciator's judgment was in question, the Pierreville community (including management) was quick to cover up such denunciations. At the same time, distinguishing theft from homer activities was necessary to maintain the morality of homer-making. The criteria used to make this distinction appeared to be largely agreed upon by the members of the Pierreville community. Moreover, when specific skill development was involved, homers could be depicted as an exercise in skill training, and therefore deemed more legitimate. This points to a certain morality of homer-making, evidenced by accepted rules around what could or could not be done.

In between theft and the more tolerated practice of retirement homers, a full spectrum of homer activities is still open for analysis. Chapter 6 explores the variety in meanings associated with these more common homer activities that constitute neither pure theft nor publicly tolerated retirement homers, but what can be labeled the gray zone of homer-making. Though clearly bound at both extremes (by retirement homers and homers gone wrong), this gray zone still contains multiple shades of meaning, and by extension, layered moralities. Understanding what drives these shades of meaning is the subject of the next chapter.

6

Shades of Homer Meanings:
Occupational Variations

THE ANALYSIS of retirement homers and of homers gone wrong suggests distinct ways to narrate homer activities. A close reading of the interview transcripts, triangulation with the archives, and the exchanges I had with the retirees at the Labor Council and in the factory museum lent further salience to these distinctions. The question, then, becomes: what drives such distinctions? This chapter partly answers that question by examining the variations in the occupational identities of gray zone participants. Participants, in this case, encompass the homer initiating, creating, and receiving parties, as well as the facilitators, such as members of the plant hierarchy. In this chapter, participants' occupational identities are shown to color the meanings of homer interactions. Homer activities in which craftsmen represent both the homer-makers and recipients, for example, reveal distinct meanings of respect and recognition. This strong interplay between occupational identities and meanings of homer interactions is further evidenced by examples of missteps that break the patterns of meaning. Ultimately, these different meanings build distinct moralities within gray zones. Although craftsmen might find respect and recognition in specific gray zone activities, others might understand the same activities very differently.

Distinct Meanings of Homer Activities

Leaving aside theft (discussed in the previous chapter), four broad categories of meaning emerged from the data regarding homer activities. As detailed in appendix A, "Data and Methods," these meanings initially emerged from iterative reviews of the interview transcripts. Main themes were culled from the narratives homer activity participants shared with me during the interviews. The participants' ways of describing homer activities were then cross-checked with other available data, mainly from the Pierreville archives and my observations.

Once patterns were established, I returned to my interview data to make sure that I had not overlooked any trends in ways of describing homer interactions.

This process revealed four categories of meaning: respect and recognition, collegiality, jobs or regular work, and exchanges, each of which is described here. These categories were determined based on the perceived nature of the practices that led to the production of the homers studied. These artifacts (i.e., the concrete outcomes of the practices) were often suggestive of potential meanings, but ultimately, the form of the relationships between participants is what enabled narrators to assign distinct meanings to the practices. The following categories should be understood as ideal types. Though a category was usually made more salient in any given homer narrative, other categories frequently also informed that same narrative.

Respect and Recognition

The first category of meaning associated with homer activities, respect and recognition, became salient when participants depicted homer interactions as a form of recognition of an individual's professionalism or skills. These interactions were inherently imbued with respect. Respect and recognition were observed in four forms: (1) as exhibited by those who engaged in the production of homers toward those who received the homers (i.e., the homer-makers showed respect toward the recipient); (2) as experienced by the homer recipient (i.e., the recipient felt respected); (3) as perceived by those who engaged in the production of homers (i.e., homer-makers felt respected because of what they did); and (4) as voiced by recipients and onlookers who knew given craftsmen had produced specific artifacts (i.e., recipients and onlookers respected homer-makers for what they did). In the ideal scenario, the homer-maker felt respected for his skills while at the same time demonstrating respect for the recipient. The recipient, in turn, felt respected by virtue of being the object of the homer-maker's efforts and voiced respect for the homer-maker. Illustrations of some of these forms of respect and recognition follow.

First, respect and recognition were exhibited toward an intended recipient by those producing the homer. In this first narrative, a former craftsman talks about his neighbor, also a coworker, and the homer gift he made for him. The coworker, being the older of the two men, left Pierreville first. (Though this particular instance is in reference to a retirement homer, other generic homer activities were described similarly.) Crafting and giving this homer was a way for the former craftsman to show respect for his more senior coworker's skills. "One of my colleagues was a fitter by trade. This guy used to be able to drill, to shape on a wheel, to fit. He knew all the machines. We decided to make him a gift that recognized his skills." Homer recipients—specifically craftsmen—were often quick to pick up on this form of respect. They felt respected when they received such a homer. A craftsman who received several homers from his colleagues—a fairly common occurrence among craftsmen at Pierreville—remarked that the homers were "unique pieces that were made to specification" for him and "embodied [his] professional life." Homers were described as tributes to the relationships between the homer-makers and the recipient; they were each perceived as separate recognitions of the recipient's professionalism and skills.

Moving away from the recipient, homer-makers also symbolically benefited from participating in homer activities. The next example is of an individual who felt respected and recognized because of the homer work in which he engaged for others. Philippe, a craftsman skilled at welding aluminum, participated in many homer projects. His remarks clearly express the pride he took in his skill when engaging in homer activities. "At the time, people knew they could bring me anything—be it a piece of an oven or a broken cast iron stove, I would weld it. If it was a piece of split aluminum, anything, nobody else at Pierreville knew how to repair it. That's because I was interested in it. I learned. . . . I did not really learn, I taught myself how to do it." At that time, few at Pierreville knew how to weld aluminum, and Philippe knew he could do it. In some ways, this form of perceived recognition evokes the desire to be useful that was previously identified in the case of the draftsman caught subcontracting his skills (chapter 5). But unlike the draftsman, Philippe knew he should not ask for monetary compensation for his work (and appear to profit from it); thus his activities remain in the homer realm instead of drawing suspicions of theft. He exemplifies the perceived skill-based recognition that the homer-maker achieved at the plant.

Other plant members echoed this sentiment by expressing respect and recognition for homer-makers' skills and professionalism. The names of the "great homer-makers" (often nicknames) were widely circulated throughout the plant. Though artifacts were not signed, their producers were often well known. Numerous independent recommendations from plant members often converged toward these homer-makers. Within the already highly respected group of craftsmen, they formed an "aristocracy." The following quote is from a worker, an onlooker who also sometimes received homers made by Pierreville craftsmen: "It was always the same thing; these were the most skilled people. In order to make a homer, and I don't mean to just weld a piece, these kinds of homers [decorative and functional pieces] . . . not anyone could do it. There was a real aristocracy. This was unique work. These were people who completely mastered their tools."

The main participants in homer activities (whether the homer-makers or recipients) were described in great detail in narratives about homers that conferred respect and recognition. The artifacts supplied pretexts for describing the relationships. The main participant in a homer activity of this kind could invariably name the other main participants, specifically the recipient. This was not the case in all homer activities. As we shall see, the meanings and levels of familiarity with other participants greatly differed in those interactions that only conferred a sense of collegiality.

Collegiality

Homer narratives that acknowledged membership in or appreciation of the Pierreville "family," but not the professionalism, skills, or behavior of any particular individual, are characterized as conferring a sense of collegiality. Unlike homer narratives that evoke respect and recognition, narratives that confer collegiality did not presume intimate knowledge of the recipient's regular work at Pierreville. It was important that the homer-maker and the initial homer recipient knew *of* each other, but not that they knew each other very well. Narratives of collegiality recognize existing positive relationships between the homer-makers and the initial recipients. In homer activities characterized by collegiality, sometimes the initial recipient of a homer kept the resulting artifact, but other times the homer was passed on to someone else.

Craftsmen characterized homer activities narrated as collegiality as "easy." Some craftsmen remarked that they were not "really homers," but more like "small gifts." Such homer practices were often in response to prompt requests for help with tasks that usually did not require much time (such as welding a broken metal piece or brazing metal barbecue grills). René, a respected craftsman to whom many people came for both generic and retirement homers, showed me one he created. "This one [similar to one given to another Pierreville worker] takes only three or four hours to make. They're part of a series I made. You get a batch of scrap blades, a few welding points, and the trick is done. These things we made didn't do much for me." Nevertheless,

René was happy to participate since making the homers enabled him to please his coworkers and maintain or sometimes build relationships with other members of the Pierreville community. In short, they allowed him to be collegial. Homer narratives that confer collegiality reflect shared, albeit somewhat generic, relationships. Regarding René's batch, two workers explained, "We all had these homers. He gave them to everybody." Each collegial narrative could be repeated with little risk of dilution since a large number of recipients could be treated in the same manner.

Although such narratives also signal a recipient's membership in the Pierreville community, the focus—in the eyes of the homer recipient— is as much, if not more, on the artifact as it is on the person's relationship to the homer-maker. One recipient, for instance, complained that a given homer-maker made many homers, but only gave him one. Collegiality—unlike respect and recognition—was not measured by how the artifact was made, but rather how it looked or how many the recipient could obtain.

Paradoxically, although homer activities framed as collegiality generally implied that the homers were easier to produce, it often was more difficult to get homer-makers to commit to these projects. The lament of an unskilled Pierreville worker who wanted a wooden box exemplifies this and further illustrates the emphasis on the artifact as opposed to the relationship in these collegial homer narratives. "It's hard, because you need to go through someone who knows the person. 'Hey! Would you mind asking him?' 'Oh, sure, I wasn't thinking about him.' For instance, I asked a pal to ask his fellow craftsmen to make a wooden box for me. I didn't go directly to the craftsmen. You don't get priority. You take your ticket in the waiting line, and six months later you get your box." This worker did not know who ultimately made the box for him, and did not really seem to care. The collegiality component of the interaction was present, but minimal and indirect.

A fairly frequent "collegiality" narrative at Pierreville involved welded metal roses. A welded rose could easily be made from scrap metal shavings and did not require much time. A craftsman at Pierreville known for making these roses frequently offered them to female office workers. No clear recognition of the main participants', including the homer-makers' and the recipients', distinct professionalism or skills attended these narratives. Both the rose-makers and the recipients characterized these practices as small signs of appreciation and shared membership in a community. On both sides, investment in these interactions seemed minimal. What also made such practices collegial was that homer-makers freely consented to them.

Jobs or Regular Work

Other narratives described homer activities in much the same way as jobs or regular work, save that the outputs were homers, not official company products. This category is consequently termed "jobs or regular work." Participants describing homer activities that fell into this category referred to "commanded work" or the "placement of orders." These narratives often included a precise accounting of hours spent on the job. Since many Pierreville members were required to complete time sheets for official work, accounting for hours spent on a job reinforced the conflating of homer interactions and regular work.[1]

A practice involving the same artifact could be categorized as respect and recognition, collegiality, or regular work. (The artifact alone did not impart meaning onto a homer practice.) The following quote illustrates how narratives about the same object can shift in meaning depending on the events leading up to its creation. It also illustrates how typical jobs or regular work narratives were expressed. The person recalling this episode was showing me an artifact he created when he worked at the plant. "We made a small batch of toy replicas of the Concorde [a commercial airplane] and passed them around to some friends. A few days later, the shop manager saw one of them and liked it. He asked for a whole batch, we were reluctant. He finally ordered us to make the batch so he could give them out as corporate gifts. It didn't feel right. We weren't happy about it. We made them because we had to, but they weren't really homers anymore; [it was] just another job like all the others." This narrative initially framed the production of the batch of Concordes in terms of friendship (evoking collegiality or perhaps even some respect), but when a higher-level member of the plant hierarchy ordered more of the homers, the activity quickly assumed the characteristics of a job or regular work. Categorizing these activities as other than voluntary homer work does not change the observed phenomenon: producing homers. As Roger, a blacksmith, put it: "Homers can't be an imposition. If so, it doesn't work." It is not that homer interactions narrated as jobs or regular work were not completed, but that the meanings associated with these interactions differed from those associated with the interactions narrated as respect and recognition or collegiality.

Jobs or regular work homer narratives often involved more organized coordination and more detailed artifact specifications than the other types of homer narratives conveyed. Moreover, preset completion dates were the norm in these types of activities. They mimicked regular work in almost every way. Whereas many homer practices might exhibit sequential interdependence (one homer-maker passing an object along to another for the next step), regular work homer interactions frequently involved synchronized teamwork: "If the job that was ordered was important, we would work on it as a team." These homer practices usually shadowed the official work in which the participants were customarily engaged: "It was done like a normal motor piece. They had all the elements to work on them since they used to make prototypes for us."

At times, homer practices narrated as jobs or regular work resembled almost a full-time position, although this was probably only the case for the most skilled craftsmen. Broadly speaking, however, the boundaries between official work and homer activities blurred whenever a craftsman was given precise orders or when a worker was asked by his boss to get new materials from the stockroom for homer production. The case of René, who could weld, shape, and repair both metal and wood, exemplifies this type of homer work scenario. René described his homer projects as if he were reciting a list of jobs he had held: making metal candle holders, building small motors, cutting aluminum window frames. His supervisors requested these homers in large numbers and René would simply make them, as if homer-making was part of his official job description. As he recalls, "in my department, I was often the person people came to. I was often stuck with it [homer-making], so I made them."

I heard one of the most evocative examples of a regular work homer narrative from a Pierreville member who explained how he could inconspicuously incorporate homer jobs into official work. When he supplied a batch of ten drawings to an AeroDyn subcontractor for execution, he would occasionally insert a drawing that was for a homer. The fact that it was a homer job was unknown to the subcontractor; it was treated as any regular job and "hidden" in plain sight. Since the contractor's invoice did not detail the number of drawings executed, Pierreville's accounting department was also unaware of the practice. In homer activities narrated as jobs or regular work, the norms of acceptability regarding what homers entailed also tended to shift. Parsimony in the use of one's time, restrictions on the use of new materials, and prioritizing official work over homer work lost some of their saliency. Repairs made to directors' private cars, as well as window frames and garden gates manufactured from new materials, are among the examples cited in homer interactions narrated as jobs or regular work. With respect to company property, the standards were somewhat more lax in these narratives than in the respect and recognition or collegiality ones.

Exchanges

Although the previous three narrative categories involved some level
of exchange (e.g., exhibiting respect and recognition toward a recipient
for the experience of being respected and recognized by the recipient),
the exchange component of homer interactions gained saliency when
the expected returns were made explicit in the narratives. When participants voiced a debit and credit mechanism for these exchanges, the
synchronized trades became central to the homer interaction.

Exchange narratives entailed give and take, a "buy and sell" pattern,
usually involving some kind of currency. An example of such a narrative is that of a craftsman who explained how he traded homers for
English language translations. Roger, the craftsman who engaged in
this exchange, received written materials from the United States related to one of his hobbies. He gave the documents to a secretary who
translated them into French for him. In exchange, he gave her small
artifacts she requested. However, Roger could not bring himself to
frame these exchanges in a purely instrumental manner, saying that
she also wanted to "please" him and he wanted to be "of service to
her." Moreover, almost to excuse his behavior, he added that the secretary also engaged in "work that had nothing to do with her daily
work" during work hours (i.e., she engaged in homer work as well).
Nevertheless, a gift and counter-gift mechanism was at play.

In at least one instance, the existence of an actual hard currency used
to keep track of these exchanges made this mechanism explicit.
Homer-makers and homer recipients both used a currency that was
officially introduced by AeroDyn for other reasons (to keep track of
work time). This official trading currency was used at AeroDyn's
Terre-Neuve plant, a facility located a half-hour from Pierreville. Frequent communications and personnel transfers took place between
Terre-Neuve and Pierreville, and several Pierreville informants confirmed the account shared by a former Terre-Neuve worker. In the
1980s, this large, fifty-person workshop relied on a currency exchange
system that involved "time-checks." A time-check (a perforated paper
card) equated to one or more hours—or even several days—of work,
and each worker was required to submit one upon completion of a job.
Each time-check corresponded to the time required to perform a specific job. Thus, a worker who had to produce fifteen pieces during the
course of a week, each of which required two hours of work (based on
a workload assessment conducted by the methods department), would
receive a time-check for thirty hours. Under this system, speedy workers would be able to hold on to their time-checks and slower ones

would run out of checks before completing their tasks. One former participant in the time-check system explained, "When we made good time up front, we could spend the extra time however we wanted, either doing homer work or not doing anything at all."

This time-check system, discontinued at the end of the 1980s, though obviously open to some abuse, was intended to motivate workers. During its decade of operation, workers regularly exchanged time-checks for homer work. Unskilled workers who needed homers (often those who found it hardest to hold on to their time-checks) gave their hard-earned checks to a craftsman, who could "help them out." Smaller checks (one- or two-hour checks) were preferred over larger checks (fifty-hour checks); because craftsmen could use them in small amounts when it suited them, small currencies were worth relatively more than their face value. Bicycle and motorcycle repairs and creating decorative home pieces typify the homer work executed under this system.

Instances of unskilled workers or office employees purchasing homers with regular currency (i.e., cash) were also reported at Pierreville: "Some engage in homers to make money. I, for instance, bought these lighters. The guy would take real coins and insert them on these lighters as a decoration. He used to do this on his evening shift and sell them." Openly profiting from homer activities rendered the homer-maker suspicious in the eyes of the community, but some circumstances seemed to mitigate the stigma—most notably when the customer was a lower-status Pierreville member (as was the case just described). In the absence of other craftsmen, the morality could shift. One "customer," or homer recipient, an unskilled worker describing such homer exchanges, added, "Anyhow, as I told you, each time we would pay him [the homer-maker] something, under the coat of course, and what we gave him was always less than we would have paid outside." In this last instance, a market-price minimizing strategy was pursued—a strategy that fit well into the exchange narratives.

Occupational Identities and Patterns of Meaning

The varied narratives associated with homer activities reveal diverse meanings in what initially appeared to be a fairly defined and uniform practice. These meanings sustain the multiple moralities that emerge in gray zones, and are further discussed throughout this book. Having established these distinct categories of meanings (respect and recognition, collegiality, jobs or regular work, and exchanges), the next step is to explain the variation in their occurrence (in terms of frequency). To determine the extent to which each category of meaning emerged, I conducted a search of the interview data for any narrated homer events that involved more than one participant. (The rare accounts of homers manufactured by individuals for themselves without external assistance were excluded from the analysis.) The two sections that follow show how the patterns of meaning in these narrated homer events depend on the participants' occupational identities. Their occupational identities are shown to partly dictate the meaning attached to the gray zone interactions.

Participant Occupational Identity and Meanings

From the seventy interviews, 135 narrated homer events involving more than one individual were identified. Of these, fifty-eight (43%) were narrated as respect and recognition, twenty-nine (22%) as collegiality, thirty (22%) as jobs or regular work, and eighteen (13%) as exchanges. For the purpose of this analysis, the occupational identities of the participants in these interactions were coded in three categories that reflected the craftsmen's perspective. Craftsmen constituted one category; all higher-level staff, including supervisors, executives, and engineers, formed the second category; and all lower-level Pierreville members such as office employees and unskilled workers constituted the third and final category used for analysis. All of the narrated homer events included at least one craftsman.

Coding homer narratives by category of meanings and participants' occupational identity revealed clear patterns. Interviewees primarily narrated peer-to-peer homer interactions among craftsmen in terms of respect and recognition (66%). To a lesser extent, they were narrated as jobs or regular work (17%) or collegiality (11%). It probably helped that craftsmen and the peers with whom they engaged in homer activities often had an existing rapport with one another. "Suppose we worked in the same workshop," observed one, "slowly we would have gotten to know each other quite well." As such, they knew *what* to respect and recognize.

Homer activities that took place between craftsmen and lower-level Pierreville members were narrated quite differently, framed by the participants who recalled them in interviews mainly as collegiality (42%) or exchanges (55%). Monetary compensation, highly frowned upon in dealings among peers (in this case, other craftsmen), was more tolerated in homer activities involving lower-level plant members. Homer practices that involved higher-level staff tended to be narrated mainly as jobs or regular work (64%) and, to a lesser extent, as respect and recognition (16%) or collegiality (16%). These variations in meanings shed new light on what might initially appear to be quite similar gray zone practices.

Although participants' occupational identities largely informed these narratives, the fact that such narratives also shaped the participants' occupational identities should not be discounted. Complex homer pieces made by craftsmen reflected the same attention to detail and flawless execution as official work pieces, and this great care taken in homer production probably influenced the way they saw themselves in the factory. Scale drawings were kept to ensure the manufacture of perfectly executed homers. Small barbecues, chimney shovels, and car parts were all crafted according to precise, self-imposed specifications. In this sense, homer practices often reinforced the professional self-image of the craftsmen who participated in them. "The [homer] ashtray that you saw [at Pierreville]," a former craftsman explained to me, "increases the sense of value of the guy [who made it]." But it was not only the occupational identity of the homer-maker that mattered; the occupational identity of the recipient of the ashtray also shaped the meaning of these homer practices.

Recipient Occupational Identity and Meanings

Having established participant occupational identity as critical to understanding observed patterns of homer meanings, the analysis can be taken a step further by also examining the impact of the recipient's occupational identity on these meanings. To control for the homer-makers' occupational identities, only homer events involving two craftsmen were analyzed, and the identity of the recipient was noted. Again, the recipient was coded as being a craftsman (either one of the two homer-makers or a third craftsman), a higher-level plant member, or a lower-level plant member. This reduced the sample size of homer events from 135 to 81.

The analysis suggests that collegiality was almost exclusively reserved for homer activities engaged in by two craftsmen for a lower-level Pierreville recipient. The majority (78%) of these occurrences were framed as collegiality. If the homer recipient was a craftsman, and two craftsmen were still involved, the interaction was usually narrated in terms of respect and recognition (96%). Finally, if the recipient was a member of Pierreville's higher-level staff, but the homer activities still occurred between two craftsmen, the homer activities were usually narrated as jobs or regular work (78%) and, to a lesser extent, as respect and recognition (11%) or collegiality (11%). The previously cited example of the miniature Concorde airplanes illustrates the effect a recipient's occupational identity had on the meaning of the homer event, which shifted from collegiality or perhaps respect and recognition when the recipient was another craftsman or a lower-level plant member, to a job or normal work when the recipient was a supervisor.

Miniature replicas of engines, airplanes, and cars more generally illustrate the effect of the recipient's identity on meaning since replicas were widely distributed to people in various positions and occupations at Pierreville. A craftsman who made many (and often similar) homers with his fellow craftsmen, including such miniature replicas, explained the distinction he drew in his practice with respect to the recipient's identity. When the recipient was a peer, the replica was "something of high precision" that his peers recognized as uniquely associated with the homer-maker's and the recipient's abilities. The homer-maker was specifically sought out for these homer-making tasks. But when the recipient was a boss, the piece, often a very similar replica, was said to be "made on demand." Though the homer-maker might pay as much attention to the task as he would to a homer for his peer, instead of completing the task alone, many of his colleagues would often work with him on the replica interchangeably (with no risk of modifying the meaning of the activity). For lower-level employees, homer-making was "open to anybody [to do]"; how they were manufactured did not seem to matter. There were crazes for given artifacts, such as "small portable barbecues that stood on four feet." But after these crazes, "nothing of the homer activities was really left." These homer practices among craftsmen, even if they involved the same craftsmen that were involved in homer-making for peers and bosses that produced very similar outcomes, were not narrated the same way. Their meanings were quite different.

Another illustrative account, one involving trained mechanics in the Pierreville garage, strengthens these findings. The mechanics described homer activities they engaged in for their bosses as jobs or regular work, and homer activities with peers that generated similar output (repaired automotive parts) as respect and recognition. When they worked on a car for a boss, it did not matter if it was an official or private car. Ultimately, it was just another job or regular task. In these instances, the mechanics hardly made the distinction between homer and official work. However, when they engaged in car or motorcycle repairs for their peers, the same practices took on another meaning. The skills of the mechanic working on the homer were emphasized ("He could undo and rebuild the entire motorcycle"), as opposed to the results of their actions (a repaired car or motorcycle). Thus, the occupational identities of all homer participants, including the recipients', dictated the meaning derived from a homer activity. Activities between two craftsmen assumed different meanings depending on the recipient. The patterns that emerge from these shifts in meaning point to a complex yet fairly stable social system in which membership in occupational groups provides some regularity.

Meaning Missteps

Instances in which the meanings of homer events broke down or deviated from the established norm further clarify the patterns of meaning linked to participants' identities. Unlike the cases of homers gone wrong (depicted in chapter 5), where there was doubt about the actual homer quality of the artifacts, the following missteps illustrate moments in which the category of meaning assigned to the homer interaction is questioned. These missteps do not entail refusals, denunciations, or suspicions of theft; instead, they point to cognitive dissonance in selecting the proper homer meaning category. One of these examples involves a moment of meaning incongruence during a visit to a dentist's office; another, a failed attempt to (re)frame a homer event up the meaning spectrum (toward respect and recognition); and the last example is a sudden realization of a shift in the meaning of a homer practice. Together, these missteps allude to the stability of the above-described patterns of meaning.

The first misstep suggests a meaning incongruence, or a moment when conflicting cues do not add up to an expected category of meaning. Richard, a supervisor at Pierreville, went to his dentist's office not far from the plant for an appointment. He was accompanied by his spouse. Upon entering the office, the couple's eyes locked on an object behind the dentist's desk. Richard recalls: "And there I see a propeller on an oak wood base. This is exactly the type of thing we make when someone retires. It's a very classic piece. I'm thinking he must have gotten it as a gift. So I ask him, 'Did this come from my factory?' 'Oh, yes,' he answers, 'Mister Poulot gave it to me.' [Pause]. We were a bit surprised." The supervisor's spouse, who also worked at Pierreville, concurred: "When we see this at a dentist's [office], someone who never worked in aeronautics [pause]. Let's say . . . in my home. . . . [She nods her head to signal agreement.] I'm in that field, so it wouldn't seem so odd. But here, in this context, and moreover, such a huge piece [pause]."

Meaning was not usually derived only from the artifact itself, but this homer was so distinctive and required so much work that, in Richard's opinion, it could only suggest respect and recognition. Richard suspected that because the dentist was not a plant member, the homer activities leading to such an artifact were probably more akin to exchanges. But the homer "looked" like respect and recognition. To see such a homer in a dentist's office undermined the prevailing association of respect and recognition with peer-to-peer interactions. The homer-makers might have experienced their work as a form of respect and recognition. (Respect and recognition narratives involved mainly craftsmen as recipients, but on occasion other recipients were mentioned.) Nonetheless, Richard saw this as a meaning misstep.

Missteps also occurred when homer participants perceived homer activities in different ways and failed to convince each other to adopt their own framing. This was the case with an office employee who asked a craftsman she knew to make a retirement homer for her boss. She phoned the craftsman and described her boss and the kind of artifact she wanted. But the craftsman was reluctant. She expressed the respect she had for her boss, and tried to frame the interaction between the craftsman and her boss as respect and recognition as well. The craftsman (who narrated this event) called her back a few days later and told her he was willing to do it, but that it would cost her fifty euros. She was surprised, and declined the offer. The office employee framed the homer activity as one of respect and recognition, but interactions between craftsmen and lower-level Pierreville members were usually framed as collegiality or exchanges. Though the office employee seemed to want to ignore this rule, by putting a price on the request the craftsman reminded her of the meanings typically ascribed to such homer activities.

A final illustration of a meaning misstep involved a recipient's sudden realization of a shift in the meaning of a homer interaction. The scenario was narrated by a supervisor, also a former craftsman, who was retiring from Pierreville. He worked in different AeroDyn plants during his career, and he received a retirement homer upon his departure from Pierreville, where he had returned after holding multiple positions. He received the homer from former colleagues and interpreted their efforts as a sign of respect and recognition. Though he was retiring as a supervisor (i.e., higher up in the hierarchy), prior "peer" relationships he had developed with the craftsmen drove his assumption of respect. Several days after the retirement ceremony, when he learned the artifact he received had been ordered by the Pierreville communications department, the homer suddenly lost its meaning (or, in his words, its "value"). The homer interactions in which his colleagues took part were merely jobs or regular work, and did not suggest respect and recognition. Whereas many recipients prominently exhibited their retirement homers in their homes, he stored his in the basement.

A sudden shift in framing from the respect and recognition he hoped for to regular work changed his reading of these homer activities. In an attempt to imbue respect and recognition onto homer activities between his two craftsmen colleagues—who were, in fact, producing an artifact for a higher-level plant member—the supervisor discounted the more common meaning associated with this particular homer participant combination—the one associated with jobs or regular work.

This chapter first documented four broad categories of meaning associated with homer activities (respect and recognition, collegiality, jobs or regular work, and exchanges). The occupational backgrounds of the participants, including those of recipients, inform much of the observed patterns of meaning. The examples of missteps discussed point to the robustness of these patterns. These meanings also start to inform the potential moralities of the homer gray zone. Specific participant combinations (depending on the participants' occupational backgrounds) call for distinct meanings, and each combination also suggests a distinct morality of the practice. For instance, homer interactions involving two craftsmen, specifically when the intended recipient was also a craftsman, more often than not were imbued with respect and recognition; as such, the participants perceived the activities as highly moral endeavors. Pierreville craftsmen were particularly receptive to such associations. In the shifting context of the Pierreville plant (described in chapter 7, "The Rise and Fall of Craftsmanship"), craftsmen found it increasingly difficult to locate sources of respect and recognition. The distinctions in meanings documented in this chapter, particularly the potential for finding respect and recognition, provide the basis for a system of hidden symbolic incentives to operate in the plant (detailed in chapter 8, "Trading in Identity Incentives"). The trades between management and craftsmen that often occur in the homer-making gray zone here find their basis and partial explanation.

7

The Rise and Fall of Craftsmanship

> I joined AeroDyn in 1963.... The company had a good
> reputation. I started as a fitter. Unfortunately, the fitter
> trade started to lose some of its value. With technical
> changes, new technologies were able to take over the work
> of a fitter. Work really wasn't very rewarding [anymore]...
> it had nothing to do with what we had trained for in the
> technical schools, when we used to do dovetails and
> complicated stuff.
> —ARMAND, *retired Pierreville worker*

SOME HOMER INTERACTIONS carried very desirable meanings for craftsmen. They both expressed and conveyed a peculiar form of respect and
recognition that played into their occupational identities. Why would
such interactions become so valuable? And how is it that craftsmen
seemed so attached to these specific homer interactions? An examination of the shifting occupational dynamics at Pierreville provides insight into the interactions' desirability. As new technologies at the
plant increasingly marginalized the craftsmen's skills, homers offered
one of the last available venues in the plant to sustain their occupational identities.

This chapter begins by explaining why craftsmen and engineers were
historically attracted to AeroDyn. The perceived opportunities to pursue and develop one's craft initially encouraged many Pierreville members to apply. The chapter also depicts the gradual decline of such professional development opportunities for craftsmen. A subsequent
review of union archival data illuminates the implications these shifts
in opportunity had for the occupational identity of craftsmen. The chapter ends with a discussion of the career of a retired Pierreville craftsman
named Thomas. Thomas's words epitomize the craftsmen's struggle for
professional relevance in the plant and the occupational identity threats
they faced. These threats are discussed, not to excuse the breach of official rules that occurred in the plant as a result of homer activities; rather,
they elucidate the apparent tolerance of this homer-making gray zone
at Pierreville and help to explain it. The growing disconnect between
the Pierreville craftsmen's desired occupational identities and the actual

work they performed at the plant sets the stage for their pursuit of desired identities within gray zones.

The Historical Pursuit of Craftsmanship

Many retired Pierreville members joined AeroDyn after World War II, during an era when its mission was to develop turbojet airplane engines for the French Air Force. Craftsmanship was highly valued at that time, given the challenge AeroDyn faced. Recent studies suggest that France's aeronautic inferiority in relation to Germany's capabilities during World War II may have been overstated. Nevertheless, the prevailing belief in the postwar period was that France's defeat was secured, in part, by the relative abundance and efficiency of German aircraft.[1] The awareness of this weakness led the French government to pursue aeronautic collaborations with the British between 1935 and 1939, and to acquire American planes between 1938 and 1940.[2] It was in this context that AeroDyn was asked after World War II to build turbojet engines, nearly from scratch.

Many of the engineers and craftsmen who joined AeroDyn through the late 1960s were inspired by this pursuit. Though the salaries and benefits at AeroDyn were also attractive, the notion of developing a product "from the ground up" attracted many AeroDyn—and Pierreville—members. As one retired Pierreville engineer recalled: "After the Liberation of France, we didn't have any people able to take on the task of building new engines. The British, the Germans, and the Americans all had programs to develop turbojet engines, but we were completely short on engine design and development."

In the wake of World War II, AeroDyn developed new engines, drawing from what others had done abroad as well as on initial domestic attempts, and mainly by trial and error. Craftsmanship was a necessary part of this process since the stabilization phase of the industry, which allowed for the mass assembly of engines, had not yet been achieved. During this period, the tasks of the engineers and craftsmen were probably less distinct than they are now. Many members who retired between 1970 and 2000 worked during a time when the technological challenges AeroDyn faced in developing engines were still quite immense and/or worked alongside engineers and craftsmen who had been present during the initial years of Pierreville. Craftsmen and engineers who worked during the early decades at Pierreville (from the 1940s to the 1960s) recall having to tackle basic questions about whether the engine they developed could actually fly, and even if it could, how the prototype could then be scaled up to meet growing military needs. The art of engine development was much more relevant than the industrialization of the tasks. For those who joined AeroDyn with these ideals and images in mind, the shift in focus from the craftsmanship to the mass production of engines would be quite stark. The ideals and images of inventors and builders pursuing a critical, national challenge hand-in-hand would soon become somewhat obsolete.

Narrowing Opportunities for Craftsmen

As the evolution of the Pierreville workforce indicates, starting in the late 1970s, Pierreville craftsmen were slowly marginalized (see fig. 7.1). The craftsman population was essentially concentrated in the worker's hierarchical category and, to a lesser extent, in the technician's category. Craftsmen represented a large and historically central subcategory of workers (estimated at approximately half of the total workers by Labor Council members), a category that fell from 29 percent of the total workforce in 1977 to 15 percent in 2001. During this same period, technicians were gaining representation in the factory (from 36% in 1977 to 45% in 2001). (Technicians worked in workshops or offices, often with computers, and performed tasks that involved less manual work than those craftsmen conducted.) Most of the increase in the technician population was the result of new recruits—not internal promotions. The new recruits were trained as BTS (*Brevet de Technicien Supérieur*), and due to their difference in training and relative youth, the craftsmen did not consider them part of their group. Thus, even though some craftsmen were internally promoted to technicians, most of the increase in technicians did not benefit craftsmen.[3] Newly hired technicians and craftsmen did not mix. Engineers and executives were also a growing presence in the factory; their combined representation reached 30 percent in 2001, up from 18 percent in 1977. Pierreville was slowly being transformed into a more "upscale" research and development facility.

Over this period of time, the interesting experimental work had migrated to the computer. Technicians and engineers could design and test engines using computer models without input from craftsmen until much later in the development process. For instance, when the metallic curve of an engine was assumed to provide less resistance to air with a new slope, a few modifications via computer model were sufficient to collect sound enough data to make a fairly good call about

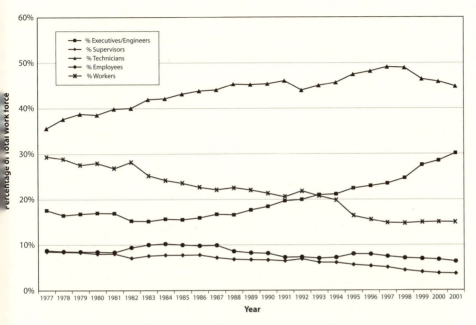

Fig. 7.1. Workforce evolution at Pierreville, 1977 to 2001. *Note*: This diagram shows the distribution by hierarchical employment category. The following English translations of the French categories were adopted: "cadre" = executive and engineers; "maîtrise" = supervisors; "technicien" = technician; "employé" = employee; and "ouvrier" = worker. Craftsmen were mainly concentrated in the worker category and, to a lesser extent, in the technician category. *Source*: Pierreville Annual Social Reports.

the modification's suitability. At the same time, many tasks that were previously performed in-house, such as developing new tools or manufacturing specific engine subunits, were slowly outsourced. Precise outsourcing figures are considered proprietary company information and therefore could not be accessed. However, a more recently adopted AeroDyn accounting reporting format indicates an increase in the amount of outsourced purchases. Outsourced purchases as a percentage of total sales grew from 35 percent to 41 percent between 1998 and 2001 (the years for which data became available).

Human resource policies reflected the plant's declining need for craftsmen. For example, the policies set a cap on the qualification level members could attain in the workshops, and they introduced incentives for craftsmen's early retirement. Each job was assigned a level, and in order to climb above a certain level, workers needed to take a new job, often in an office outside the workshop. Though this mobility translated into higher pay, it did not translate into higher social standing among peers. In fact, moving from a craftsman role to an office job was sometimes labeled as "selling out." Craftsmen also referred to these moves as "one-way tickets," since the probability of returning to the workshop after accepting a new office job was slim to none. Most of the office positions AeroDyn offered to craftsmen involved preparing the logistics for the mass-assembly workers. Preparation jobs encompassed making sure all necessary tools and materials were available for assembly work, thereby ensuring the proper production workflow. Alain's move, described in the next section, was typical of individuals who chose to move "up."

In the late 1940s, after passing a fitter test, Alain was hired for a position at another AeroDyn plant where he learned to operate a large threading machine. By 1965, Pierreville was looking for workers to occupy the newly created experimental workshop, and Alain was asked to join. It suited him well since his other option was to go to the more assembly-oriented Terre-Neuve plant. Alain wanted to continue in a skilled occupation; he enjoyed the autonomy of his position at Pierreville. By the early 1980s, however, he had reached the highest employment category in his workshop, so his wife encouraged him to move up. As she put it, his "unwillingness to do office work" was the reason he was stuck at his given pay level. She advised him to apply for an office job, which he did reluctantly, and he was hired for a position preparing logistics for assembly work. The only reason he applied, he said, was for higher pay, but he had "a hard time leaving the workshop." Later, his former colleagues from the workshop tried to do the same, but many of the positions had already been filled. When I met Alain and his wife, he hardly spoke about what he did during his seven years in the office. He wanted to talk only about his time in the workshop.

For craftsmen who decided not to graduate to office positions or who were not able to make the move once they decided they wanted to, the likelihood of ending their careers conducting unskilled labor was high. This being the case, when the plant offered incentives for early retirement, many decided to leave. This trend is particularly evident among blacksmiths in the experimental workshop. In the mid-1960s, there were fifty blacksmiths at Pierreville. By the early 1990s, that number had fallen to less than twenty, and by 1995, when the experimental workshop was transferred from Pierreville to Terre-Neuve, not one blacksmith could be found at Pierreville. This marked the end of the reign of the Pierreville blacksmiths.

For those craftsmen who avoided moving to an office position—but were also unwilling to regress professionally by engaging in less appealing assembly tasks considered menial—early retirement was a seemingly attractive option. Such departures generated mixed feelings, though. The idea of not having to work long hours anymore and having a free schedule was appealing, yet also sometimes upsetting. The social connections inside the factory meant that work was often more than merely the sum of the technical actions required to manufacture a piece: work was a community that maintained a member's cherished identity. Jacques's departure from Pierreville embodied the mixed feelings that accompanied many like it.

Jacques joined AeroDyn in 1962 and left in 1994. When asked if his departure was voluntary, he answered "no," that he "was let go," but he admitted it was not a surprise. Many of his colleagues were let go before him. Because he was hesitant to go, however, he waited for his superior to ask him to leave. But when he saw his name on a rank-ordered list of potential departures that his supervisor drew up, and noticed he was too far down on the list to leave in the next round of departures, he argued with his supervisor about how the list was ranked. Jacques, unconvinced by his supervisor's explanations, threatened to shirk his duties if not put on the list of the next departures. He was quick to add, however: "All this [threat of no work] can only be momentary because you can't really say 'I'm doing nothing from now on.' You can't stop for very long. The anger disappears and you go back to work." Jacques talked about his work with genuine excitement. He even showed me pictures of engine pieces he manufactured. At the same time, though, he complained about having to be at work at six in the morning. Overall, he concluded that he did not miss not going to work every day, but he also never went back to the factory again after he left. He did not want to return; it was "finished" for him. It was "disheartening" to be let go when work meant so much to him; yet staying on when "no longer needed" was painful as well. By and large, he expressed very mixed feelings about his departure: something he simultaneously wanted and feared, regretted and welcomed.

For craftsmen who were not promoted to more administrative functions or did not leave the workshops, engaging in homer activities, preferably ones that recognized their skills, was a source of validation of their occupational identity, even when the homer requests came from the hierarchy. The craftsmen's ability to independently create artifacts from scratch was a key element of their identity. Perhaps the homers made for supervisors, executives, and engineers did not provide as much identity validation as those made for peers, but they still offered a way for craftsmen to both maintain and showcase their desired identity. In doing so, craftsmen were able to stay connected to the critical elements of their identity—their manual skills and independence.

Philippe, a craftsman who built small models used in wind tunnel tests, recalls making such models for directors who exhibited them in their offices or homes. Though the models were ordered and refusing to make them was out of the question, Philippe described the pieces with great animation: "They were half wood, half metal. I used to do all the assembly, everything inside. It was fascinating for me, and I loved it. It was almost like a game." Philippe was known to make models of planes and engines, including detailed elements such as small reproductions of the pilot and his ejector seat. Reflecting on his decision to join AeroDyn in 1949, Philippe said he would have liked to pursue an artistic career, painting or drawing, but that it seemed financially impossible at the time. At Pierreville, Philippe jumped at every opportunity to build a model, be it an official one or a homer. As he built these models, he applied a concerted effort to develop and pick up new skills. He described the models as "precious"—a word that could easily be applied to Philippe and his value to the Pierreville community, since he did what few others were capable of doing.

Thus, as the work that maintained the craftsmen's occupational identity slowly lost relevance at the plant, craftsmen had to make difficult career choices, none of which were very appealing. The craftsmen's desired identity no longer matched the options they faced. Retiring often meant leaving friends behind, staying in the workshops often meant engaging in less appealing work, and being promoted to office work equated to a loss of status. In this context, select homer interactions could help soothe the identity threats craftsmen faced. (Whereas other venues, outside the plant, such as work conducted at home or hobbies, might also sustain these identities, the focus here is on what is happening inside the plant.)

Union Support for Craftsmanship

Individual attempts to reclaim identity and status echoed broader discussions regarding the future of the experimental workshop that were slowly gaining momentum at Pierreville. In 1995, AeroDyn management decided to physically transfer the experimental workshop to Terre-Neuve. Though the official impetus for the transfer was technical, many Pierreville members saw it as a way for the company to dispose of the craftsmen's old guard. In addition, some Pierreville members described the transfer as a way to eliminate a last pocket of potential for labor unrest, since the communist CGT union drew many of its most outspoken members from the experimental workshop. Thus, by relocating the workshop, union members would be isolated from other Pierreville members, and might opt for early retirement given that a change of environment at such a late stage in their careers was hardly attractive. Regardless of AeroDyn's intentions, this transfer was perceived by many Pierreville members as a direct blow to craftwork.

In many ways, the archived leaflets the unions (both the CGT and the CFDT) printed and distributed to oppose the transfer evoked the "respect and recognition" narratives that became salient in craftsmen's peer-to-peer homer activities. As early as 1978, rumors of a potential workshop transfer to Terre-Neuve triggered union reactions. Approximately seven hundred people were working in the experimental workshop at the time. Though the transfer did not occur until later, the workshop was placed under the supervision of the production department head, who was physically located in the Terre-Neuve plant. Previously it had operated under the supervision of the research and development technical department head at Pierreville. What the CGT feared was that over time, such a transfer would reduce AeroDyn's research and development capabilities and transform AeroDyn into a subcontractor for larger aeronautic manufacturers. The experimental workshop epitomized craftsmanship—an activity historically separate from the mass assembly or production of engines. In defending the "interest and expectations of salaried workers, the CGT is also spearheading a fight for the independence and the development of the [national] aeronautic industry," commented one union leaflet from that time period.[4] The risk of becoming merely a manufacturer instead of an airplane engine designer was what the union feared most. Moreover, issues of de-skilling of the workforce were rampant. The usually more moderate CFDT union also expressed its fears for the future: "The Technical Department has been amputated of its most essential tools: The experimental workshop. . . . It is the company's capacity for innovation, study, and research that is at stake."[5] (See fig. 7.2.)

In 1983, the labor situation had become so tense that the CFDT felt compelled to issue a policy paper entitled, "A New Experimental Workshop for the Engines of Tomorrow," in which it warned Aero-Dyn's management of the impending crisis in the experimental workshop. The union spelled out its goals for developing the company's "technical and human capabilities. . . . Professions will undergo capital transformations—at this time, AeroDyn needs to set adequate training targets."[6] The policy paper went on to document the experimental workshop crisis. As proof of it, the paper reminded readers that subunits (such as the materials research group) had already been placed under the supervision of the Terre-Neuve production department head, and that the blade research group had been dismantled and its

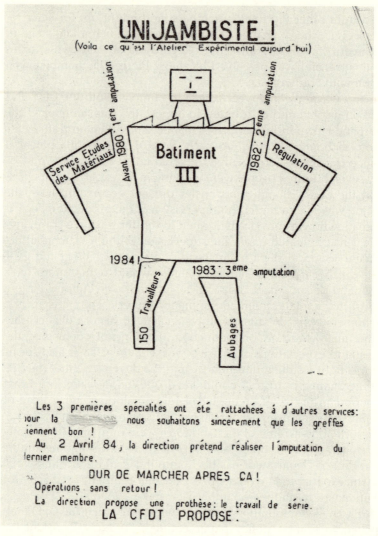

Fig. 7.2. Union leaflet denouncing labor cuts in the experimental workshop. Translation: "A ONE-LEGGED MAN! (That's the experimental workshop today.) Before 1980: first amputation (the material study unit); 1982: second amputation (regulation unit); 1983: third amputation (blade unit); 1984: 150 workers [number of proposed cut]. The first three areas of specialization have been attached to other units. For AeroDyn's sake, we sincerely hope the transplants will hold! As of April 2, 1984, management wants to amputate our last unit. HARD TO WALK AFTER THAT! This is an operation with no return! Management is offering us an artificial limb: mass assembly work. The CFDT [union] offers . . . " *Note*: The leaflet continues on the back page, not shown here. Photo by author.

personnel reassigned to other units. Pierreville's transfer of this last group was depicted as "a fatal blow to the experimental workshop" that meant the "know-how [had] been lost by AeroDyn."[7] The union's reaction echoed the craftsmen's view of assembly work as demeaning, asserting such "batch-assembly work" to be "unfit for an experimental workshop." Though the union recognized the growing importance of computer technology in engine design, the experimental workshop was still thought of as essential to manufacturing and testing engine blocks. Thus, with their 1984 policy paper, the CFDT opposed the transfer of AeroDyn workers. It predicted the consequence of the transfers would be a "disappearance of motivation." Moreover, in order to preserve the workers' "know-how," the know-how needed to be "continually updated" and "used."

By framing the 1983–1984 debates in terms of the future, the unions voiced their members' concerns regarding their continued relevance in the plant. These workers were struggling with their diminished role in the development and production process. In 1984, Pierreville workers marched beneath the Parisian windows of the Ministry of Defense, historically one of AeroDyn's largest customers. "Our problem," wrote the CFDT in a leaflet distributed at the march, "is not an employment problem today, but a problem of choices for tomorrow! We expect the Ministry of Defense to understand that [our march] is about allowing AeroDyn to maintain the professional capabilities necessary to face tomorrow's challenges."[8]

The craftsmen's narrowing options crystallized in their struggle against Pierreville's transfer of the experimental workshop. The transfer threatened the most meaningful kind of work—experimental, unique, nonassembly craftsmanship. For craftsmen who had often imagined themselves as key to AeroDyn's success, this reality was hard to face. It directly threatened the part of their identity that was derived from their occupation—and left them with homer-making as an alternative to the truly meaningful work.

A Tale of Lost Work and Identity

Thomas was a Pierreville retiree I met on several occasions who, in the later part of my fieldwork, personified the shifting dynamics of occupational identities and meanings at Pierreville. His tale both summarizes and gives voice to some of the key dynamics in this book: the waning position of craftsmen, the threats to their occupational identity, and the ways in which some gray zone homer practices tamed this decline. Thomas was born in 1943. He spent three years in the French

Air Force before joining AeroDyn in 1963. He was a fitter by trade
(with a CAP) and started working as early as he could to support his
siblings. As the eldest sibling, his parents expected him to contribute
to the household early on. Thus, after his military service, joining Aero-
Dyn was a first step in what would become a successful career as a
craftsman. Though he enjoyed many good years of work, the end of
his career was not as happy a period of his life:

> It's true that when I left [Pierreville], part of me wanted to leave and part of
> me didn't. But I decided on the spur of the moment. I was called on a Friday
> morning. Management called me Friday morning. But I also wanted to leave
> because in the previous year and a half [he left in 1998] the orientation had
> completely changed. In a sense, we found ourselves a bit removed; at the
> periphery. We were not doing anything interesting anymore. Fine, they
> wanted us to work on computers, the warehouse to be computerized. Fine,
> but what can I say? I spent 35 years doing something else . . . so, we were a
> bit compelled to leave. So they transferred me to another factory. I was called
> on a Friday morning at 9 or 10 a.m. I was told, "Sir, you need to give us your
> decision by Monday." The choice was to be transferred or to leave. [I chose]
> to leave.

Once Thomas left the plant, he tried to engage in other activities and
hobbies, but he missed his job. Perhaps what made him more attuned
to the interplay of his work and identity was that, as he was leaving
the plant, his son was finishing his studies and wanted to work in a
profession where finding a job proved very difficult. Thomas went on
describing what happened to him.

> I had come to a conclusion. . . . It was Friday. I told myself I was going to
> leave, and that I didn't want to stay there . . . and go around in circles in the
> workshop. . . . There wasn't anything interesting left to do. When you were
> transferred from my old workshop to the new one I was assigned to, many
> considered it a dead-end job. We told ourselves there was nothing left to do.
> The new workshop didn't have any specific reputation, but when we were
> transferred there, it meant life in the old one was dead. There isn't anything
> left [in my old workshop] . . . a naked workshop is frightening. Everything
> was set aside, the machines and everything else. . . . We barely had any de-
> velopment work left. We only had three engines at that time: we had almost
> nothing left. So, we told ourselves, we don't serve any purpose anymore.
> We're going to a larger workshop, and we have nothing to do. A good sev-
> enty of us were in my old workshop at that time, and everybody was walk-
> ing in circles. . . . So on Monday I said I would leave.

Thomas proceeded to link his departure to his sense of worth. The rewards he enjoyed from his work suddenly eluded him. He described

his impressions of moving from a craftsman's job to an administrative position, since a few years before being let go he had accepted a promotion to become a technician. He underwent what he considered a double indignity: first confined to administrative work, and then encouraged to retire early.

> I worked hard, for sure, we worked. We put in fifteen-hour days sometimes . . . and always in development. More or less, we did it with pleasure. It was not too complicated, not too hard . . . and so rewarding. It was something when we did tests, when we saw the engine being launched, when it was running a bit. . . . We told ourselves: "Shit, good job!" So when day in and day out you end up dealing with backorders in the basement, no, it's not exactly the same.

Thomas finally weaved homers into his story. He even spoke about some he made himself. He then mentioned a fellow craftsman he knew very well. Describing other plant members' homer activities in detail without disclosing their names was a common way for retirees to speak more freely about homers. The slight distance it introduced helped lessen the potential stigma associated with homers. Thomas's reference to his coworker best illustrates what peer-to-peer homer interactions meant to craftsmen.

> When my coworker was sent to do assembly work, it almost broke his heart. So when he could escape from the assembly work to actually work on machines, it was nirvana for him. People liked their jobs, there's nothing much to say about that. And it's so nice to take a piece of square metal, [not even a square] whatever piece of metal . . . even a piece of rusted metal, and make an artifact out of it. Something that will function, that will be useful, that will serve a purpose. . . . It really is a creation; there's no doubt in my mind.

Thomas's tale is fairly representative of many others that were shared with me by plant retirees. Two caveats, nonetheless, deserve to be noted. First, though the union's position was that AeroDyn was losing its capabilities by doing away with craft-based experimental work, to this day, AeroDyn continues to produce engines and remains competitive in the industry. The question of whether craft-based experimental skills are essential to manufacturing new engines is therefore an open one. Also, the notion of de-skilling might be relevant to craftsmen, but perhaps confined to this particular group of plant members. Over time, AeroDyn sought to develop new skill sets at the plant (as evidenced by the company hiring technicians). A closer, longitudinal examination of the technologies used and produced at Pierreville would enable an assessment of any potential de-skilling occurring at both the company and plant levels. By many measures, and given the competitive pressure imposed on aeronautic manufacturers, AeroDyn is still considered a success story.

The second caveat is AeroDyn's reputation as a responsible employer. AeroDyn remains at the forefront in France in terms of salary, benefits, and complementary health coverage for its employees. Many employees joined AeroDyn specifically for that reason, and not a single retiree I met voiced dissatisfaction about any of those aspects of their employment. In more difficult times, layoffs were often planned, and involved financial incentives rarely found in other industries. Pierreville's addition of a museum was conceived as a venue to enable interested retirees to stay involved. As such, the museum also illustrates the stewardship AeroDyn exhibited toward its retirees. They were offered access to the plant canteen and the opportunity to take part in outreach educational programs at the museum. Thus, many retired Pierreville members—including Thomas—remain connected to their former employer.

Discussion of these caveats puts Thomas's comments in context. He never claimed that his skills were absolutely necessary to AeroDyn or that AeroDyn mistreated him. However, Thomas did not feel the organization lived up to his expectations of certain important aspects of work that meant the most to him—hence his impassioned depictions of homer activities. Thomas's delight in engaging in complicated, useful homer work echoes Armand's position, cited at the beginning of this chapter, that "work really wasn't very rewarding [anymore]" and that he longed for the dovetails and the "complicated stuff" he once did.

Relevance through Work

Relevance can come in numerous forms, at and outside of work, officially or unofficially, repeatedly or sporadically. Previous studies in industrial settings document the craftwork male factory workers carry out at home (mostly in their garages), which positively contributes to their desired senses of self.[9] Because these pursuits are valued and considered important in these men's social settings, this craftwork provides them with relevance. Pierreville craftsmen might have engaged in these kinds of activities as well. Many of the retirees I visited seemed to have spaces set aside in their homes, either in the basement or garage, for specific manual activities. But they were probably not able to gain as much relevance from these activities as they had from their work in the plant.

Historically, the craftsmen's skill set aligned with the core mission of the plant: designing from the ground up and manufacturing airplane engines that would enable military (and later civilian) aircrafts to fly safely. In many ways, craftsmen stood at the heart of what Pierreville represented. The fact that they often used to work side-by-side with engineers on the most pressing technical problems of the time speaks to their relevance to the entire plant membership. Moreover, their skills were in high demand, making them individuals management had to court.

Between 1970 and 2000, craftsmen lost their relevance at Pierreville. Modeling engines on computers rather than in workshops saved AeroDyn a considerable amount of time and money, and allowed for more frequent testing. Thus, the craftsmen's particular skills became less essential to AeroDyn's success. Their degree of recognition in the plant was still theoretically high, but undermined in practice by the assignments they were given and the skill sets they were required to utilize in the new positions they occupied. For instance, even if a craftsman was known as an excellent welder, on a daily basis he could be asked to align the required materials for assembly. Mixed messages further blurred their standing in the plant. The museum still praised their knowledge, and it often relied heavily on their advice and free guidance during off hours to restore old engines. But engineers who had not worked with them in the past and newly hired technicians rarely sought their advice. Craftsmen were less conversant in the critical challenges Pierreville now faced. In more recent years, the challenges AeroDyn faced in the market were linked more to performance issues (e.g., lighter engines with higher thrusts, less pollution, and less noise) than feasibility issues. AeroDyn now knew how to build safe, functional engines. The new challenges also seemed less exciting to craftsmen than the ones they had solved in the past. Taking on these challenges paled in comparison to their past collective "achievements" of flying airplanes. The days when the entire workshop stopped to anxiously watch a pilot test a brand new engine were long gone. The focus of Pierreville had now shifted toward areas of expertise that were often out of the craftsmen's realm. The technicians were becoming the interlocutors of choice whom engineers consulted regarding issues they encountered.

An intriguing episode illustrates this shift, but at the same time shows AeroDyn's efforts to praise the craftsmen and note their importance. As a sign of appreciation of its craftsmen, AeroDyn invited a resident metalwork artist to work in one of its plants alongside some craftsmen. The project was meant to showcase to the broader community AeroDyn's expertise in craftwork and the skills of the craftsmen who helped the artist. The experiment, a first in the history of the plant, lasted nearly two years and was widely covered in internal company bulletins. Though the project occurred in the fairly nearby Terre-Neuve plant, it was rarely mentioned by any of the Pierreville craftsmen I spoke to. Large sculptures that were hard to miss, some of which were erected at Terre-Neuve and gained national press coverage, were the result of the project. Yet the Pierreville craftsmen treated it as a non-event. In the official publication released by AeroDyn during the inauguration of the sculptures, connections were clearly drawn between the sculptures and the craftsmen in the plant: "the worker [the craftsman] shared his know-how and techniques with the artist," claimed the leaflet. "I taught him [the artist] to hold the blow torch to weld . . . I helped him weld tubes on the back of the sculpture. It was a beautiful moment," read a craftsman's quote. This attempt illustrates AeroDyn's efforts to maintain the craftsmen's relevance. The resident artist experiment was well intentioned, but the Pierreville craftsmen's silence suggests unease. It might have been that AeroDyn simply chose the "wrong" plant—Terre-Neuve, instead of Pierreville. But it might have been that what remaining respect the craftsmen commanded in the plant was handed to an outsider who would benefit from it. Though they played a part in the artist's creation, they were in supporting roles in a pursuit that was no longer their own.

In this context, the satisfaction Thomas expressed when he described homer activities and Armand's comments about longing for dovetails cannot be taken as the expressions of isolated disgruntled workers. Such longings were shared by many craftsmen in the plant and are to be expected from workers who no longer engage in the activities that make them relevant. The notion of relevance also evokes that of usefulness: usefulness of the tasks, and by extension, of the people who execute the tasks. The reaction of another craftsman, this time in the United States, further clarifies what a quest for relevance might entail. The independent blacksmith's reaction was documented in 1973 by the man who commissioned him to make a fire tool.[10] The blacksmith "was pleased when I asked him to make some kind of tool, because he considered that type of work to be a real 'old time' blacksmith task," the man said. The tool the blacksmith made was topped with a very complicated spiral that was difficult to draw; yet it possessed great utility. The fact that the tool would be utilized, and not merely exhibited as decorative art, greatly pleased the blacksmith. The blacksmith also may have cherished the opportunity to make a tool because it brought back memories of his apprenticeship (similar to that of the Pierreville apprentices), during which he was taught to build his own tools. Specific tasks such as the one just described—and making homers—carry

highly valued meanings when they express and shape the maker's occupational identity

---

This chapter began by highlighting the historical importance of craftsmanship at Pierreville, and subsequently documented the diminished
work options available to craftsmen at the plant. The choices they were
left with undermined their independence and manual skills—two elements crucial to their occupational identity. The chapter also stressed
the linkages between these difficult individual choices and the broader
institutional context, as depicted in the union leaflets. The Pierreville
unions' discourse illustrated how these individual struggles aggre-
gated into a more collective effort to save the experimental workshop
and its craftsmen. Thomas's words illustrated these shifting dynamics
and the craftsmen's reliance on homer activities to maintain their
threatened occupational identity. "A man's work," observed Everett
Hughes, "is one of the things by which he is judged, and certainly one
of the more significant things by which he judges himself."[11] When the
doors finally closed at the Pierreville experimental workshop where
many craftsmen worked, the remaining craftsmen, unable to perform
their traditional tasks in a redesigned production process, were left
mainly inside the plant, with homer activities to enact their occupational identities.

Beyond the folklore of homers, deeper struggles emerge. Homers reveal the craftsmen's agency, however constrained, and their reliance
on these practices to attach select meaning to their work experiences.
Whereas homer activities might have provided craftsmen with the relevance they sought, they were also tolerated because management
found them appealing. The next chapter details the practices' appeal
from management's perspective, and the many trades in which participants in this gray zone engaged.

8

Trading in Identity Incentives

WHAT HOLDS a community of homer-makers, homer participants, and informed bystanders together? How does the community sustain homer practices? Given our knowledge of the boundaries of homer practices at Pierreville, the shades of meaning associated with such practices, and the craftsmen's diminishing prospects for professional development in the plant, a partial explanation of the sustainability of homer-making can be offered. This chapter discusses three readings of homer-making. Together, these readings provide a conceptual framework for understanding what homer practices and, more broadly, many gray zones are about, and why they persist in organizations to this day.

The first reading frames the interactions as trades—defined as exchanges occurring between gray zone participants. Essentially, these trades concede craftsmen the ability to fulfill their desired occupational identities in exchange for enhanced managerial control. These trades temper the craftsmen's growing discontent with their changing status in the plant, and simultaneously render them partially dependent on the plant's management in order to enact their desired identities. Aero-Dyn leverages these desires of identity enactment to build compliance with managerial will.

A paired, second reading positions homer-making as part of the broader compensation package offered to Pierreville craftsmen. Specifically, some homer interactions can be understood as identity incentives.[1] Such identity incentives are targeted toward specific individuals and, at times, depend on performance, though other criteria also apply. As such, they are more flexible than official incentives (which, at Pierreville, were offered only once a year and applied to broad categories of employees). Leniencies around homer-making constitute part of the plant's incentive system; the combination of official pay and homer tolerance form a compensation "package" for workers. This allows the organization to perform while maintaining or even enhancing the workers' self-images. Paradoxically, the apparently subversive practice of homer-making also benefits the organization. Ultimately, the homer system builds managerial control by engaging plant members in a tacit agreement with management.

Last, this chapter discusses the pockets of situated moralities that emerge within and are surfaced by these gray zones. This third reading of homers as moral pursuits is analyzed from the vantage point of both craftsmen and management. Gray zones "confuse our need to judge," as Primo Levi wrote.[2] Nonetheless, they constitute moral pursuits in their own right—pursuits with which some bystanders might disagree, but that participants deem morally worthy. By unveiling the mechanisms that support these three readings of homer practices, this chapter makes evident their embeddedness (and sustainability). Homer gray zones are part of complex social systems, not merely folklore on the side of a system left intact; they involve trades with the hierarchy, pertain to the broader compensation package offered in the plant, and reveal the situated moralities of these communities.

Trading in Identities alongside Homers

Whereas, historically, homer interactions were framed in the context of labor rebellion and resistance toward management, the analysis of the Pierreville plant suggests a more nuanced relationship, one evoking less contentious trades between participants.[3] At Pierreville, management generally seemed fairly tolerant of these forms of "rebellion," and from management's perspective, some homer practices carried positive connotations. Similarly, craftsmen engage in these trades with an eye more toward affirming their desired occupational identities than rebelling against management. The articulation of clear distinctions between theft and homers helps make this tacit agreement possible, and the continuous border patrol between homers and theft probably accounts for Pierreville's high tolerance of homers. Thus, a tacit labor–management agreement emerges around homer trades.

The main, concrete outcomes—in this instance, manufactured artifacts—might seem prized, but the true currencies of these trades are not the artifacts. Instead, the meanings associated with them form the appreciated currency. At Pierreville, trades in material currency around homers were probably the least common. Few homer activities exclusively involved the acquisition, transformation, and transfer of material in exchange for other material currencies (such as money, other services, or material rewards). Even homer interactions narrated mainly as exchanges were hard to conceptualize as exclusively material trades. If a set of ten homer key chains is really worth a bottle of wine, then why is it that ten bottles of wine sometimes cannot get a person even one key chain? In many instances, trades in which the artifacts are valued purely for their material worth are considered al-

most taboo. Such trades occur at the margin of homer gray zones, oftentimes between craftsmen and unskilled office workers or outsiders,
and are not actively sought out by craftsmen. An illustration of this
taboo was narrated by a Pierreville supervisor who noticed some
welded metal lamps in a furniture store near the plant. When he inquired about whether he could purchase some, the store clerk said they
did not have them in stock right then and that it could take some time
to order more. The clerk then added that the wait time varied since
someone at Pierreville was making them. His reply made it unclear
whether the plant member was producing the lamps on the job or not,
and with or without the consent of his supervisor. Nonetheless, this
framed the practice as a seemingly material pursuit, specifically one
involving non-Pierreville members, and was deemed off-limits by the
supervisor. The apparent profit motive, reminiscent of the distinction
drawn between homers and theft (see chapter 5, "Homers Gone
Wrong: Delimiting the Gray Zone"), troubled the supervisor. Additional lamps were ordered but never delivered, and the culprit was
never identified. All homer trades seem material at first, but the form
is deceiving; the artifacts are a distraction from the locus of action.

Supervisors, engineers, and executives often ordered homers
(framed as jobs or regular work) in exchange for permitting craftsmen
to engage in their own homer activities. However, the artifacts that
resulted from the latter activities were not the primary representation
of the workers' share of the company's tolerance. While artifacts belonging to workers were often brought home, it was not so much the
acquisition and transfer of the artifacts as their meanings that were a
source of satisfaction for them. What mattered most was that the way
in which craftsmen made these homers echoed their occupational
identities. When Pierreville craftsmen showed me the homers in their
homes, they more frequently spoke about what each piece represented to them and rarely about a piece's material value. Only one
person, an outlier in my interview sample and probably in the plant,
openly boasted about the savings he incurred by purchasing homers
at the plant instead of buying commercial items outside. (From the
data I could gather, it seemed he had few close acquaintances at the
plant.) Evidently such material comparisons were made on occasion,
but they rarely prevailed. Thus, describing homers only in terms of
their material value would not do justice to the majority of the accounts I gathered.

A parallel can be drawn between these homers and the white arm-
shells (akin to bracelets) and long red shell necklaces traded by the
Trobrianders (the inhabitants of the Trobriand Islands) of Papua New
Guinea.[4] These shells are a pretext, in many ways, for the rituals and

ceremonies later enacted. As Annette Weiner further clarifies in her discussion of these shells (and banana-leaf bundles and skirts also exchanged), "Trobrianders, like people in other parts of the world, give meanings to things that make them worth more than their cost in labor and the material of which they are made."[5] Returning to Pierreville, less material currencies—specifically respect and recognition—were the important ones traded in this process.

Respect and recognition—or, more simply put, dignity—was perhaps the currency most sought after by craftsmen. Dignity, understood as finding "a sense of meaning and accomplishment in work and the creation of positive and supportive coworker relations," was here achieved through the recognition of craftsmen's membership in a valued occupational community.[6] During the period of study, maintaining dignity was a pressing concern for craftsmen, given their increasing marginalization at Pierreville. Though members of a dying occupational group such as the craftsmen's might be more likely than those of a rising group to seek dignity in their work, their quest is probably typical of that of many contemporary workers.[7] Regardless of one's dignity baseline, this pursuit is universal, and may be realized through the enactment of prized occupational identities.

In some instances, craftsmen achieved such dignity simply by manufacturing—under the watch of supervisors and peers—homers that they kept for themselves. These instances showcase the manner in which homers may preclude trades in material currency and still retain great value. What was traded in these cases, more than anything else, was the ability to enact a given identity before others. One craftsman who clearly understood this kept a photo album of the homers he created, readily and proudly showing it to inquisitive coworkers. Other workers spoke of fully articulated miniature engine reproductions certain craftsmen built for themselves in almost legendary terms. ("He once made a miniature engine that was so perfect that it could run.")

Homer artifacts that were not circulated were testimonies to the fact that trades around homers were not only material; instead, meanings were circulated. In her fieldwork, Weiner also documents instances of rarely circulated yet highly valuable shells (labeled *kitomu*).[8] The mere possession of the artifacts allows their owners to gain status in the circle of exchange, even when the *kitomu* are not circulated. At Pierreville, the most respected homer-makers were known for making artifacts they hardly ever gave away or traded. A craftsman once brought such a homer to the Labor Council for us to see. It was wrapped in cloth like a jewel and kept safe in a cardboard box. The ceremony surrounding the craftsman's display of his homer (a miniature replica of a workstation) commanded respect. Arguably, their absence of material equivalency did not render these homers worthless; quite the contrary. Trades in meanings were the norm at Pierreville.

These trades entailed the exchange of meanings that could be made similar or distinct through homer interactions. The multiplicity of meanings associated with homer interactions allowed plant members to participate in the trades on their own terms; namely, they could view the interactions differently, yet still engage in them without these asymmetries blocking the trade.[9] (Following Mary Douglas's argument on the sacred, it is perhaps precisely because homer interactions had multiple meanings that they retained their "sacred" quality in the eyes of craftsmen. Ambiguous distinctions between the sacred and the profane are what make the sacred prized to believers, who see what others cannot.)[10] Primarily, trades among craftsmen involved similar meanings of respect and recognition; but distinct meanings often coexisted in trades across occupations. For example, a craftsman might offer what he deemed akin to collegiality to an unskilled or office worker, while the recipient might perceive the interaction as a form of respect and recognition. Similarly, a craftsman could engage in what he considered regular work for a supervisor, and the supervisor might see it as a form of respect and recognition.

The key element of homer activities entailed trading, regardless of the symmetry (or lack thereof) of the traded meanings. However, in order to facilitate the process, trades followed a somewhat expected pattern, but retained enough flexibility to allow for some multivocality in meanings.[11] Venturing too far beyond this framework led to taboo trade-offs, such as when a craftsman found himself selling a homer to another craftsman. These situations were probably exceptions. Trades that violated the deeply held normative intuitions regarding the patterns such interactions should follow were, for the most part, avoided.[12] Overall, most of the trades provided a smooth and informal regulating mechanism in the workshops. There were few denunciations, limited refusals, and a largely accepted distinction between homer activities and theft. The trades that occurred within homer activities offered a unique way to integrate the behaviors of relatively autonomous actors, which is, in essence, the definition of organizing.[13] The trades accommodated the coexistence of very contrasted meanings. In some instances, respect and recognition could be found alongside other meanings, such as when a craftsman engaged in complex homer work for a boss (regular work) or was paid by an office worker to craft an extremely elaborate artifact (exchange). Implicitly, the craftsmen's ability to enact a desired identity was fundamentally at stake in these homer practices.

But why did other Pierreville members participate in these trades? Specifically, why was Pierreville's management so tolerant of this gray zone? These questions first require an understanding of what management and, by extension, the organization gained by tolerating such practices. Examining these gains helps explain the sustainability of these gray zones. Paradoxically, the more opportunities craftsmen were given to engage in homer activities on their own terms and trade in meanings they found most beneficial to their quest for relevance in the plant, the more dependent their occupational identities became on management's tolerance. Craftsmen's reliance on organizational leniencies to reinforce, if not generate, their identities came at a cost: added compliance to managerial will. As Marcel Mauss reminds us in his essay on gifts, the etymological root of the word "gift" is the same in both German and Greek, meaning "poison."[14] The close association between these two words derives from the obligation to reciprocate a gift. A gift accepted (say, the latitude to engage in homer work) is accompanied by the expectation of a gift reciprocated (added engagement in official production or added loyalty to management). In this way, homer interactions that on the surface may, from a corporate and managerial perspective, appear counterproductive, might in fact benefit organizations. These interactions certainly seem aligned with management's goals—goals, in theory, also partly aligned with those of the organization.

Controlling Craftsmen through Identity Incentives

Historically, from management's perspective, craftsmen were an important constituency to please. Though craftsmen at Pierreville would never dream of sabotaging plant production, other expressions of discontent could become problematic. The craftsmen knew the safety of passengers was a paramount concern, and as they worked, this concern was constantly in the back of their minds. Plant members often discussed airplane accidents, whether or not they involved AeroDyn engines. (Visiting the home of one retiree revealed shelves of videotapes of airplane accidents that he watched in order to gain insight into what went wrong in each crash.) The quality of their work was rarely compromised. A more common expression of discontent was to delay the speed of development and manufacture of engines. Discontent among craftsmen could rapidly become challenging; they were highly united and strongly unionized, and they could complain collectively when they were dissatisfied. A craftsman who worked in the experimental workshop recalled: "Whenever we had a problem in the work-

shop [he whistled to indicate a call to action] . . . all of us were in the
workshop manager's office. If it didn't go well with the workshop
manager, we headed up to the department head. If that didn't work,
we went to the head of personnel." Work stoppages were not an unknown at Pierreville. Because craftsmen could control the speed of testing and the delivery of engines, their cooperation was extremely important. Management was therefore accustomed to courting them.

But even when craftsmen started losing their key role in engine development, the erratic schedule of aircraft engine deliveries continued
to make them important players in the plant. The timing of deliveries
could see extremely idle periods quickly alternate with nonstop work
weeks, necessitating extra shifts. Historically, the irregularity of demand was a source of considerable uncertainty for Pierreville management. In order to manage this unpredictability, many Pierreville members considered themselves "on call," like surgeons or emergency
responders, when official production needed to be "cranked out."
They were well aware of the fluctuation in demand, and most fully
accepted it as part of their job. Workshop supervisors and other executives or engineers therefore relied on craftsmen to ensure that the manufacture of official AeroDyn products did not derail, specifically under
tight deadlines. By giving them slack to manufacture homers, the hierarchy could expect in return greater flexibility in official work, efforts
on ordered homer work, or even reactivity to other requests. The recollection of this blacksmith illustrates this give-and-take mechanism:
"The workshop heads said almost nothing [when they noticed ho-
mers]. They'd let it slide. I had one boss, but I didn't give a damn about
him. In my [official] work I had nothing to be ashamed of. I used to
do my work in such a way that nobody could complain. That way, if
one day I needed to make a homer, no one could hold it against me."

Often it was the most skilled workers in the factory who received
greater latitude to engage in homer work. They were less concerned
with their bosses' opinions since they knew they were needed in the
factory. By the same token, their official work had to be beyond reproach. As a blacksmith and frequent homer-maker recalls, "As far as
[regular] work was concerned, deliveries were always on time. Work
was well done; there was no reproach to be said about the work."
Thus, in a way, leniency for personal homer-making activities was
framed as "compensation" for doing well on official or ordered work.[15]
Turning a blind eye to homer activities that did not directly benefit
supervisors or executives meant potentially benefiting later from the
craftsmen's skills. Though the Pierreville retirees I interviewed and
came to know rarely brought up internal organizational politics, there
was nothing keeping factions in the hierarchy from selectively enforc-

ing rules to their own advantage.[16] Competing factions of management could rely on selective enforcements to consolidate their power and build loyalty among their troops. Perhaps the high reliance on seniority as a deciding factor in one's potential for promotion in the plant tamed such internal politics. Nonetheless, the potential for the politically motivated use of leniencies cannot be entirely discounted.[17]

Since homer activities were often hard to ignore, most Pierreville supervisors were aware of what was happening in their workshops. When craftsmen worked on drawings that did not correspond to an official engine piece, supervisors knew homers were being made. Rarely did workers intentionally hide their homer endeavors; a hidden homer suddenly discovered could be a pretext for disciplinary action. But if a supervisor had seen a homer, it was a sign of tacit approval. "The way in which the [workshop] boss participated [in homer-making] was to see without saying anything, but clearly make it understood that he knew," explained a craftsman. In doing so, management implicitly approved of the practice.

However, not all homer-makers were given as much leeway. As one craftsman recalls, "People would get caught. . . . He [the homer-maker] got a one- or two-day suspension. . . . But otherwise, you could get fired on the spot." Cases of homer-makers who were disciplined for their actions attest to this. An analysis of records from the Pierreville archives from a ten-year period (1970 to 1980) yielded only seven cases of individuals who were disciplined for homer-related activities, but these case were well known among plant members. (For a discussion of some of these cases, see chapter 5.) The fact that many more cases of larger homers made during that period (such as the case of the garden barbecues or the discovery of the room full of homers) went unpunished suggests a selective enforcement of rules.

When craftsmen are in a position of strength, leniency toward homer activities can be seen as an engagement between the organization and a specific group of workers. It can also be conceptualized as an efficiency wage; that is, a salary above and beyond what the market would dictate, with the expectation of higher productivity.[18] In a sense, management feels compelled to negotiate, but also looks forward to negotiating with craftsmen to ensure their satisfactory performance on official production and on other requests. Tolerance of homer-making is a hidden incentive. Supervisors grant "good" workers more leeway to engage in homer work, and the workers know what is expected of them in return.

Whereas official incentives, which tend to be more explicit, force the articulation of broader agreed-upon principles to account for pay discrepancies, homer incentives support the creation of local, more situated arrangements. Official wages at Pierreville were regulated by multiyear collective agreements that associated salary levels with legal employment categories and job coefficients. Plant members gained their job coefficients mainly through seniority and training. Within a given employment category, such as the French "workers" category (*ouvriers*), the coefficients could account for a doubling of the average monthly salary. While this might seem like an important figure, the fact that these coefficients were based on objective measures—mainly outside the purview of managerial discretion—severely hampered their usefulness as managerial tools. Strict union enforcement of these collective agreements ensured limited room for managers to exercise discretion. Besides, historically, AeroDyn's dominant culture was not one that encouraged pay discrimination. From 1970 to 2000, when the retirees I interviewed were working in the plant, the multiple between the average monthly salaries of the top 10 percent and the bottom 10 percent of the workforce (in salary levels) was approximately three. Though salary differences could clearly be found between and within categories, they rarely qualified as managerial levers to distinguish among plant members on an individual basis.

In contrast, both supervisors and, to some extent, coworkers had a hand in assessing who received more leeway to engage in homer work. Although such instances were rare, any plant member had the ability to alert the guards that a coworker was leaving the factory with a homer or producing an illegal artifact. When this happened and management did not want to or could not defend the culprit, he or she could incur financial costs (unpaid leave) and face termination. Targeted and distinct tolerance levels around homer-making could be enforced for specific individuals. The burden of regulation was thus shared within the group (encompassing supervisors and workshop members) rather than at the plant or corporate level, and supervisors had an important say in setting those levels of tolerance. Such arrangements around homers offered venues for more nuanced regulation than corporate, company-wide policies might ever allow. They provided management with influential ways to distinguish among their workers beyond what employment categories and coefficients would allow for—something difficult to achieve with official salaries alone (given the context of Pierreville). Thus, by engaging in homer-making and accepting a reward in this manner, a worker entered into an implicit contract that conceded management significant additional control.

Tolerance of homer-making was not the only form of hidden incentives at Pierreville. Managerial tolerance of workers taking time off during official work hours, by taking extended lunch periods or sick days when they knew they were not needed in the workshop, also constituted forms of hidden incentives. It is difficult to document whether sick days were granted for reasons other than legitimate sickness; nonetheless, upper management became intrigued by what was perceived—rightly or wrongly so—as excessive leniency. A well-intended yet probably ill-advised upper-level manager once tried to regulate this practice by enforcing a new internal company rule regarding sick days. The rule stated that any plant member who missed more than ten days of work during the previous year would not be eligible for a salary increase the following year. (Union work, official holidays, and weekends were excluded from the number of days considered, but all other days off, specifically sick days, were taken into account.) The manager's intention was to increase the presence of workers at Pierreville. A very large protest involving most of the Pierreville workforce ensued, which then led to demonstrations in Paris. Aside from the fact that this new rule was at odds with French labor law, which often strongly protects workers' rights (not to mention the rights of sick workers who might require more than ten days off in a year), the manager who spearheaded the reform overlooked a crucial labor-regulating mechanism in the plant.

For the most part, plant members were more than willing to help when needed, but in exchange expected leniency when they required time off. The somewhat loose accounting of lunch periods and sick time was probably, in some instances, a way to compensate workers for being available at other times. As this episode regarding the sick day policy illustrates, the ongoing maintenance of the craftsmen's involvement in official production—despite the unpredictability of demand—was crucial. It is possible that one avenue by which management encouraged this ongoing involvement was through the creative use of time, but probably more commonly through its tolerance of homer activities, particularly during idle periods.

A likely consequence of this tacit labor–management agreement must be pointed out. Workers engaged in gray zones might be less inclined to voice their discontent (and claim their desired identities) in more confrontational manners. Gray zones have the capacity to temper such concerns. Whether these findings inspire joy or sorrow is for the reader to conclude. From a radical viewpoint, these findings are probably a deception; what might be imagined as a potential seed of revolt (i.e., homer-making) simply becomes absorbed in the broader patterns of Pierreville labor relations. From an individual organization member's perspective, this might seem reassuring. Gray zones offer alternative venues for enactment of valued identities. Organizations are powerful entities that enable and constrain individual action; finding local venues where such enactments are permitted is, to some extent, soothing.

Situated Moralities

When operating in a gray zone, management continually makes decisions regarding specific practices as they may apply to given individuals. With every such occurrence, managers allocate and reallocate discretionary and, often less visible, hidden incentives. Concurrently, craftsmen decide what they can or cannot do. All these decisions require constant judgment and the creation of what I refer to as "situated moralities." Situated moralities result from the multiple, sometimes competing evaluations participants make in these gray zones. Organizational regulation requires a shared, local understanding of what is appropriate. An external normative perspective on homer-making might thus require some revision. At minimum, an attempt should be made to understand the internal moralities of these arrangements and their potential for competing moral interpretations. Moralities are akin to "everyday rules in use" that participants agree to follow.[19] Given the nuances inherent in homer practices, judgment should not be made with haste.

From the workers' perspective, homer-making is not seen only as a liberating activity. Management's tolerance of homer-making positioned the homer-maker as having little leeway to reject a request from above. Outside of official production, supervisors, executives, and engineers sometimes relied on their formal hierarchical power to coax participants into working for them. In the process, the official social structure of the plant was reinforced; homer interactions resulted in members' consent to the plant hierarchy.[20] The form of consent in which craftsmen engaged when making homers was also somewhat deceiving, because although they often enjoyed the work, they did not directly benefit from it since their bosses were the main recipients of the ordered homers they made. Given this likelihood, homer interactions are not exactly liberating: in this gray zone, they reproduced a microcosm of the broader labor dynamics and official hierarchy that prevailed in the plant. In these instances, the hierarchy might be suspect of holding dubious moral grounds since they could abuse their authority. But before reaching any hasty conclusions, another dynamic ought to be explored, that which arises between craftsmen and lower-level plant members.

Engaging in homer interactions with lower-level plant members can be seen as a way for craftsmen to share their higher status—collegiality at its best. Craftsmen perhaps had the greatest degree of freedom at Pierreville: strong union representation and, until recently, many coveted skills. Engaging in homer interactions with office employees and unskilled workers was perhaps a way for them to share the rewards of their position. But craftsmen who accepted monetary or other compensation for their services also benefited from their position (as did higher-level plant members who requested homers). When they delayed requests from lower-level plant members, craftsmen were also reinforcing their standing in the plant. In the case of the time-card currency exchanges that occurred at the Terre-Neuve plant, the use of a uniform currency initially hinted at equality among participants, but the fact that unskilled workers were the ones spending most of their time cards and craftsmen the ones accumulating them suggests an uneven flow. These episodes of craftsmen "profiting" from and delaying homer interactions with lower-level plant members point to layered moralities. What is the moral justification for a craftsman to delay a homer request from a lower-level plant member? If nothing other than the power imbalance in the relationship explains it, how justified is it? In interactions narrated as exchanges involving craftsmen and lower-level plant members, the craftsmen's morality might be deemed tainted since they benefited from their relative position in the plant to dictate the terms of the engagement. In the example of the craftsman who put a price on an office worker's homer request (see chapter 6), what if the office worker really needed the homer and the price had been doubled? How might the craftsman's behavior be judged? Social limits apply to a craftsman's discretion, but are these limits acceptable to all involved?[21]

Finally, interactions narrated as respect and recognition involving only craftsmen—even when the materials transformed are scraps—might be construed by outsiders as theft, because company property is used and the activities are performed during work hours. Craftsmen might consider these respect and recognition interactions at the core of their occupational identity (rooted in skilled manual work and independence), but outsiders might be dubious of such claims. To illustrate this point, consider the proposition that "a little larceny can do a lot for employee morale."[22] This suggestion, though not in reference to gray zone practices per se, implies that some level of theft might generate positive individual benefits—and possibly positive organizational outcomes, since high employee morale is assumed to benefit the organization. All things considered, limited theft might serve a worthy cause. When an industrial psychologist formulated this proposition based on his research, some reviewers were not even remotely willing to entertain the notion of theft as permissible; theft is theft, and it should not be allowed under any circumstance. While he reported his findings in another outlet, the *Harvard Business Review* rejected his article, and in a letter, spelled out the issue reviewers had with his findings: "To be perfectly frank, the consensus is that your conclusions—especially the idea of a tolerable amount of theft—aren't consistent with the ideals of *HBR* [*Harvard Business Review*]." Evidently these ideals, though not clearly articulated in the letter, did not allow for any endorsement of theft. Gray zone practices by craftsmen would probably generate similar reactions among some outside observers. Nothing would redeem the theftlike characteristic of the practice since company material and company hours are being stolen in the process.

Overall, many moralities exist within homer practices, and the normative interpretation of them requires a close look at the meanings of the practices and the trades being conducted. Situated moralities, moralities that make sense and exist only within given social contexts, abound in these gray zones.[23] The historical, scholarly interpretation of homer interactions as rebellion against management probably better reflects the observers' hopes than the empirical practice of homer-making.[24] The Pierreville homer analysis finds, in place of rebellion, a high potential for labor–management complicity, and layered moralities. The majority of homer interactions seem to produce occupational identities and organizational control, even though instances of (concomitant) exploitation (by management, but also by craftsmen) cannot be entirely discounted. The benefits that specific occupational groups derive from the enactment of these moralities are further explained in the next chapter.

Though craftsmen often spoke more openly of homer activities than the hierarchy did, they still knew that the morality of their practices might not translate well to external settings. Consequently, many normalizing narratives were used to render these situated moralities more acceptable to external audiences.[25] The three most common strategies used to normalize the practices were conceptually distancing homer activities from theft; stressing the relative inconsequentiality of homer behavior; and playing up the potential organizational benefits of homer practices. All of these strategies point to a need to justify the integrity of the practice to external observers. None acknowledged the intertwined social regulation achieved through these practices; instead, they emphasized the economic returns (or absence of economic loss) linked to homer-making. Chapter 5 already detailed the first normalizing strategy, which consists of differentiating homer interactions from theft. The main distinctions are that homer-making involved scraps (rather than new materials), a transformation of materials (rather than mere repossession), and no monetary profit (unless the combination of participants tolerated it). The first and third of these three distinctions inform the second normalizing strategy: the argument around inconsequentiality.

Because most homers are made from scraps, which, by definition, have little to no market value, they can generate only minimal profit, or constitute only petty theft. (However, this narrative disregards the fact that scraps of expensive materials still attract high secondary market values.) As Johnny Cash eloquently describes in his song about building a car for himself from parts at General Motors, where he is supposedly employed: "Now, I never considered myself a thief. GM wouldn't miss just one little piece, especially if I strung it out over several years."[26] Other, more consequential gray zone behaviors at Pierreville were often offered by craftsmen as a comparison to emphasize the inconsequentiality of homer interactions. The "slush" entertainment funds to which some high-level executives were entitled, paybacks certain executives supposedly secured when negotiating contracts with foreign countries, and insider trading reported in the French national press involving AeroDyn stocks were all presented as similar practices with hidden incentives, involving much larger sums of money. Depicting other Pierreville members as engaging in more consequential pilfering contributed to the exoneration of homer-makers, but by association, also slightly tainted them (since they all worked for the same plant). Thus, outsiders with less of a connection to the plant were sometimes enrolled in this normalizing process. The scrap metal merchant who frequently visited Pierreville was an easy scapegoat. Identifying this "profiting" scrap metal merchant, a Pierreville outsider, as a counterexample to homer-making was a common strategy. Homer-makers would assert that he made a "fortune," while Pierreville members realized only marginal material benefits from homers. The consequences of homer-making inherently depended on the selected reference point.

A final, more intriguing normalizing strategy emphasized the trickle-down benefits of homer activities to the organization. These benefits were not explicitly framed in organizational terms, but instead referenced measurable outputs, such as patents. Several informants suggested that technical issues with which Pierreville staff struggled were resolved through homer practices, and possibly led to patents for AeroDyn. One example of a "patentable" invention linked to homer activities was the development of a specific tool, which allowed one to work inside an engine without actually disassembling it. The fact that I was not able to document this or any other patent linked to homers does not render the strategy irrelevant. Rather, what these normalizing narratives suggest is an awareness of the situated moralities of homer arrangements and the potential stigma risked, were the arrangements to be disclosed outside the workshop or plant.

Trades in identity incentives, the possibility for added organizational control, and the creation of situated moralities all contribute to the sustainability of homer gray zones. Various meanings are constructed and traded through homer activities. Homer gray zone interactions serve as social enablers, relying on hidden identity incentives to facilitate the regulation of activities between management and craftsmen as well as within the workers' community. In the process, situated moralities embedded in a given community are voiced and built. Their meanings are confined to the Pierreville community in the same way they might be confined to a specific neighborhood or a given street.[27] Moreover, many moralities coexist, some of which reinforce rather than reshuffle the existing social dynamics in the plant. What some might characterize as immoral (akin to theft) is shown to be perceived by others as highly moral (since it enhances their occupational identity).

"Small and shabby objects" deemed too trivial to warrant attention are often powerful revealers of complex social struggles, wrote Walter Benjamin.[28] Homers would probably fit his definition; they uncover profound regulating mechanisms in the Pierreville plant that both generate and sustain occupational identities, organizational control, and situated moralities. In retrospect, tolerance of homer practices might be a small price to pay for such critical social outcomes. The puzzling question, then, becomes, how can organizations operate without gray zones? The real paradox, in that case, is the absence rather than the presence of gray zones.

Part Three

THE IMPLICATIONS

9

Organizational Gray Zones as Identity Distillers

THE HOMER PRACTICES that are the focus of this book might seem slightly esoteric to those unfamiliar with industrial settings, yet many organizations harbor their own distinct gray zones. Though rarely documented, gray zones are present in many and varied work settings. This chapter takes pause from homer-making at Pierreville to discuss some examples of other organizational gray zones, and to describe the occupational dynamics at play within each setting. An exploration of disparate work environments—ranging from hospitals and restaurants to docks and postal services—demonstrates the prevalence of gray zones and the pervasiveness of identity pursuits within these zones. Though these gray zones occur in environments different from Pierreville, they ultimately rely on mechanisms similar to those described in the aeronautic plant.

Beyond the peculiarity of each example, commonalities emerge: gray zones are shown to be particularly apt venues for enacting and revealing occupational identities. Gray zones first command the attention of participants (and observers) and, as such, create a focused audience that open settings often lack. In addition, gray zones present opportunities for inappropriate enactment, thus carrying the potential for friction between participants to emerge (around what is proper or not). Given that friction often reveals contrasting identities, gray zones provide opportunities for these differences to become salient. These commonalities, discussed at the end of this chapter, further link the sustainability of gray zones, more generally, to identity dynamics.

Specifying the Gray Zone

Organizational gray zone activities differ from criminal activities in that their outcomes do not necessarily occasion external prosecution. Their "grayness" is defined relative to internal organizational rules rather than external laws. Moreover, criminal activities can be perpetrated by lonely individuals, whereas gray zones require, at the very least, the tacit involvement of supervisors. Gray zones have been defined throughout this book as areas in which workers and their supervisors together engage in practices that are officially forbidden, yet tolerated by the organization. This means that two components are required for a gray zone to emerge: (1) the breaking of official company rules, and (2) the supervisors' explicit or tacit approval of the violation of these rules. For example, retail store clerks who, without supervision, decide to close the store ten minutes before the official closing time are not engaging in a gray zone practice. However, if these same store clerks were to do so with the approval of their direct supervisor, they would be engaging in a gray zone practice. This last example also illustrates that not all gray zone activities risk external prosecution. Nothing in the law states that a store cannot close before its official closing time. If these same store clerks were to leave work ten minutes early (regardless of whether or not they closed the store), then perhaps a criminal prosecution could be pursued for "theft of company time." In general, however, many gray zone practices are not criminal.

The fact that contemporary organizations might rely on more elaborate employee monitoring mechanisms could appear to endanger the existence of gray zone practices. Factory workers, for instance, still produce homers, but perhaps less so than in the past. Airline flight attendants on extended stopovers who, with the tacit approval of the cabin chief, help themselves to onboard alcohol for private consumption also engage in gray zone practices.[1] Again, this might seem harder to pull off in a contemporary organization that relies more heavily on rules and monitoring mechanisms to control behavior.[2] For instance, whereas in the past truck drivers could pick up passengers en route, today a video camera is often used to monitor the driver's seat. In some instances, a driver can lose his job if he picks up a passenger (a practice that goes against company rules but often used to be tolerated).[3]

However, two important reasons suggest that gray zones are here to stay. First, gray zones involve tacit managerial approval. Thus, it is not because employees are more highly monitored that gray zone practices will disappear; instead, employees are now made more aware of their supervisor's tacit approval. The risk that a supervisor's manager might more quickly notice what is happening locally and have stronger evidence to document the practices might threaten the local supervisor's ability to deny knowledge of the practice (in cases of legal pursuits), but not his ability to tolerate it. New monitoring systems might in fact broaden the boundaries of the gray zone "open secret": more people at various levels are now in the know.[4] In other words, what Georg Simmel referred to as the open secret participants' "particular kind of shading and togetherness" attracts new members. Assuming this "togetherness" does not get diluted in this process, contemporary gray zones might call for enrolling participants beyond a traditional core group.[5]

Second, the extent to which the homer analysis at Pierreville revealed gray zones as venues in which identity pursuits play out suggests that gray zones will remain prevalent. Independent of work setting and historical period, many gray zones seem to offer ways to fashion desired occupational identities. Even flight attendants' consumption of alcohol, which might seem disconnected from any occupational dynamic, warrants closer observation; maintaining composure during flights is core to their occupational identity (characterized by engaging in emotional labor), and to the extent that alcohol consumption facilitates maintaining composure on subsequent flights, it informs their occupational identity.[6] What might initially be labeled as theft takes on very different undertones. The practice of stealing alcohol from one's employer, though generally reprehensible, can be seen in this specific case as helping to compose an occupational identity—one in which accommodating the airline passenger's slightest whim is endured during the flight, with the expectation of being able to completely "let go" once the flight ends. Aside from any potential health hazards such practices might cause if abused, they also influence how flight attendants see themselves. Today, the cabin chief might be better able to monitor the level of "theft." However, this does not mean that she is less likely to tolerate it. Thus, there is little reason to believe that such gray zones will cease to exist. Moreover, regardless of the perceived base level of identity status (be it of truck drivers or tenured university professors) and the conditions experienced (those of threatened or rising occupations), identity pursuits remain rampant at work.

This does not mean that the nature of contemporary gray zones will not evolve. More specifically, assuming monitoring increasingly focuses on company materials, and other individuals (aside from direct supervisors) are put in charge of such monitoring, gray zones involving tangible company material appropriation might gradually be replaced by gray zones that involve less tangible appropriation. It is probably easier for a supervisor to decide locally about gray zone practices without having to involve an outside monitor. A first set of examples of gray zones without tangible company material appropriation, reviewed in the next section, might exemplify a class of more contemporary gray zones. Gray zones such as these in which company materials are not clearly appropriated (but instead, for instance, company time is diverted) are probably also less likely to be viewed as theft by external observers. But this does not mean that more traditional gray zones (i.e., involving appropriation of company materials) do not exist today. A second set of examples of these latter gray zones (including instances of appropriation of cargo and medicine) is also discussed in this chapter. Together, these examples provide insight into contemporary gray zones in work settings other than factories, both with and without tangible material appropriation.

Gray Zones without Tangible Company Material Appropriation

Monitoring organizational gray zones is not easily achieved in the following examples in which material appropriation of company property is hard to recognize. These examples, with settings ranging from the U.S. Postal Service to ambulances, further clarify the linkages between gray zone practices and occupational identities. They also point to the prevalence of gray zones in what are perhaps more familiar settings.

Since their delivery routes and tasks are highly controlled, the choices postal carriers make about delivering mail are fairly constrained. However, a carrier who wishes to deliver mail to a given home earlier than the official schedule dictates is often encouraged to do so by his supervisor, albeit without any official endorsement of changes to the delivery route schedule. Carriers who participate in such activities and finish their routes before the workday officially ends often engage in "hiding." Hiding—when carriers go home or leave their posts before the end of the official workday—is an important part of the work routine that, while generally tolerated by management, is unlikely to ever earn official endorsement.[7] The carriers operate in a gray zone—their supervisors are well aware of the official rule breach, yet impose no disciplinary action. They are able to end their day earlier by modifying the schedule of delivery, but by doing so, they also please the customer. Though annual tips might be perceived as an incentive to please customers, carriers play down such motives, insisting instead that they are responding to a sense of duty. Supervisors are also well aware of this sense of duty. They know it looks best if their carriers "hurry and get their routes done right." "This makes them look like they are hurrying and not lazy and the customer gets his mail early."[8] One of the core elements of carriers' occupational identity is to bring all the mail, on time, to each and every customer. Tactics such as finding shortcuts (e.g., jumping over fences) to optimize the timely execution of their routes or turning over their mailbags when they return to the post office to ensure no mail was forgotten show how important it is to carriers to be viewed in that way. The practice of hiding, which allows them to add some flexibility in the execution of their routes, helps them get home earlier, but also enact their occupational identity.

Mail carriers are not alone in alerting us to the interplay between gray zones and occupational identities. The behaviors of construction crews, paramedics, and emergency medical technicians also showcase this interplay. Threatened with delays in the work schedule by property owners who insist that machinery and workers remain strictly in the right of way (e.g., the area around railroad tracks that is legally open to such work), members of a pipeline construction crew might arrange with their supervisors to offer property owners some simple labor in exchange for the latitude to get their job done quickly.[9] Such arrangements, of course, are outside company rules, but ultimately reinforce the crew's sense of occupational duty. Periods of idleness are detrimental to the crew since they want to get the job done quickly, ideally with overtime wages, and move on to the next job. Skilled pipeline crew members are particularly in demand during construction's high season (from June to August), and gain recognition during this period by going from job to job, working overtime at each, and building enough income to withstand the slower periods of the year. The financial incentives for adopting this work pattern are numerous, but the ability to work nonstop during the high season also informs the occupational identity of pipeline crews. The most skilled crews work as teams, going from job to job without stopping, as long as the weather permits. Bending rules with the approval of supervisors might be necessary to ensure the proper completion of work, but it also acknowledges the way these crew members see themselves, namely, as "hired hands" completing as many jobs as possible during the peak work season.

Paramedics and emergency medical technicians (EMTs), often the first medical responders to arrive at the scene of an emergency, provide another illustration of occupational dynamics at play in gray zones. These individuals are charged with delivering patients to a certified emergency physician as quickly as possible. Officially, few medical procedures deemed necessary to a patient's survival are authorized at the scene or in transit. Most require the explicit approval of a physician. But physicians often afford paramedics and EMTs considerable leeway to "play doctor" or "experiment" with certain drugs and dosages when they believe it critical to a patient's survival (in their words, when the patient is going to "code" or "crash"). Physicians tolerate such practices so internal rules do not prevent rescue workers from "doing what is necessary" to save a life.[10] Paramedics and EMTs, on the other hand, operate in these gray zones because it is what their jobs are about: saving lives.

Gray Zones Involving Tangible Company Material Appropriation

Gray zones that involve the appropriation of tangible company materials are more easily identifiable, and perhaps more easily monitored. These gray zone practices are also more likely to be labeled as theft given that materials are being diverted. The following examples further reveal the linkages between these gray zones and identity dynamics, while extending the range of examples of work settings that harbor gray zones.

Consider the case in which hospital nurses take general supplies, over-the-counter medicines, and non-narcotic drugs—with the tacit approval of their peers and supervisors—for personal use. Supervising nurses often dismiss discrepancies in inventory as errors.[11] A closer look at the kinds of medicines and drugs taken and the circumstances considered fair game for personal appropriation helps us understand the relation with occupational identities. Nurses often see themselves as caregivers whose job is to help patients at any cost. Thus, when the patients no longer need them, general supplies, over-the-counter medicines, and non-narcotic drugs can be appropriated. Leftovers that were not distributed or excess prescriptions are the preferred conditions for such appropriations, as patients are not harmed by the practice. Moreover, nursing is a physically demanding occupation, so theoretically, appropriating remedies for personal use allows nurses to continue carrying out their jobs effectively. In contrast, narcotic drugs, due to their potency and the fact that they are usually prescribed in only the necessary amounts, are deemed off-limits for appropriation. The nurses' ability to distinguish which practices affect patients and which might increase their own alertness to better treat patients is what allows them to engage in these practices. Though these rationales could be depicted as mere ex-post justifications for behaviors forbidden in hospitals, they are also explained by the occupational identity of nurses. (Knowing what patients need and being alert enough to deliver a high level of care are core to nursing.) Paradoxically, the nurses who care best for their patients and are most committed to performing their jobs might be more inclined to engage in these gray zone behaviors since they know what *not* to take and strive for peak personal performance.

Restaurants and dining rooms offer similar opportunities for "fiddling." For example, head waiters sometimes collude with waiters to remove some of the items paid for by customers from recorded receipts, and then distribute the extra revenues among the staff according to complex sharing procedures. The head waiter is expected to defend the waiters if anything goes awry. Thus, an order of three coffees might be recorded on the books as only two coffees—even though the customer's receipt lists three coffees—and the payment for the extra coffee is shared (obviously fiddling pricier entrées is more lucrative than coffees).[12] The fiddle can be seen as a self-defined "tip," the amount of which is determined partly by the head waiter. More important, fiddling reflects the ability of the head waiter to coordinate with his staff. Moreover, the power of the head waiter over his staff is reinforced in the process. That kind of coordination, both integral to and ensuing from the collusion, is precisely what is required to provide customers with a high-end dining experience. Ultimately, the customer is not directly harmed since the bill received corresponds to the order placed. The restaurant owner loses revenue, but also probably gains in the staff's quality of service. Being able to execute a "fiddle" is a testimony to the occupational "competence" of the head waiter and the dining room staff.

However pricey an entrée might be, it probably still pales in comparison to valuable cargo arriving or departing on ships. Longshoremen loading and unloading merchandise sometimes "hone in on 'rootless' cargos, in transit between large, impersonal firms, which are covered by insurance, and which are always fair game." "Individual cargos, like personal baggage," are not considered appropriate items to divert. That these workers engage in this behavior consistently and are bothered only when the level of "theft" exceeds accepted norms hints at the high likelihood that supervisors are tacitly aware of the activity.[13] This gray zone is part of the occupational routine of dockworkers— almost a sign that they are operating normally and the team is sufficiently coordinated to deliver results (even if the results mean the theft of selected goods). Further probing shows that the most highly skilled workers are also the ones who control access to the goods and manage those without access; these individuals are entrusted with coordinating the fiddling for the group.[14] Time after time, a respected longshoreman can load and unload merchandise. Consistency is also expected of them professionally. Thus, on the docks, the manner of fiddling points to professionalism, which enhances the occupational identity of longshoremen as reliable employees. It is not only what they fiddle, but also how they fiddle that longshoremen care most about. The proper practice of loading and unloading is at stake.

Additionally, consider garment shops that allow supervisors and cutters to earn extra money "under the table" making and selling items from the shops' extra material.[15] These workers are usually careful to pick property of "uncertain ownership." Their ability to make elegant clothes out of extra (scrap) sections of fabric is a testimony to their occupational competency. Also, the proximity between these forms of transformation and the rewards for good work are evident; garment workers are being implicitly recognized by their supervisors for their ability to produce. The major axiom in the industry is "the more work you do, the more work you get back"; garment workers who master their craft are also the ones who could benefit most from gray zone practices. They are sought after by supervisors because of their abilities and take pride in showcasing their skills. Thus, the implicit assumption is that "the more work you get back," the better the seamstress you are.

Finally, reflect on the senior investment banker who covers up some potentially questionable expenses for the junior analysts working for him or her. Using a company-paid car service to return home from the office after a certain hour (for instance, 10 p.m. at some New York banks) is a commonly authorized practice. But instances of analysts expensing cab rides before the officially authorized hour (say, at 8 p.m.) are also found.[16] With their salary levels, even junior analysts can likely afford cab rides on their own. Managers' recognition of analysts as individuals worthy enough of commanding such services perhaps carries more value in analysts' eyes, though, than the monetary worth of a cab ride. In an occupation in which identity is often determined by the amount of revenue one generates, repeated managerial leniency regarding company expenditures on aspiring investment bankers is a crude proxy for perceived worth and identity.[17]

These examples demonstrate the existence of gray zones across varied settings. They also suggest that there might be more to the practices than just the appropriation or transformation of organizational resources. From the outside, these examples of organizational gray zones with tangible appropriation of company material might conjure associations with theft, but they also involve practices that act as profound occupational identity distillers. Moreover, whereas the organization is de facto losing medicine, revenue, or material, complex social systems are also being sustained, the potential benefits of which are more difficult to assess.

In all of the cases just mentioned, the employees' gray zone practices potentially mirror their performance on official work. The organizational gray zones in which nurses operate deal with their competency around drug selection and administration; those in which flight attendants operate involve their ability to temporarily relieve stress so they can later maintain composure during a flight; for waiters, the seamless coordination of the guests' dining experience is inherent to their gray zone practice; for longshoremen, the consistency in loading and unloading goods is core to their performance and self-image; for garment workers, the ability to create sought-after clothes from small bits of material is a test of their occupational competence; and for aspiring investment bankers, generating expenses mirrors their ability to produce high revenues. Most of these gray zones therefore involve key elements of these workers' occupational identities.[18] The material elements of these practices act almost as pretexts for the enactment of their identities.

Gray zones are thus populated by hospital nurses, restaurant workers, garment workers, mail carriers, pipeline crews, investment bankers, dockworkers, paramedics, and emergency medical technicians, among others, in a host of occupations and in a wide range of settings. Direct material rewards are likely to first come to mind as the main motivation for such arrangements, but the former examples, such as the mail carriers and EMTs in particular, should provide pause and dissuade the observer from making a hasty judgment. In the context of the occupational constraints and hopes of workers, what might initially appear to be immoral warrants closer examination, especially with respect to the occupational dynamics involved.

Attentive Gray Zone Audiences

Why do these occupational dynamics not play out more openly? In other words, why do participants operate in the realm of gray zone practices when their occupational identities could be more visibly acknowledged? Occupational identities might indeed seem more visibly enacted out in the open, without the risk of being fired for breaking organizational rules. This might be true, but display is only part of the puzzle. Gray zones offer something open venues can rarely provide: a captive audience. What is done out in the open is for everyone to see and observe, but this also means that people can choose *not* to pay attention. Unlike open settings, gray zones force participants to become active observers.

Understanding how occupational identities are constructed helps us understand the importance of the audience. Occupational identities are identities from which members derive valued "self-images directly from their occupational roles."[19] These identities are "constructed and reconstructed in daily interactions with others as people learn to view themselves from the point of others." This perspective builds on the fact that individuals both project their social identities onto and derive their identities from social interactions.[20] It posits that people come to know who they are through interactions with others, and therefore rely on relational self-identities to fashion their self-images.[21] Occupational identities are often enacted in small group interactions in the workplace. They result not only from the enactment of practices, but from the rhetoric that surrounds these enactments, which comes to life in social interactions.[22] Workers mobilize a variety of occupational rhetorics to justify their jurisdiction and who they are. In doing so, workers fashion their occupational identities, which are socially, temporally, and spatially situated. Moreover, these identities are associated with specific tasks. Yet, the execution of tasks by itself is insufficient to maintain identities. A person who engages in a task that allows for occupational enactment might not find as many rewards as a gray zone participant that engages in the same task. For instance, in a study that observed French community gardeners, the gardening activity (an easily imagined solo endeavor) is shown to only partially contribute to the gardeners' views of themselves as honorable citizens.[23] Instead, their interactions with other gardeners, the ways in which politicians and employers discuss gardening, and the family interactions surrounding the activity are all instrumental in assessing gardening—and, by extension, its participants' identities, as being honorable community members. Identities are inherently relational; audience members are not merely uninvolved bystanders. They recognize and actively construct identities. The examples of gray zones discussed in this chapter further inform the relational aspect of the described occupational identities. For instance, nurses could easily only enact their occupational identity in the official tasks they provide when caring for patients, and not in the gray zone practices of selectively medicating themselves. When open and gray zone tasks coexist, what, then, makes gray zone tasks so attractive?

Examining the audiences of these gray zone practices illuminates their appeal. The ability to interact with an attentive (ideally expert) audience—one that is able to recognize and reinforce an occupational identity—is an attractive proposition. In the same way that chess tournaments provide opportunities for players to build their identities as capable players, each interaction with the appropriate counterpart provides an occasion for occupational enactment.[24] Consider the supervisors' leniency at Pierreville described previously—granting sick days as recognition of employees' efforts on official production work or efforts on other managerial requests (see chapter 8). This gray zone practice would not be nearly as attractive if the supervisors and coworkers were unaware of the justification for allowing the sick days. A worker who takes a sick day without an audience aware that he is not really sick but is actually resting for having done a "good job," will experience his idleness quite differently than one who pretends he is sick but shares the truth with others. Most likely the latter experience will contribute positively to how the worker sees himself, whereas the for-

mer one will, at best, not affect him. Thus, the presence of an audience
in the gray zone is what fuels occupational identity enactments.[25] As
we have seen, gray zones force the attention and often the collaboration of key audience members. In most of the gray zone examples described in this chapter, both peers and supervisors are involved. These
two audiences are particularly well suited to assess occupational competence and the consequent occupational identities of participants.
Recognition occurs within a community of practice.[26] (Longshoremen,
nurses, and waiters, for instance, all engage in gray zone practices before their peers.) It is therefore not only the task at hand, but also other
participants' and observers' attention to the task that renders gray
zones so apt for occupational identity enactment.

Frictions as Identity Revealers

Assuming identities are not static constructions, but are instead the results of relational "frictions and errors across social settings and disci-
plines," gray zones are highly appropriate settings in which to sustain
occupational identities.[27] As participants and meanings collide, distinctions among groups and group members emerge. As Harrison White
points out, identities beg for attempts to be restricted since the contes-
tation of their boundaries reinforces them.[28] Similarly, Annette Weiner
notes that among the Trobrianders, when individuals link themselves
to other individuals, tensions between "autonomy and domination,
desire and refusal, can never be fully resolved without entering into
dangerous confrontation in which security and retreat are no longer
possible."[29] These confrontations are inherently part of the process of
linking individuals to identities. In contemporary Western societies,
specifically in work environments such as those in the United States
where threats of legal action are relatively high, the opportunities for
frictions in open work settings might appear limited. Though cases do
exist (such as those of executives engaging in open conflict with one
another or public tensions erupting between occupational groups),
they are probably not the norm.[30] Open, formal settings probably do
not offer nearly as many opportunities for frictions as do gray zones.

Under the watch of coworkers, and with fewer defined rules to follow than in open settings, many of the individual decisions made in
gray zones constitute tests of occupational norms and identity. Numerous unwritten rules permeate gray zones. At Pierreville, as we
saw, homer-making was not a free-for-all. The boundaries of gray
zones were constantly patrolled, and non-normative behaviors within
gray zones were rapidly identified, often leading to the stigmatization

of the "offenders." Similarly, the longshoreman who appropriates personal cargo—versus more impersonal cargo that is in transit between large corporations—is immediately called out, as is the nurse who takes narcotic instead of nonnarcotic or over-the-counter drugs from patients and the mail carrier who "hides out" before rather than after completing the assigned delivery route. It could probably be said that these offenders are also de facto losing membership in their respective occupations when they travel outside the boundaries of expected gray zone practices.

Despite the existence of strong norms within gray zones, more experimentation probably occurs in these settings than in open ones. The expected behaviors in gray zones are not clearly articulated and require trial and error. Unsurprisingly, some of the most active gray zone participants at Pierreville were also the most respected workers. These individuals knew the norms of gray zone behavior and could enact the proper occupational identities within gray zones. They possessed sound judgment of what was appropriate. But not all gray zone participants saw things as clearly. Gray zone participants might easily be tempted by practices or shortcuts that "true" members of the occupational group would deem improper. Consider the case of the unskilled Pierreville worker who showed me a small decorative homer he crafted at the plant—something he "made with his own hands." He later told me he had used a nail file to carve and polish it. With this added piece of data, I understood that the artifact had been a much more tedious endeavor than it initially seemed. I asked a craftsman what he thought about using a nail file to make such a homer, and he said he strongly disapproved; other available tools would have produced the same outcome in a much shorter period of time. Thus, the homer-maker just described (who was not a craftsman) was wasting time. By mimicking what resembled a legitimate homer practice (building something with his own hands), he was in fact enacting the practice inappropriately. He had failed the test despite his best intentions, and lost the coveted association he sought with the craftsmen's identity.

These tests not only assess the boundaries of occupational groups, but also the standings of specific individuals within the groups. Let us consider open settings permeated by officially endorsed organizational rules (such as labor divisions between occupational groups). These official rules are meant to be generic; finer distinctions among participants are harder to draw. In general, official rules apply to all members regardless of management's potential desire to discriminate. In gray zones, under the gaze and control of coworkers, the boundaries of a proper occupational enactment are continuously redrawn and can be tailored to individual participants. The extent to which an EMT can play "doctor" is a distinction that not only applies to EMTs in general, but also to each specific EMT. Levels of tolerance are assessed on a case-by-case basis in gray zones. The suitability of a behavior is loosely defined, with numerous possible individual delineations. Because these boundaries are not clearly spelled out in gray zones, the rules can vary from one worker to another; one EMT might receive more leeway than another. In that sense, within gray zones, distinctions (and potential frictions) can be created between participants even within the same occupation.

Gray zones not only mix participants with various occupational backgrounds, they also distinguish among participants in a given occupational group. Moreover, they also allow for competing readings of interactions to develop among participants. No unique official reading of a practice is offered in these gray zones. Gray zone participants co-exist with one other, and sometimes they confront one another by attaching very different meanings to gray zone practices. When flight attendants leave the plane with alcohol for private consumption, despite official regulations forbidding it, frictions might ensue. For example, ground crews who do not have access to similar goods might be jealous of the flight attendants' distinction. But even among flight attendants, the amount, the type, or the timing of alcohol appropriation might become a source of contention. Some attendants might find it inappropriate to take alcohol from the airplane at the end of a rotation as opposed to during a stopover (in order to regain composure for the next trip). Furthermore, discussions around which types of alcohol to pick (the most expensive ones or the ones customers rarely ask for?) force an articulation of the occupational identity of flight attendants. These frictions are what set flight attendants apart from other occupational groups in the same setting, and what differentiate "good" flight attendants from "bad" ones. Whereas, for the most part, open settings offer venues for generic, less contentious distinctions, gray zones ultimately also allow for distinctions, but perhaps via bumpier and more individualized routes.

There are probably few organizations and occupations that are entirely exempt from gray zones; homer-making by craftsmen in factories is but one example. Be it an aspiring investment banker expensing potentially questionable cab rides with the tacit approval of her manager, or a journalist writing an article at work for a competing publication with the tacit approval of her editor, gray zones permeate work environments. They might involve the appropriation of company material, thereby resembling theft, yet what is really also at stake is not only the material appropriation per se, but the meanings attached to the gray zone practices.

Whereas ideally thieves want their actions to go unnoticed, many gray zone participants seem to almost strive for the attention of other participants and observers. Open settings rarely allow for such focused attention, and perhaps are less suited for revealing frictions. Gray zones, in contrast, require a constant reaffirmation of boundaries, and occupational identities undergo repeated testing. In addition, they allow for individual distinctions to emerge between members of the same occupation. These qualities make gray zones attractive—not only to individuals who can no longer enact their valued occupational identities in open settings, but also to those who, more generally, desire to enhance their self-images. These bumps in the road, or the frictions that result from testing, are precisely what allow participants to fashion their occupational identities and assess their standing within their occupational groups. The qualities of a "good" nurse can be assessed by analyzing the selective "theft" of medicine he engages in and the ways in which he justifies the practices. Gray zone activities can act as identity distillers; not only do they distill frowned-upon theftlike identities, but they can also distill strongly desired and respected identities within given occupational communities.

10

Identities, Control, and Moralities

NEARLY A CENTURY after the introduction of scientific management, gray zones are still rampant in organizations, raising the question of how they are sustained. When gray zones become public, moral outrage from the broader community often ensues with little understanding of the distinct moralities of these arrangements. Why do rationally designed and professionally managed organizations permit gray zones to develop? This study of homers addresses that question by refraining from hasty judgment and, instead, attempts to understand the full depth and impact of the social dynamics at play. At the broadest level, this book provides evidence of how gray zones can enrich our understanding of occupational identities and organizational regulations. Far from being anecdotal arenas, gray zones provide powerful venues for the enactment of occupational and organizational imperatives, allowing for control to exist while images of the self are maintained or enhanced.

Focusing on the dynamics of one practice occurring in one occupation in one plant might not do justice to the entire range of gray zones found in other work environments. However, some general conclusions can be drawn. These findings around homers extend research on organizations and occupations in at least three ways: first, they force the reappraisal of gray zones as mere relaxations of a constraint; second, they extend the repertoire of available forms of organizational controls by introducing the notion of identity incentives control; and third, they call attention to the use of morality as an occupational boundary marker. These contributions are detailed in the following sections.

Gray Zones as Identity Pursuits

From the organizational perspective, gray zones have been shown to be not remotely as subversive as their outputs might suggest. Participating in homer activities has similar implications to those Michael Burawoy noted regarding participation in regular labor interactions; participation equates with "consent to the rules."[1] With the benefits of involvement come many costs for homer makers, the most important probably being that in exchange for tolerance, compliance with managerial will and efforts on official production are implicitly expected. The gift/poison tension is inherent in gray zones. At least in some ways, organizations seem to benefit from gray zones more than participants do since managerial control over workers intensifies with gray zone tolerance. By participating in gray zones, workers put themselves at the mercy of their hierarchy, but also become dependent on their coworkers. When official jobs, or for that matter, unofficial jobs, need to be done for the hierarchy, refusing is difficult for those who have previously taken part in gray zone practices. Moreover, once a worker turns a blind eye to the fact that a coworker is engaging in gray zone practices, that coworker becomes indebted, as well; strongly binding future expectations are created, as is an imbalance—gray zone participants now owe something to their supervisors, to other coworkers, and to their organization.

The surprise regarding gray zones is that participants are not always required to participate, yet often still do. The declining position of craftsmen at Pierreville challenged the way the workers saw themselves. Shifts in industrial processes and labor trends help explain why craftsmen were willing to accept such a deal. The craftsmen devolved from highly skilled, independent individuals to extra hands the organization struggled to put to use. This shift threatened their occupational identity. Yet, in limited instances, mostly when interacting with their fellow craftsmen, respect and recognition were partly restored or enhanced through homer activities. While gray zones harbored numerous distinct meanings, under the guise of similar-looking homer interactions, craftsmen were able to express and build their waning occupational identity.

Craftsmen attached different meanings to similar-looking practices depending on the participants and recipients. In doing so, they exhibited more than consent. Though it could be argued that these craftsmen were left with few choices, they still selectively constructed distinct homer meanings on their own terms. With these gray zones, they attempted to fashion their own identities as able craftsmen.[2] No data were collected on the overall frequency of occurrence in respective meanings, making it difficult to assess how often these workers engaged in rewarding gray zone practices versus ones that were less so. Regardless of the frequency of these events, those instances around homers framed as respect and recognition were highly valued by craftsmen. Craftsmen initially constituted a high-status occupational group in the plant and, therefore, might have had more leeway than other groups to fashion their identity. When engaging in homer activities, craftsmen were implicitly agreeing, on some level, to more constraining control, while simultaneously obtaining, on another level, a say in their experience of those controls. When gray zones manifest and enhance occupational identities, their presence in organizations has the potential to benefit all parties involved.

Such a reading of gray zones that combines identity pursuits and managerial desire for compliance complements the views of gray zones developed in classic organizational sociology. These views of gray zones, discussed either from workers' or management's perspectives, but rarely from both, have historically been fairly well documented. For example, Alvin Gouldner writes about the "indulgency patterns" by which supervisors in gypsum mines tolerate practices forbidden by internal codes of conduct.[3] As he notes, these indulgencies dispose "workers to react to the plant favorably, and to trust their supervisors"—as such, they constitute forms of control.[4] Similarly, Burawoy vividly captures workers' experiences of "making-out" (or turning attempts to fulfill daily quotas into games) and shows how they ultimately lead to a higher degree of organizational control.[5] In most of these classic accounts, however, the implicit assumption is that gray zones selectively buffer participants from an organizational constraint (even if they sometimes then reinforce a new, less visible form of constraint).

Whether in a gypsum mine, a law enforcement agency, or a factory, initially, the main benefit nonmanagerial employees derive from these leniencies is assumed to be greater freedom from constraints. In Gouldner's work on informal nonenforcement of rules, or what he refers to as "mock bureaucracies," the emphasis is on organizational patterns "where rules are usually neither enforced, nor obeyed."[6] The identity benefits participants might derive from "mock bureaucracies" as distinct from greater freedom are not directly addressed. At most, gray zones are depicted as sometimes generating a positive attitude toward the employing organization, but nothing beyond that. Similarly, managerial leniency toward employees who do not report bribe attempts (despite explicit rules prescribing that they do so) is depicted by Peter Blau as the selective relaxation of a constraint that facilitates the work of the (law enforcement) agency.[7] The possible links between the occupational identities of these law enforcement officers and the organizational tolerance of the rule violation are not pursued, except when noting that reporting such bribe attempts might taint the reputation of the agents.[8] Also, in Donald Roy's account of "banana time," an unauthorized daily break devoted to snacks and jokes among machine operators, again the emphasis is on escaping organizational constraints.[9] Hence, a lot is assumed about what leniencies disable (i.e., the initial organizational constraint), but very little about what they might enable, aside from reinforcing loyalty or a less visible form of constraint.

This book challenges that assumption by suggesting that management might pursue gray zones and workers might embrace them for reasons beyond the initial relaxation of a constraint. Without falling into an instrumental view of social life, it offers an alternate reading of these gray zone practices: one that depicts craftsmen with more agency than classical views suggest. As the tale of lost work and identity in chapter 7 makes clear, this study does not downplay the frictions between craftsmen and management; positive collaboration at work is not suggested as a norm. Instead, this book presents a reading that explains the engagements between management and workers on grounds other than a normative human "cooperative" motive.[10] This reading highlights the judiciousness of both workers and management to engage in these gray zones.[11] At Pierreville, gray zones are shown not only to initially relax an organizational constraint, but also to engage participants' desired occupational identities. Identity incentives are also at play as a result of managerial leniency. Gray zones inherently contribute to regulating behavior within organizations. Whereas control and identity are the two outcomes made most salient in this reading of gray zones, they should not force an overly instrumental reading of gray zones. Instead, they are meant to suggest that multiple explanations and dynamics may simultaneously exist within these organizational gray zones. Moreover, a darker side of gray zones cannot be discounted. As previously suggested, it is possible for management to use its selective tolerance of gray zone practices to further personal ends.

Identity Incentives as a Form of Control

A second main focal point of this book is to more broadly highlight an often ignored form of organizational control: identity incentives control, or the reliance on the selective positive arousal of identity feelings to induce action or efforts. To date, much of the classic literature on organizational control equates control with constraint, and usually assumes that control is achieved through the power to impose constraints.[12] These formulations assume that an organization member's aspirations for human freedom, dignity, and well-being compete with the organization's implicit need for control.[13] This conflict of interest explains the necessity, from an organizational perspective, to implement stick-like controls to curb behavior. Studies of members' resistance and of covert political conflict in organizations are consistent with this view of control.[14] Classic control, therefore, is mainly a matter of constraining behavior; voluntary engagement is neither sought nor assumed to be necessary to achieve organizational control.

However, constraints are only one form of organizational control. Another type of organizational control that may be more effective than imposing constraints is the reliance on members' voluntary engagement.[15] This alternate form of control requires participants' buy in, thus obliging the organization and participants to construct the control together. To co-create it, complying members voluntarily act in a manner favored by the organization. Members' voluntary engagement can be achieved by various means, most notably through financial incentives or the promise of a fulfilling job.[16] A less widely acknowledged way to elicit voluntary engagement is to create opportunities for the enactment of desired identities. Organizational research has shown that organizations can shape members' identities, but the possibility that such identities might also be desired has not been fully examined and raises the prospect of new forms of incentives.[17] For example, in the U.S. boxing world, neighborhood training gyms help shape fighters' identities, but the gyms' reliance on the fighters' desire to engage with this identity is also an incentive to train.[18] Such identity incentives—defined as the selective positive arousal of identity feelings to induce action or efforts—can be used to exert organizational control.

The theoretical notion that identities can serve as incentives to action has been formulated, but not explicated or detailed. For instance, Harrison White proposes that "identities are the only source of intentional efforts," and adds that identities and control are inherently intertwined.[19] Similarly, George Akerlof and Rachel Kranton argue that "the ability of organizations to place workers into jobs with which they identify and the creation of such identities are central to what make organizations work."[20] Though they do not spell out what these identities might entail or the processes whereby actions might proceed from identities, these authors theoretically advance the notion that identities might function as incentives in organizational regulation.

Empirical evidence of the importance of identities in organizational regulation is scarce and typically confined to settings that offer only inspirational identities, such as social movements, public agencies, and highly regarded organizations. Literature on social movements explicitly discusses identity incentives when specifying elements that engage participants. The "collective identity" of a social movement organization is assumed to drive its members' engagement.[21] The appeal of "identity pursuits" is also invoked in a study of the expectations of public managers whose authors find that managers "participate in political activities that are primarily about the pursuit of identities rather than specific organizational outcomes."[22] The context in which the authors of this study employ the term "identity rewards" is volunteer firefighting. They posit that volunteer firefighting probably offers greater identity rewards than other types of work. Members' esteem for an organization seems to implicitly condition the existence of identity incentives. A study of Amway distributors (selling household products) illustrates this point: the high esteem in which they hold their employer also explains their engagement and their observed organizational identification.[23] The appeal of identity incentives in organizations with highly inspirational identities is also apparent in detailed discussions of West Point cadets and military personnel.[24]

A first limitation that can be drawn from these empirical accounts of identity incentives is that not all organizations offer highly inspirational identities. A second and more crucial limitation is the potentially diluted potency of identities as incentives when all members of an organization can claim the coveted identity equally; no discriminatory (controlling) intra-organizational sorting can occur. Consider, for instance, a group of workers who are given the official opportunity to contract, outside of working hours, with external factory clients to produce machines. (Such a case is documented in Hungary.)[25] The ability to earn extra income by engaging in valued occupational activities is identity-engaging in the sense that it allows the workers to pick the work they want to do and the partners with whom they interact. But managerial discretion cannot be exercised since the practice is open to all employees. Officially forbidding this same practice, but tolerating it, would allow management to regain discretion.

Selective tolerance, rather than official acceptance, is therefore a precondition for identity incentives to operate. If such tolerances are offered unilaterally and to all employees, identity incentives lose their capacity for control. This loss is evident in the democratization of such an incentive among French glassblowers. Traditionally, glassblowers in France were entitled to keep the last glassblowing of a given series for themselves, which often occurred at the end of the workday. Typically a gray zone practice, this tolerance was considered almost a due or an implicit right, but management did not always tolerate it. However, glassblowing in France constitutes a well-organized occupation, and glassblowers were historically powerful partners in the manufacturing process. By 1972, the national labor convention that governed their employment conditions explicitly stated that any leftover glass paste unused in official production could be used by the workers for their own production.[26] By translating this tolerance into a practice open to all, workers gained the ability to enact their desired identity. At the same time, however, the discriminating nature of the gray zone was lost.

Thus, within a given organization, reliance on identities that are selectively allocated by management, rather than automatically granted, is likely to prove more discriminating.

Though members of organizations may desire many different identities, prior research suggests that occupational identities are important levers, both of engagement and control.[27] For instance, studies of engineers, high-tech professionals, and even crack-house managers all suggest that organizations can build on their members' desired occupational identities to exert control. Research on engineers has shown that their desire to be seen as professionals provides for effective control.[28] Among high-tech workers, too, identity is a key element of organizational control. High-tech workers decide how to divide their time between work and nonwork activities, but their employers rely on their desired occupational identity to ensure that their decision-making tilts in favor of work.[29] Even in multi-site crack-house operations, the organization relies on each site manager's desire to be recognized as a respected drug dealer to ensure sufficient revenues. Crack-house site managers, appointed by the head of operations, are not obliged to reach specific sales targets. Even so, they pursue new business not only to increase earnings, but also to earn occupational respect.[30] All three occupational groups are willing to comply with engaging as opposed to constraining forms of control in order to sustain or build desired occupational identities for themselves. Organizations, through the job practices they offer and the ensuing social interactions, can allow individuals to shape positive self-images. Alternatively, organizations can withhold from workers the opportunities or resources necessary to shape these images.

The study of homer practices at Pierreville exposes a selective process of allocating identity incentives. Besides paying an employee to perform certain tasks, management allocates "hidden" incentives to select employees.[31] The currencies of these hidden incentives are identities, not monetary. The fact that such occupational-identity-engaging interactions occur despite their official proscription highlights the managerial discretion in this process. By allowing participants to enact their desired identities, leniency around homers manufactures control. Similar to tight-knit communities in which "a certain amount of one thing may be exchanged for a measure of another," in the Pierreville community, trade-offs are being made.[32] As such, this study illustrates an alternate form of organizational control: identity incentives control.

Thus, a main implication of this book is to shed light on the role of gray zones in regulating organizational behaviors, and to articulate available forms of control found at work. All three classical forms of control—simple, technological, and bureaucratic—are present at

Pierreville. [33] These three classic forms of control encompass the
following:

1. Simple control, or the direct, authoritarian, and personal control of
work and workers by the organization's owner or hired supervisors. Hired
helpers in small family-owned businesses such as retail shops often experience this form of control.

2. Technological control, whereby the physical technology of the organization generates control. The moving conveyor belts still used in some factories exemplify this form of control.

3. Bureaucratic control, based on the systematic rules observed within organizations. The requirement in retail banking that a supervisor approve
loans above a specified amount exemplifies bureaucratic control.

None of these forms of control requires any active engagement on the
part of employees; instead, they restrict behaviors. In contrast, this
book highlights a more engaging form of control that rests on identity
incentives. Managers at Pierreville could order work to be done (exercising direct control), make sure the pace of production did not allow
for much down time (technological control), and spell out all the tasks
that craftsmen needed to complete to do their jobs (bureaucratic control). They could also selectively tolerate the practice of homer-making
(identity incentives control). From management's perspective, the informal rule allowing for the selective violation of official rules is an
implementation rule, or a "rule about a rule."[34] Selective tolerance,
under the threat of disciplinary action, is what makes this leniency an
effective form of control. The fact that Pierreville management could
forbid occupational-identity-engaging interactions and that opportunities to enact such interactions in official work were waning probably
increased the strength of such a control. A less potent form of control
could entail providing select employees with opportunities for more or
fewer occupational-identity-engaging interactions without the added
leverage of disciplinary action. For instance, the allocation of interesting work or special projects to select individuals might constitute such
a form of control. The allocation of advanced modeling work to mathe-
maticians employed at financial institutions in exchange for extra effort on less engaging projects exemplifies how this form of identity
incentives control might play out in other work settings.

Identity incentives forms of control need not be limited, though, to
occupational identities. Identity incentives control can rely on any desired identity whose arousal requires managerial intervention. For instance, identities linked to gender, ethnicity, age, disability, or sexual
orientation, increasingly valued by employees, could play into such
control.[35] Discussions of identity regulation in organizations implicitly

downplay the attractiveness of certain identities by depicting organizations as imposing identities on their members; however, identity incentives control points to a voluntary process of engagement with certain identities.[36] Whether such incentives have the potential to lessen the importance of other organizational incentives (such as financial ones) remains an open question. Evidence suggests this might occur, for example, when biologists accept lower-paying job offers from employers who allow them to publish in scientific journals (a typical identity incentive for biologists not offered by all employers).[37] At the very least, identity incentives control complements other forms of organizational control, both engaging and constraining in nature.

In his analysis of an industrial bakery alluded to in the introduction of this book that involved the selling of pilfered bread, Jason Ditton concludes that such practices (an example of a gray zone) produce a "can't win" situation for workers. The workers are faced with incompatible demands not to steal, yet to make up their wages. This double-bind creates, according to Ditton, "added power that accrues to the employer."[38] But it might partly empower the workers as well. Tolerating gray zones in contexts in which identity dynamics might play out provides participants with symbolic rewards in addition to material rewards. Thus, workers may achieve gains above and beyond the quantity of diverted labor or materials. For instance, the bakery truck drivers might offer customers they like reduced prices on the loaves they deliver, thus discriminating among their customers. In doing so, they might consider themselves providing "better service" to these customers, an experience that could feed into their occupational identities as drivers and salespeople. An assessment of gray zones requires that all forms of costs and benefits—material and symbolic, incurred and experienced—be taken into account.

Organizational Conditions That Favor Gray Zones

Assuming gray zones can act as identity distillers, their presence in organizations might be more common when identity incentives control is seen as tempting, both for workers and management. Such control might appeal to workers who belong to a larger valued collective (i.e., those who have internalized adequate codes of conduct, beyond what official rules prescribe), such as an occupational group with a strong collective identity. Physicians, librarians, and accountants constitute such examples. These workers may be more tempted by identity incentives control—rather than simple, technological, or bureaucratic controls—since the latter forms rely less on their sense of identity. Thus, the presence of a valued collective—one could also imagine, for example, an ethnic group—might warrant the use of identity incentives control.

Second, identity incentives might also strongly appeal to employees whose desired identities, specifically occupational ones, are not or cannot be affirmed by official work. Limited opportunities to enact occupational identities in official settings due, for instance, to de-skilling might set the stage for the use of such incentives.[39] The fewer official opportunities offered, the more attractive occupational identity incentives might prove to be. For example, in a study conducted in the late 1950s of young professionals drafted in the U.S. Army, the vast majority (seventy-nine out of eight-four subjects) occupied jobs requiring minimal or subutilization of their professional skills.[40] In these instances, one would expect identity incentives and gray zones to thrive. While the author of the study did not specifically analyze such behaviors, he noted many "outward symbols" the enlisted men displayed (such as subscribing to professional journals or changing from their uniform to civilian attire before dinner). Had official rules forbidden these "symbolic" practices, one can easily envision the men still trying to pursue them in what might have become a gray zone. A similar argument applies when a career plateaus and associated work tasks, though not yet completely obsolete, do not require the engagement they once did.[41] By extension, rising occupational groups who also experience a disconnect between their identity aspirations and their current work might also find identity incentive controls attractive. Just as games played on a shop floor (such as those that entail competition among machinists to get or finish a job) allow workers "to make real choices, however narrowly conceived," identity incentives control offers opportunities, however limited, to enact desired identities in specific interactions.[42]

Third, members' longing to engage in identity incentives control might be particularly noteworthy when organizations harbor multiple identity groups. In the case of occupational identities, members of organizations with multiple occupational groups might be more tempted by identity incentives control.[43] For example, in-house lawyers at a large corporation might enjoy fewer opportunities to enact their occupational identities since they are only one of many occupations at the establishment. (By contrast, in a law firm, lawyers probably have more leeway to reinforce their occupational identities given that all their colleagues readily understand what is most important to them.) In settings where varying occupations coexist, the unique characteristics of each occupation are rarely reflected at the organizational level with the intensity desired by each occupational group. Thus, a high degree of identity group variety in an organization might make identity incentives more appealing to the members of each of the groups.

Finally, the inability to discriminate between good and bad performers in official work might make way for occupational identity incentives. The managerial practicality of identity incentives control also conditions its use.[44] In settings where official rules and incentives cannot be used to reward outstanding performance or loyalty, managers might be more inclined to rely on identity incentives to do so.

The last point underscores the fact that if gray zones generally benefit workers, they might not benefit all workers equally. We saw that a collective patrolling of the boundaries of a gray zone is required for such a control to emerge, but gray zones also allow for greater individual entrepreneurship. Like direct control, which allows a supervisor to control the actions of each individual, identity incentives control opens the door to more targeted use: each worker can be treated differently. Whereas identity incentives control might be well-suited for some, it might spell disaster for others—namely those most unfamiliar with the boundaries of accepted behavior. The participant unfamiliar with community expectations is quickly shunned; recall the unskilled worker at Pierreville who craftsmen dismissed because he "wasted time" making an artifact with a nail file instead of the appropriate tool. But capable community members can also be recognized and given more leeway. Consider the craftsman who was the only one able to weld aluminum. His unique skill among craftsmen was recognized, and the fact that he often engaged in homer work seemed normal—a just recognition of his standing in the community. Ultimately, the reliance on identity incentives control in gray zones is also a potent sorting mechanism in organizations. The basis of this sorting, as will be shown next, is rooted in a morality that is almost a prerequisite for this form of control.

Morality as an Occupational Boundary

A second contribution of this book deals with the use of morality as a social boundary, specifically among occupational groups.[45] As Michèle Lamont reminds us in her analysis of the upper-middle class in the United States and France, social groups have mostly been defined in cultural and socioeconomic terms.[46] Whereas cultural boundaries are drawn on the basis of "education, intelligence, manners, taste, and the command of high culture," socioeconomic ones rely on "wealth, power, or professional success."[47] Her research indicates, however, that the upper-middle class also uses a third boundary—relying on morality—to distinguish itself from other social classes. This moral boundary centers on qualities such as honesty, work ethic, and personal integrity. Outsiders such as social climbers are said to lack personal integrity or morality. The findings of the Pierreville study extend her insight beyond the upper-middle class and into the realm of the workplace, specifically among craftsmen. No attempt was made to formally measure, as she did, the moral views of the plant members across occupations; nevertheless, the justifications and continuous border patrolling of acceptable homer practices suggest that craftsmen pay close attention to the moralities of their gray zone practices as well as to how these moralities reflect on them as members of an occupational group. Variations in levels of tolerance were also noted; depending on who took part in the practice and the participants' occupational backgrounds, the boundaries of morality could shift. For example, building a metal window for a home using new company material might be deemed acceptable if the recipient of the window was a boss, but the practice was highly stigmatized when the recipient was another craftsman. The artifact is de facto enrolled in a boundary-marking exercise.[48] Aside from cultural boundaries (e.g., craftsmen's education and training) and socioeconomic boundaries (e.g., their former position of high status in the plant), craftsmen also used moral distinctions to define themselves as an occupational group.

Occupations are often identified by the work participants perform; by their skills, education, and training; as well as by the official credentials required to partake in their tasks. The U.S. Department of Labor (Bureau of Labor Statistics) uses these criteria to sort individuals into occupations. Therefore, the definition of an occupation primarily focuses on *what* members of a given occupation do and what is *required* (skills, training, education, and credentials) for them to engage in the occupation—and not *how* they do it. While this technical approach has proved fruitful, it might provide only a partial picture of what occupations are about.

Research has shown that occupations are also associated with other, less obvious markers, such as specific customs or jargon.[49] For instance, when journeymen electricians apprentice, they not only learn processes and acquire skills, training, and education, but they also learn how to dress and they learn a vocabulary that binds them to the other already-trained electricians. Evidently, the task and the requirements alone are not sufficient occupational markers. Stephen Barley makes this point quite saliently with his study of funeral home directors. These individuals rely on a full range of semiotics to "elucidate rules by which members of a work culture consistently and coherently generate meaning."[50] Pending licensing issues, many individuals might be able to figure out how to organize a funeral when faced with the obligation to do so. What distinguishes funeral directors from other occupational groups, however, is the way by which they rely on "systems of signification and the rules that govern their use" when conducting their tasks. For funeral directors, one of these rules is to describe the posed corpse in terms very similar to a living, sleeping human being; in a way, the directors resuscitate each dead corpse. These semiotics contribute to the construction of an occupational morality regarding how to conduct a funeral or, more broadly, how to engage in a task. Articulations such as these of appropriate manners of conduct bind occupational communities together. In their discussion of occupational communities, John Van Maanen and Stephen Barley note the "moral standards surrounding what work is considered good or bad."[51] This moral reading applies to the evaluated work, but also to "matters falling outside the realm of work itself." The findings presented in this book document the multiple meanings and ensuing moral readings associated with practices exhibited at work, outside of official work. Here, the moral undertones are made explicit as they unfold in the practice of homer-making at Pierreville. Although the notion of shared values has been applied to occupational communities, the translation of these values into a morality of action *outside* of official work is somewhat less explored.

Consider the following examples of occupational concerns around notions of morality. In Robert Jackall's account of corporate managers, appropriately solving "moral mazes" is inherently part of these managers' occupational struggle. Their proper identification and application of "rules in use" are what earn them respect and promotion in their occupational community.[52] In William Kornblum's study of a Chicago blue-collar community, terms such as "decency and respect" are used to describe specific workers in this steel mill community, even though such terms are mainly attached to subgroups of an occupation (divided along ethnic lines), rather than to an entire occupational community.[53] Mitchell Duneier touches upon similar moral boundary issues when discussing how book vendors on New York City streets make "an honest living."[54] As we see from his accounts, not all practices are deemed proper in making an honest living. Selling books that appear to be stolen from regular brick-and-mortar book vendors gives rise to tensions among street book vendors.[55] Though selling books on the street might be the primary occupational marker of these vendors, *how* the books are sold is at least as important. In a different context, Peter Bearman's research on doormen also shows that doormen construct their occupational identity in moral terms. In a chapter tellingly titled "Crossing the Line," he documents the numerous practices doormen engage in to distance themselves from the tenants in the buildings in which they work, yet still get to know them enough to be able to serve them.[56] "Crossing the line"—and becoming too close to tenants— is highly frowned upon among doormen. Additionally, in his study of executives, Calvin Morrill highlights the existence of elaborate honor codes that allow for a distinction to be drawn between honorable and less honorable executives.[57] And finally, Rakesh Khurana shows how the beginnings of managerial education in the United States and the invention of management as a distinct occupation were imbued, from the start, with strong moral undertones, suggesting that the bound- aries of the occupation were as much moral- as task- or credential-spe- cific.[58] Thus, occupational groups also define themselves in terms of morality—not just in terms of what they do and of credentials, but also of how they do what they do inside and outside of official work.

Some studies point—alongside the benefits incurred—to the costs of boundary setting in fostering exclusion and separation. These costs should not be overlooked.[59] As noted, very few female and non-French citizens populated the workshops at Pierreville. The relative absence of minorities might give way to more easily setting moral boundaries since homogeneity in viewpoints might be stronger. (Concurrently, set- ting boundaries might be used to justify the relative absence of such minorities.) Outside public view, social dynamics can play out unfet- tered, and the inclusion and exclusion processes can be much more violent. The analysis of a group of Hungarian workers who decide to contract their services to external factory clients off-hours reveals that only the most skilled workers were asked by their coworkers to partici- pate.[60] As a result, a less open setting, such as this Hungarian factory where work is done off-hours, allows workers to define their own boundaries, which often exclude the less valued employees. Thus, the morality of the moral boundary might itself be in question. The aware- ness of the costs is entangled with the benefits participants might de- rive from the boundaries.

Cynthia Fuchs-Epstein shows that the construction of gender bound- aries at work provides many benefits, including the development of identities, and a sense of security, dignity, and honor. Given that she focuses on a traditionally underrepresented group in the contempo- rary workforce (women), the costs of these boundaries (to the majority) are not made prominent. However, depending on the perspective, the costs can clearly appear. When Joel Podolny and James Baron analyze the social network ties among female workers in the context of a high- tech engineering and manufacturing corporation, they posit that such ties might act as a support network reinforcing women's professional identities.[61] This assumes that the professional identities enacted by other coworkers (mostly men) could not completely reinforce women's professional identities or were not fully available to them. Thus, here, the creation of an occupational boundary also partly excludes female workers from belonging to it. Michèle Lamont also makes the costs of boundary setting clear with her analysis of the morality of the members of the upper-middle class she surveyed and interviewed. By definition, these boundaries also keep other participants (such as "social climbers") from entering a delimited insider group of individuals. The boundaries are particularly tested in instances of ambiguity and when articulation of the boundaries is required. Gray zones offer repeated tests of the participants' moralities. They also provide numerous opportunities for inclusion and exclusion.[62]

Defining an occupation in terms of morality raises intriguing questions about the broader role of occupations in society. In an era of increased job mobility in which 2.7 percent of employed Americans change jobs in any given month, identities that are portable from one employer to another might prove powerful contributors to social regulation.[63] Other identities, such as religious or ethnic ones, are also portable and can carry moral claims but are more static and, therefore, cannot easily be adopted. Shifting ethnicities and converting to a different religion are not simple options. By contrast, occupations technically are open to all individuals who fit the entry requirements (skills, education, training, and credentials). They define a notion of the collective that crosses ethnic, gender, and religious lines. Occupations also span national boundaries. Emile Durkheim wrote that occupational groups have the potential to curb egocentric tendencies by intercalating between the State and the individual a whole series of secondary and, in his opinion, beneficial affiliations "near enough to the individuals to attract them strongly in their sphere of action and drag them, in this way, into the general torrent of social life."[64] Evidence of such processes is apparent in public accounting firms in the United States. It has been shown that when accountants are asked to focus on profitability and client development, their occupational identities fuel some resistance.[65] Though occupations also generate segregation—for instance, between doctors and nurses—they might provide a level of segregation close enough to the individuals to provide guidance for action, yet concurrently far enough to favor a collective goal. Participating in gray zone practices forces an articulation of the moralities of occupations: a potentially vital lever of regulation in contemporary Western societies.

Next time you see a polished key chain or a metal ashtray, look at it carefully. If you should come upon such an object, do not "hurry on" as Antoine de Saint-Exupéry advises when describing the bland landscape where his little prince appears. Consider that the key chain or ashtray might be a homer. A homer, like the landscape, can be one of "the loveliest and saddest" sights in the world, crystallizing both anticipations and fears.[66] I hope that focusing our attention on homers has allowed for a clearer understanding of the tensions and the regulations between individuals and the organizations for which they work.

Ultimately, factory workers, particularly craftsmen, are not so different from nurses, mail carriers, or longshoremen; all engage in practices that, while they may be perceived as similar to theft, also contribute to the maintenance of their occupational identities. In doing so, these individuals trade in differences in the meanings of their interactions, allowing situated moralities to emerge. The gray zone practices described in this book contribute to the maintenance of identities by affording workers a comforting sense of fashioning their views of self, especially when workers feel their identities are threatened. Such threats, I would argue, are widespread, and are present in all types and at all levels of work. Investment bankers, professional chess players, and physicians are not immune to them. Whether some gray zone practices temporarily delay the inevitable erosion of these identities or actually modify participants' identity trajectories remains to be seen. At the very least, though, they can soothe the experience of work.

Moral Gray Zones has attempted to answer the puzzling question of the persistence of gray zones in organizations. In this book, many gray zones were shown to encapsulate micro-struggles for relevance that might independently appear trivial, but cumulatively provide the substance of actual and desired social life. For a majority of workers and managers with ongoing involvement in such gray zone activities, these gray zones, when patrolled, offer local venues for regulation and expression. For the supervisors who must encourage the performance of their team members, who are willing to be selectively lenient, and who are astute enough to protect their workers caught in the act, such gray zones are tempting. They offer a more flexible venue for exercising control than any formal rule provides. The hope is that this added control is put to good use.

Similarly, for those workers who can discern proper from improper occupational enactment, and who feel they can trust the judgment of their coworkers and supervisors, gray zones can be alluring. When properly executed and linked to valued, shared identities, gray zone practices are testimonies to the participants' moralities. It is striking how often we are asked, particularly in the United States, what we "do." A standard reply might be, "I am a teacher" or "a stock broker," but this says nothing about *how* we do what we do. Gray zones can provide opportunities to answer this question in practice and through the eyes of peers. They offer venues where good teachers or stock brokers are recognized, and maybe even where they are made—venues, in other words, not only for recognition, but also for accomplishment.

Surrendering one's autonomy to a group of coworkers and supervisors rather than an impersonal authority might be perceived as costly. The potential arbitrariness of group norms involves uncertainties that are sometimes difficult to predict. Yet collective action involves compromise, and the choice to surrender, perhaps only partially, one's autonomy to a small group of trusted coworkers who understand what the work involves, might appeal to workers and managers alike. Depending on our level of trust in small groups, our reading of gray zones can shift from indifference to hope.[67] As George Homans optimistically noted in *The Human Group*, "At the level of the small group, society has always been able to cohere."[68]

However, this leaves us with many unanswered questions. Far from providing an extensive description and analysis of a social system, this book only provides a window into parts of one. Nonetheless, the window—homer-making at Pierreville—sheds light on the complexity and regularities of work social systems. It partly repositions social interactions in their context; inhabiting organizations with individuals operating in and navigating social systems. As such, it also offers an illustration of one way to cohere—a local, situated, and probably imperfect way to do so, but one that over time provides many participants with a sense of agency that they might not otherwise experience. More important, this way to cohere fairly elegantly enables collective action. The craftsmanship lies as much in the concrete outcomes of gray zones as in the subtle mechanisms that sustain them.

I am tempted to believe that the greater the power of an organization, the more likely it is that gray zones proliferate. In the same manner that light calls for shadow, organizational quests for power foster the emergence of gray zones. When they expand, organizations require members' collaboration to achieve broader reach and control. The organization's quest to enroll and engage members in its expansion, alongside members' desire to resist, is what fuels the development of gray zones. That Primo Levi first employed the term "gray zone" in reference to World War II concentration camps and that gray zones were widespread in former Eastern Bloc countries suggests the affinity between gray zones and organizational quests for expansion.[69] These settings required the engagement (however temporary) of members to operate and expand.

If this proposition holds true, gray zones will not merely be sustained, but will probably also profoundly grow and transform in the decades to come. In the less contentious contemporary work settings, gray zones should thrive, as well. Contemporary organizations are known to be powerful.[70] For instance, the myth of a high-powered free-lance agent jumping from employer to employer has largely been rebuked.[71] In a context where organizations try to expand their reach, gray zones—understood as part of an *organizing* project—are bound to grow. If there is any temptation to treat formal organizational rules as efficient solutions to control, gray zones show another side of this control. If the assumption of power lies only in the formal organizational rules, it is dramatically undermined by the paradox of gray zones. For instance, consider the growth of health maintenance organizations in the United States. With their supervising physicians' tacit approval, physicians allocated a given number of minutes per patient already find many ways to circumvent official organizational rules.[72] In doing so, they contribute indirectly to the growth of the organization that employs them. Whereas homers might evoke a disappearing industrial era, they are only one manifestation of what gray zones entail. It might be difficult to predict the form of future gray zones, but their development parallel to the growth of organizations seems assured.

Another important reason to see such developments of gray zones is the contemporary high burden bestowed upon individuals to prove themselves, particularly in their occupation. The emphasis on the individual has been pointed out as a growing trend in Western society.[73] This suggests that in any given occupation, the pressure to stand out might increase. Imagine two software engineers with similar technical training, both vying for peer respect and recognition. One is located in London and the other in Bangalore. Both are likely to do similar work and may experience threats—distinct in intensity and nature—to their occupational identity. For the former, an upcoming cost reduction wave could eliminate her job. For the latter, the most rewarding work is probably done in London, and her earnings are likely to be lower than those of her London counterparts. With the arrival of new candidates from diverse backgrounds in occupations and organizations operating across geographies, it seems reasonable to expect the contest for respect and recognition to intensify. Many gray zones provide readily available intra- and interoccupational sorting mechanisms. In global labor markets, gray zones that allow for identity enhancement will likely blossom.

The main unanswered question for future exploration that this book raises is how to combine respect for individuals' pursuits while allowing for collective action. It is telling that this question of our ability, as a society, to do just that also lies at the conclusion of research on contemporary utopian communities.[74] Whether starting from what might be perceived as high moral grounds (utopias) or initially less appealing ones (gray zones), the same tension is reached: how to respectfully and capably pursue collective organizing projects. It is common to look up, instead of down, to find coherence. But coherence comes in many forms, large and small, high and low, in utopias and in gray zones.

Appendix A _____

Data and Methods

THIS APPENDIX offers a rationale for conducting an extended case study and discusses in greater detail the methods utilized to study the specific gray zone of homer-making at Pierreville. A combination of interviews, observations, surveys, and archival data seemed to me, at the time, an obvious, inductive way to proceed. Though it is much easier to make sense a posteriori of how this project unfolded, this appendix nevertheless provides insight into the development of this book.

The Rationale for a Case Study

An initial way to examine organizational gray zones might be to document variations in social systems that sustain gray zones across workplaces. However, a multi-workplace research design might have undermined the depth of data-gathering necessary to unearth these variations. Most studies of less-talked-about and, often, semicovert behaviors are conducted within a single workplace (except, perhaps, Alvin Gouldner's 1954 study, which focused more on informal rather than semicovert behaviors). For example, Bill Watson studied an automobile factory, Dodee Fennell an electronic component factory, Jason Ditton a commercial bakery, William Thompson a slaughterhouse, and Tammy MacLean an insurance company.[1] The choice of a single workplace appears to take precedence. Though site-specific variables might limit generalizing some of the findings, in this study, sufficient variation in terms of participants' profiles allows for varied experiences of gray zones from the participants' perspectives.

Robert Yin suggests that case study designs are favorable under three conditions: (1) when "how" and "why" questions are asked; (2) when the topic under study does not require control over external events; and (3) when the study focuses on contemporary events.[2] An inquiry into the manufacture and exchange of homers attempts to explain how and why gray zones are sustained. External events were sufficiently stable over the period of study, which prevented significant external disturbance of the observed phenomena.[3] For instance, both the availability of artifacts similar to homers in commercial venues outside the factory and the French labor laws regulating homer activities varied little during the period of study. Finally, retirement homers and, in more limited instances, regular homers, are still currently manufactured. These conditions render a case study relevant.

As Marcel Mauss explains: "It is moreover an error to believe that the credit given to a scientific proposition depends neatly on the number of cases one believes it can be verified in. When a hypothesis has been established in a case, even unique, but with method and care, the reality of the phenomenon is certain in a different manner than when, in order to be demonstrated, multiple but unmatched facts, curious examples are borrowed from the most heterogeneous societies, races, and civilizations."[4]

Therefore, the choice was made to conduct research at one site. The pitfalls of developing an "industrial sociology" in isolation from the rest of the economy have oftentimes been noted; but Pierreville represents a setting that is relatively common in the French economy.[5] Pierreville also exemplifies the fairly elaborate "social system" found in many other industries where the workforce's tenure is fairly long.[6] Moreover, the demographic characteristics of its workforce echo other industries found outside France, such as the automotive, defense, and steel industries in North America.

Analytic Strategy

At its most general level, the analytic strategy employed explores how the meaning of gray zone social interactions (understood as any attribute or feature of the relationship between interacting participants) varies with the participants' occupational backgrounds, and how such variations might shed light on the sustainability of gray zones. The meanings of gray zone social interactions are viewed here as the dependent variable, worthy of study in their own right.

Variations in meaning around gray zone interactions are analyzed primarily through plant members' narratives, which either disclose or hide their involvement with other members in gray zone activities. Since social interactions are fairly abstract, the research strategy the study pursues is to investigate concrete manifestations of gray zones—namely, the homers that are cooperatively manufactured by and circulated among plant members. The artifacts the workers produce are used as a starting point from which to move backward in time and reveal the gray zone interactions surrounding them. Although the present study would benefit from variations in workplace setting to explore the different meanings of gray zone interactions, the concrete units of analysis are the intra-organizational gray zone social interactions in a given workplace. Variations in meanings of social interactions are therefore analyzed within a given work environment. This focus assumes that occupational heterogeneity among participants generates sufficient variation in the meaning of gray zone social interactions to allow for a meaningful analysis.

Data Sources

This study is not an organizational ethnography since I was not granted access to the workshops. However, it utilizes a combination of methods, some of them akin to those used in ethnographies, to overcome this constraint. Interviews with retired plant members, mail surveys, observations made outside the plant gates, and archives were used to gather data.

The study assumes that reality can be interpreted as a sequence of actions influenced by social actors and their social places at any given time. Thus, using narratives, as opposed to more measure-driven paradigms, provides appropriate insight into these sequences of action.[7] Besides, narratives and stories *are* what constitute social ties and, by extension, social systems. Or, as Harrison White puts it: "One thus can speculate that it is stories which set human social action apart. Without stories, and thence networks emerging out of mere collections of ties, social action would have a monotone quality; there would not be all the 'colors' that humans observe and use in social settings."[8]

Ideally, direct participant or on-site observation methods would provide further contextual access to such narratives. Unfortunately, plant management repeatedly denied my requests to either gain employment or even merely observe workplace interactions at Pierreville. On-site observations were therefore not an option.[9] Moreover, noticeable personal attributes such as my relative youth and my manner of speaking rendered covert employment problematic. My outsider position would have easily been discovered. In that sense, participant observation was also not an option.[10] The following alternative research methods were used to collect data instead.

Interviews

Interviews were conducted with Pierreville retirees (not as prone to corporate sanctions) to help reveal the social systems and potential variations in narratives used to describe homer interactions. The interviews always began with general questions about what the person did at Pierreville, how that person came to be employed at the plant, and broad, open-ended questions about the individual's experience of work. Usually these questions were followed by more pointed ones such as: Where and how were homers manufactured? Who helped in the process? How did you cooperate with one another? How did supervisors and executives participate in this system? Moreover, each interviewee was encouraged to provide precise examples of the homers each encountered on the job. The examples were then analyzed according to participants' attributes, specifically occupational category.[11]

The retirees sometimes provided an introduction to the current workforce, but essentially they talked about past memories of the plant. Thus, the past is presented in an ethnographic "present." The units of analysis are the narrated intra-organizational gray zone interactions that developed in the factory during the time the retirees were actively employed at Pierreville. The retirees worked at the plant mainly during the time period between the late 1970s and the late 1990s. The narratives collected in these interviews were an ex-post reconstruction of the lives of the retirees during the time they spent at Pierreville.

The interview sample was first constructed as a snowball sample, and then grew through direct mail contacts with randomly selected retirees whose names were on file at the Labor Council when the survey was designed (see the description of the retirement homer survey in the next section). The initial snowball technique covered thirty interviews out of a total of seventy, and though admittedly it potentially biased the sample, it allowed for entry into the plant community. A formal call for exploratory interviews was first published in the Labor Council's newsletter in November 2002, and a survey was sent to 200 randomly selected retirees in February and May 2003. Most initial interviews originated with the Labor Council, but others came through labor union and factory museum contacts.

As in all qualitative research, the quality of the conclusions, namely the objectivity, reliability, internal validity, external validity, and pragmatic validity, drives the sample size.[12] Qualitative and ethnographic research sometimes assumes that the quality of researcher/informant interactions trumps issues of sample size. As Michael Patton notes, "Nowhere is ambiguity clearer [in qualitative research] than in the matter of sample size."[13] Thus, various authors approach this issue differently. Loïc Wacquant, for instance, relied on a limited number of informants when he explored the Chicago boxing world.[14] Brian Uzzi conducted forty-two interviews in twenty-three different New York apparel firms to uncover interfirm linkages.[15] Calvin Morrill started off with eighty-two interviews, both formal and informal, to analyze exec-utive conflict in one firm, and later expanded his sample to 228 inter-views in thirteen firms, thus averaging seventeen to eighteen inter-views per firm.[16] For an initial publication, Diane Vaughan relied on numerous documents, an undisclosed number of interviews, plus "transcripts of 160 additional interviews conducted by experienced government investigators" to research the *Challenger* disaster before drawing her conclusions.[17]

In this study, the numbers of potentially relevant respondent catego-ries (along occupational lines) determined the sample size. Because any respondent could give several homer examples, the sample size focused on the number of homer cases rather than the number of infor-mants. On average, interviews yielded two in-depth homer cases per informant. Having distinguished three main meta-occupational cate-gories among the homer-activity participants, and with a goal of twenty instances of interactions from the vantage point of each cate-gory, I planned approximately sixty interviews.[18] Ultimately, seventy interviews were conducted. This strategy of generating a sufficient number of instances per category follows the methodology of the stra-tified purposeful sampling plan used for qualitative interviewing.[19] In the end, forty craftsmen; twenty executives, engineers, or supervisors; and ten unskilled workers or office employees were interviewed.

When the informants gave permission, their interviews were taped and transcribed. When the informants declined to be taped (N = 15), extensive notes were taken during and after each interview to keep a thorough record of the discussion. The interview protocol was ex-panded after exploratory interviews were conducted in the fall of 2002 and the spring of 2003 (N = 30). Additional interviews (N = 40) were conducted at retirees' homes, or outside the factory either in a space the Labor Council provided or in the neighboring factory museum. On a few occasions, I first met the interviewees in public (safe) places, such as the central square of a town or a *café*, before being invited to their homes. Many of these people only knew me through a short introduc-tory letter I sent describing my interest in retirement homers and the accompanying questionnaire they completed. (After my initial snow-ball sample, most of the interviewees I met were obtained via the con-tact information they provided in this questionnaire.) Thus, it often took some explaining and a few telephone exchanges before I could arrange for a meeting. The design and administration of the survey and accompanying letter that afforded these exchanges is described in the next section.

Retirement Homer Survey

Restricting the focus of the survey to retirement homers was a precondition for the Pierreville Labor Council's endorsement of the survey. The survey asked about retirement gifts (including homers) and basic demographics (including occupational background). As such, it allowed testing variations along potential occupational lines in retirement homer receiving patterns. Although receiving a retirement homer is a different type of homer interaction than participating in its manufacture or than interactions dealing with more generic homers, a study of retirement homer recipients was an entry point into the community of homer-makers, since homer recipients were often homer-makers, as well. The items in the survey assessed the kind of retirement gift (if any) received, the hierarchical and occupational status of the respondent, hire and exit dates, tenure at the factory, educational background, and reason for departure. Because informants warned me that respondents would feel uncomfortable answering a question about union membership (at Pierreville, union membership is considered a fairly private matter), no such question was included. An invitation to participate in an interview accompanied all surveys.

Two separate mailings of an initial survey were sent (one in February 2003 and one in May 2003) to two sets of a hundred retirees randomly selected from 1,800 active names of retirees in the Labor Council files. A final, slightly modified survey was sent to another 450 randomly selected retirees in January 2004 (which excluded the 200 previously surveyed retirees). The combined response rate for the survey was 28 percent. Response rates according to hierarchical categories varied. From lowest to highest position in the official hierarchy in the plant, workers constituted 12 percent of respondents (versus 22%, on average, of the workforce between 1977 and 2001), employees 14 percent (versus 8%), technicians 34 percent (versus 44%), supervisors 15 percent (versus 7%), and executives/engineers 25 percent (versus 20%). The relative underrepresentation of workers is probably primarily a historical phenomenon: many of the potential respondents in the worker category retired at the start of the period under study (late 1970s) and are perhaps no longer alive. This underrepresentation might, however, also reflect distrust of institutional research; discussions of whether or not to respond to the survey were often later relayed to me in interviews. Similar issues of trust might also account for the underrepresentation of technicians.

Factory Archives

Understanding who received retirement homers was only the first piece of the homer gray zone puzzle. Getting a sense of the relative positions between recipients and nonrecipients required a more historical perspective on labor relations at Pierreville. Occupational dynamics within the plant were not always stable, but the factory archives were helpful in understanding evolving status issues that emerged in the survey and interviews. Two corporate archives were accessed: the Pierreville factory archives and the corporate headquarters archives. These archives were used to document historical trends in employment categories. They both highlighted the labor issues surrounding the transfer of a particular workshop (the experimental workshop) to another geographical location, and illuminated the ways in which unions portrayed the occupational groups affected by the relocation, since union flyers were archived. The archives also provided access to internal data on homer events gone wrong. Whereas interviews, surveys, and archives offer useful windows into social systems, observations helped in understanding some nuances in these data.

Observations

The previously described data sources were complemented by observations conducted at the Factory Labor Council and the factory museum. For a cumulative period of ten months, every Wednesday I spent time in these environments, either to conduct formal interviews or to simply "catch up" with retirees and Labor Council members and discuss factory news and happenings. During the course of a day, many people visited or passed through the Labor Council and factory museum, which made them good settings to make acquaintances. Usually, over the course of several encounters, the retirees would come to understand what the research was about, and they often would agree to a more formal interview or suggest other people they thought I should meet.

My most intensive period of fieldwork occurred during the 2002–2003 academic year, which I spent entirely in France. The fact that I had initiated contact with several Pierreville members as early as 2001 facilitated my rapid integration. Moreover, the Labor Council printed a short paragraph explaining my interest in retirement homers and an accompanying picture of me in its newsletter, which allowed people at Pierreville to recognize me. Though I was initially reluctant to gain such public exposure and feared nobody would ever talk to me again once my agenda was made public, in retrospect, this announcement helped me gain legitimacy. It reassured informants of my independence and gave them a sense of security since the person who showed up at their door was the same as the one pictured in the Labor Council newsletter. Though this announcement probably also deterred some potential retired plant members from participating, I believe its benefits outweighed its costs.

Because of my tenure at Pierreville and the widespread audience the plant's newsletter reached, whenever I was at the Labor Council or factory museum, many people approached me to volunteer stories or offer advice. This is not technically participant observation, but given the constraints of my research topic and my position vis-à-vis the field, it allowed me to get as close as I could to my informants, and in so doing, familiarized me with participants in the phenomenon I was studying.

Methodology

Given my position at Pierreville, I relied primarily on informants' "realist tales" for my analysis.[20] I knew that also keeping a more reflexive "confessional tale" of my experience would help me make sense of the data.[21] Though I rarely refer to my field journal in this book (except in appendix B, "Position in the Field"), I wrote entries in the journal whenever I went to Pierreville or met a retiree. Finally, I must add that "impressionist tales," the third type of ethnographic writing identified by John Van Maanen, also informed my research.[22] Moments I identified most with my informants occurred at awkward times in my own daily life: for instance, while swimming in the middle of the day, I felt as if I might be "stealing time" from my employer—even though my "employer" seemed arguably less controlling than theirs did.[23] Though I do not elaborate on these impressionist tales, they often found their way into my field journal.

I analyzed the multiple sources of data I collected in three overlapping steps that involved: (1) hypothesis generation and archival research; (2) statistical analysis of the surveys; and (3) systematic coding of my interview transcripts and notes. Iterations among these steps were ongoing. Hypothesis generation mostly occurred through conversations with informants, and was often complemented by archival research on the topics of interest. For instance, when an informant suggested the disappearance of craftsmen at Pierreville as a topic related to homers, I then examined the corporate archives to try to trace the craftsmen's presence or absence in the plant. Another step involved a statistical analysis of the responses to the retirement homer survey. This analysis was informed by the hypotheses that emerged from my fieldwork. It also allowed me to test some of the arguments informants shared with me in our conversations, such as the experimental workshop's position as central to homer-making at Pierreville. A third and final step involved the coding of my interview data. Interview data were analyzed according to grounded theory guidelines.[24] Once transcribed, the raw interview text was analyzed for salient attributes associated with work narratives and homers, which revealed interactions in the setting under study. Statistical analysis of my first wave of surveys allowed for further enrichment of the interview protocol. In the same manner, analysis of the interview data further informed the final survey design. This parallel combination of fieldwork and surveys was meant to increase the quality of research design, data collection, and data analysis.[25] The iteration between these two methods enabled the design of a more relevant survey and a more purposeful sampling of interviewees. Topics that were brought up during informal conversations at the Labor Council and factory museum were also often explored in the interviews.

In analyzing these data, I employed a theory-building technique that evolved from individual accounts consisting of thick descriptions, to a theory that was more abstract and analytical. I read the interview transcripts several times to cull themes and patterns in homer interactions, and triangulation with other data, when available, was conducted. Initially, I carefully scanned the data for dominant themes. As themes started to emerge—such as the portrayal of gray zone interactions as "respect and recognition" interactions or "transactions"—I took note of them and used them to organize new data. This method was used in an iterative fashion throughout the data collection period. I then organized the emerging themes into a coherent framework, and coded the narratives for data regarding (1) participants' occupational status, (2) descriptions of homer events, and (3) terminology used to narrate the interactions. After developing, exploring, and evaluating alternative frameworks, I arrived at one which, I believe, offers a strong contribution to theory without doing undue violence to the experiences of my informants. Whereas some observers have noted that such a reliance on narrative episodes might bias the data toward more extreme observable practices, this bias was addressed by triangulating narrative data with survey data and asking key informants (veteran Labor Council members) to cross-check the accuracy of certain episodes.[26]

Position in the Field

SINCE ONE of the methodological biases of this study is to posit that complex social systems are sustained and identities enacted through social interactions, it is only fair to detail my own relationship to Pierreville so the reader can make sense of how my data were collected. One's relationship to a field also has profound implications on the data analysis.[1] Given the nature of the topic under study (i.e., gray zones), this disclosure seems almost obligatory since informants might engage in more impression management than if I had studied other, more openly disclosed topics.

I never worked or spent time in the Pierreville plant before I began this research project. However, a family member of mine (who does not share my last name) worked most of his life at Pierreville.[2] Because of the relative illegality of creating homers, my link to him could not be made explicit, even though factory members knew of my family connection to the field.[3] Despite this nondisclosure (or perhaps because this nondisclosure also signaled that I understood some of the covert issues surrounding homers), the factory Labor Council and, more sporadically, the AeroDyn corporation granted me access. Excerpts of my field notes are interwoven below to make the position I held more explicit.

When I started this research project, I had spent extended periods of time living outside France, the country in which I grew up. Moreover, my studies had gradually shaped my interactions toward a group of similar-minded fellow graduate students living in cities such as Paris or New York. An impression of my growing disconnect from life outside large cities loomed over me. Factories seemed an exotic destination and, at that time, a perfect antidote to this mounting uniformity. To this day, factories still trigger my imagination.

[Field Notes (October 13, 2004):] I am on my way to Pierreville again. This morning, I thought my sweater was a bit too trendy. I needed something more sober. I finally found a turtleneck sweater, instead of a v-neck. It's more classical . . . more factory like? My biases resurface. I engage in what has now become my customary stop at the gas station before going to Pierreville. It usually allows me to get my ideas together, and to transition from my life to this other one that clearly is quite strange to me. Though I grew up in France, I had gone off to China and marveled at the Great Wall, then to India and its crowds, Hong Kong and its towers, Shanghai and its markets. But it's here and now that I discover exoticism—exoticism of the faces, of the hands, of the words. I need to decompress between the 10th district in Paris where I reside and Pierreville [an hour away]. In a way, the gas station stop plays that role.

Thus, my research is not an insider's view on a given work community. If anything, it started off as an outsider's perspective on it. Many of my actions made my disconnect salient, specifically when I was talking to retirees. The following entries from my field notes provide a contrast in terms of the way I was perceived to fit in (or not fit in) with the informants I met. The first woman, Madame Xavier, is the wife of a now deceased high-ranking engineer. Her sons pursued higher educational degrees and, early on, she considered me a peer ("educated" like herself) and reinforced this by suggesting I not waste my time interviewing less educated people.

[Field Notes (February 11, 2004):] I am here to see Madame Xavier, the widow of a former Pierreville engineer. I ring the doorbell at the agreed-upon hour, and the maid answers and tells me that Madame will soon entertain me. I am led to the living room. Madame Xavier is still talking on the phone somewhere else in the house; I can hear her voice, it's a very firm and direct voice. The maid tells me again to wait a bit.... Finally the widow arrives, and the conversation can begin. Two and a half hours later, as we are about to separate, I ask her again about an intriguing person she talked about—the scrap metal merchant many Pierreville retirees referred to. He passed away, but I still wanted to meet his family. Perhaps his kids knew something about him? "He's dead," she abruptly interjects, and "his kids . . . don't waste your time," she adds, "they have no education."

The next entry relates a visit to Hervé's house in a popular district of Paris and my impression that my beverage of choice, water, stood in stark opposition to my imagined association between factory work and alcohol. Hervé was a former welder and in his mid-seventies when I met him. The perceived disappointment I thought I detected when I requested water illuminates as much his social routine as my own.

[Field Notes (February 2, 2004):] Hervé receives me in his house in the 13th district of Paris, two rooms up in a tower, in what is now Chinatown. He asks me if I want beer, tea, water, or something else. Bad choice as usual, I thought after my visit, remembering his moment of surprise: I had asked for water. Tea was probably the worst choice I could have made. I look at his fingers—they are rugged, with a broken nail, blackened—which evokes steel mills in my mind. (I'm not sure why.) He was a welder. We talked for more than an hour. We then talked several more times over the phone.

The final entry depicts my encounter with Jean, a retired worker living in a fairly small village an hour away from Pierreville in the opposite direction of Paris. While attempting to engage in small talk to get to know each other, our differences became obvious. He talked about redoing his tile floor; I about having someone put carpet in the studio I lived in. I remember pushing myself to find an interest in his tiles.

[Field Notes (February 4, 2004):] I am supposed to meet Jean at his house in a small town fairly far away from Pierreville. As I walk into his house, the discussion focuses on his tile floor. He goes to great length to describe the choice of tile and the work he put into tiling his floor. Then the conversation turns to the carpet: colors, density, and general resistance. I mention that I am currently having the carpet where I live redone. He is redoing his own: slight difference, we both know. At that moment, there is a clear collusion between us around home improvement, but also an understanding of our differences. He adds that he tiled his floor only after his daughter finished her studies, because school is expensive even though it's worth it. He assesses the cost of supporting his daughter: 3,000 French Francs per month. Am I not a student, too? I feel the need to explain how my research is funded via scholarships, that we also teach classes, and in general, counter his impression that students are subsidized by their parents. After an hour and a half of conversation, I need to go. He tells me I cannot leave without having a drink with him. I must drive, I say, so I can only drink one glass. Pastis, wine, cooked wine? Sure, cooked wine sounds good. Wrong choice: that's the one with 15 percent alcohol content. I feel every drop go down my throat.

Aware of these cultural differences and my perceived relative standing in terms of fitting in socially or not with informants, I sometimes made extra efforts to fit in; the beverage choice was one of the many small strategies I employed, often to little avail. Sometimes I would let my informants choose their drinks first (when I remembered), and then follow their lead. Another such strategy was to refer to workshops by their numbers, a practice workers employed, instead of using their official names, which management and headquarters used. Very gradually, I started feeling comfortable enough with my position in the community to let go of my defensiveness and accept their biases as well as my own. Nonetheless, I tried to familiarize myself with "native" experiences, such as the one described below, and attended the Paris annual Air Show several times to get a feeling for the aeronautic industry.

[Field Notes (February 25, 2004):] I tried to engage a bit in some of the local customs by going to Castorama [a large French home improvement retail chain] to buy some hooks for the place I was living in. I was impressed to see so many men interested in home improvement and shopping at lunchtime for materials and tools I knew nothing about. I had this weird impression that I was surrounded by Pierreville retirees. And I had this strange feeling of being somewhere I shouldn't be. I always thought of myself as someone who hated engaging in any kind of handy job at home. Who knows, perhaps I will slowly learn to enjoy it.

At the same time, it would be unfair to depict myself entirely as an outsider. The fact that a relative of mine worked at Pierreville and the discovery, when I first stepped foot inside the factory in June 2002, that the facility more closely resembled a scientific laboratory than a moving assembly line allowed me to connect with Pierreville retirees on different levels.[4] Moreover, my tenure in the field helped me build a rapport with my informants (this study lasted almost two years).

When I began my research, my family member was still working at Pierreville. He retired from the plant toward the end of this project. At the time, his spouse was also a Pierreville employee, and she talked with me about her work. Thanks to them, not only did I understand the configuration of the factory (drawing maps of the factory and trying to understand the production flow was one of my favorite ways to spark discussion), but I was also made aware of the emotional toll geographic transfers and the lack of promotions took on them. She had spent several months in another AeroDyn plant before returning to Pierreville, and he had been considered for an overseas appointment, but decided not to leave. Spillover between work inside the factory and life outside was constant for my relative and his spouse. Thus, learning about their day-to-day lives provided a window into the lives of Pierreville members.

Moreover, I was made aware, partly by the official visit to the factory, of a white-collar population in the plant with whom I could relate more easily. I understood their training system better and could more quickly grasp their practical occupations. This meant I could rely on them to gain access and data, but at the same time, I needed to distance myself from them in order not to bias my analysis of the data. The Labor Council's endorsement of my research project in October 2002 exemplifies the costs and benefits of my position: sufficiently well positioned to gain an official endorsement, yet not too much so to be fully accepted by management.

The Labor Council that endorsed the project was headed by the labor union (CFDT) typically associated with technicians and executives, rather than blue-collar workers. In retrospect, the labor union seemed to have little to lose in revelations about the workshops, where their membership base was less represented than in other plant settings (such as the offices where the technicians and engineers worked). Indeed, this research points to the fact that homers were mostly manufactured in one specific workshop (the experimental workshop), which had been relocated to another site that was under the jurisdiction of another labor union (CGT). This meant that, initially, when I sought access to the core homer-makers, I was unknowingly sponsored by the "wrong" union. However, I might never have gained broad access to the site had I approached the CGT instead. Moreover, the majority union at Pierreville (CFDT) had previously expressed a desire to document the social history of the plant. Homers, when thought of as craft pieces, can be seen as symbols of pride. On another occasion (1984) in a different plant, the same CFDT helped organize and endorsed a retirement homer exhibit.[5] This precedent, probably combined with my social connection to the CFDT, was instrumental in convincing the Labor Council to endorse my research proposal.

In some ways, any official endorsement would have undermined my ability to collect data. At the same time, however, I needed broad access to be able to sample informants and get the full picture of homer activities. A Labor Council endorsement was a compromise, and I knew that associating with the CFDT coupled with my semi-outsider position could sometimes be held against me. The following entries deal with some situations in which my position was openly questioned. In the first entry below, Hervé, the aforementioned welder (who made me choose between tea, water, and alcohol), once reacted quite violently to a paper I wrote about homers, and labeled me a "bourgeois." Similar categorizing, though often unspoken (illustrated by the second entry), occurred on other, limited occasions as well.

[Field Notes (February 2, 2004):] As I was preparing to leave, Hervé asked me if he could read something I wrote. The conversation had gone well; our exchanges were quite open, and since he was reading Le Monde [a French newspaper] when I arrived, I thought he would enjoy reading something on homers. My experience and academic training suggested that this was a very bad idea, a clear way to influence informants and bias future conversation, but I was happy he was interested in what I was doing. I gave him a copy of an article in French titled "Factory Homers: Understanding a Highly Elusive, Marginal, and Illegal Practice." That same evening, he called me at home, furious, to tell me I did not talk about the real work going on at Pierreville. Then he personally attacked me, asked me if I was a bourgeois, or more specifically, to confirm that I was one of "them." I remembered my poor beverage choice [water] when I first met him. Bosses also steal, he told me, officially and much more than employees. He then quieted down and told me to further explore work at Pierreville. Later we had several quieter conversations.

[Field Notes (February 10, 2004):] I finally decide to call a friend of Hervé's for a third time. He was a famous leader of the communist labor union at Pierreville. He already had declined twice to meet me, mostly on what, I presumed, was the pretext of being too busy. With this new introduction from his friend, I naively believed this could change. When he answers the phone, he asks me if I am a member of the communist labor union. I answer no, that I am an academic. As if it is not possible for a person in academia to be a member of the communist union! I think I just messed up and shot myself in the foot. He reluctantly suggests a group discussion, that I should follow up with him. This group discussion never happened. He was too busy . . .

However, these instances of direct questioning were limited. Though I initially imagined I would have to overcome the stigmatized image of a transatlantic academic researcher in a more technical and less cosmopolitan context, the fact that I did not yet have a "real job" was a constant concern for many factory employees and retirees. In a context of high unemployment and because these individuals had regular incomes or pensions and high levels of health benefits, I was often classified as a person in "need" of assistance. Thus, my imagined stigma, more often than not, was fully reversed. Not only did the retirees facilitate this project, but many of them also inquired about my future job prospects.

Finally, issues of secrecy were often raised as a reason not to share information with me. AeroDyn corporate headquarters was extremely slow to grant me access to any corporate information, often citing a need to uphold secrecy. In order to facilitate access, anonymity was offered to the organization, the factory, and its employees, but this did not change my institutional relations with AeroDyn.[6] It is possible that my affiliation with a U.S. institution in a climate of economic rivalry with the U.S. aeronautic industry proved problematic. AeroDyn's main competitor was American, and Pierreville was classified as "secret defense" in addition to being the main AeroDyn research site. At another, similar French aeronautic company, the Pierreville equivalent was called "the thing" (*la chose*) due to the secrecy surrounding it.[7] My joint affiliation with a French research center (starting at the end of 2002) translated into a breakthrough in terms of qualitative relations with the

Pierreville retirees, but from the AeroDyn headquarters' perspective, I remained a researcher who was much too independent.

In the few instances my position was questioned (as "foreign" researcher, as a "bourgeois," as a "corporate mole," etc.), informants were also implicitly commenting on the legitimacy of my endeavor. This is something I struggled with often: how to find the right way to convey the data I collected and be true to informants—or more specifically, since I did not fully belong to the community, how to ensure I did not betray them.

> [Field Notes (November 28, 2002):] Near Pierreville, in the beet fields that surround the factory, dense fog tends to settle in quickly. I always have to be careful driving there. Because of the fog, I sometimes get the impression of being in an enchanted environment, filled with fairies and witches. This reminds me of a sentence written by Pierre Bourdieu: "Therefore, when he simply does what has to be done, the sociologist breaks the enchanted circle of collective denial."[8] Am I here to break the enchanted circle, or rather, to sustain it?

In these moments of doubt, what grounded me most was the fact that if I did not document part of Pierreville's social and labor history, few would, and in that regard, a basis for discussion, however controversial it might be, is better than none. And second, as my fieldwork progressed, I cannot say I became an insider, but I grew attached to several informants with whom I developed a rapport. It is not up to me to say if this experience was reciprocal. What I noticed, however, was that when I walked into the workshop that was attached to the factory museum—the workshop many retirees visited on Wednesdays to repair old engines—some of them would tease me by shouting, "Here is the homer-maker!" ("*Voilà le perruqueur!*") Moreover, when I ate with them at the factory canteen (where the retirees sometimes invited me to join them when I was near the plant), active employees would call us (myself included) the "old ones" and smile at me. Despite my social and occupational oddness at Pierreville, the Pierreville members made a place for me.

Ultimately, the depiction of my position vis-à-vis the field is meant more as a disclosure than an explanation of certain methodological choices or findings. The dynamics described previously (such as the outsider/insider status, social class divides, and the French/foreign label) cannot be fully dissociated from my data collection process and analysis. Making these dynamics clear is my attempt at also breaking potential enchanted circles of—in this case—individual rather than collective denial. My initial outsider position allowed me to approach with a fresh eye what a lot of Pierreville members might consider obvious. Over time, however, I gained my unique position within the Pierreville community. My position enabled me, in many instances, to gain access to various informants and data sources, and in other limited instances, identified me as an outsider. Fieldwork involves compromises; an awareness of these compromises ideally allows for a better appreciation of the research design and findings.

Notes

Introduction
The Persistence of Organizational Gray Zones

1. This interview was conducted for a separate project I worked on.

2. Michel de Certeau, *The Practice of Everyday Life* (Berkeley: University of California Press, 1988), 25.

3. Miklos Haraszti, *A Worker in a Worker's State: Piece-Rates in Hungary* (New York: Universe Books, 1978), 9.

4. For examples of how artifacts provide insight into social systems, see Arjun Appadurai (ed.), *The Social Life of Things: Commodities in Cultural Perspective* (Cambridge: Cambridge University Press, 1986); Stephen R. Barley, "Technology as an Occasion for Structuring: Evidence from Observation of CT Scanners and the Social Order of Radiology Departments," *Administrative Science Quarterly* 31, no. 1 (1986); Beth Bechky, "Object Lessons: Workplace Artifacts as Representations of Occupational Jurisdiction," *American Journal of Sociology* 109, no. 3 (2003); Fernand Braudel, *Civilisation Matérielle, Économie et Capitalisme: XV\u1d49–XVIII\u1d49 Siècle*, vol. 1 (Paris: A. Colin, 1979); Michel Callon, "Some Elements of a Sociology of Translation: Domestication of the Scallops and Fishermen of St. Brieuc Bay," in *Power in Action and Belief: A New Sociology of Knowledge*, ed. John Law (London: Routledge, 1986); Igor Kopytoff, "The Cultural Biography of Things: Commoditization as Process," in *The Social Life of Things: Commodities in Cultural Perspective*, ed. Arjun Appadurai (Cambridge: Cambridge University Press, 1986); Chandra Mukerji, *Territorial Ambitions and the Gardens of Versailles* (Cambridge: Cambridge University Press, 1997); Fred R.V. Myers, ed., *The Empire of Things: Regimes of Value and Material Culture* (Santa Fe, NM: School of American Research Press, 2001).

5. Haraszti, *A Worker in a Worker's State*, 142.

6. Certeau, *The Practice of Everyday Life*, 26.

7. Workplace folklore is rarely documented. For a noteworthy exception, see Robert H. Byington, ed., "Working Americans: Contemporary Approaches to Occupational Folklife," *Western Folklore* 37, no. 3 (1978).

8. Primo Levi, *The Drowned and the Saved* (New York: Vintage International, 1989), 42.

9. The bakery drivers' case is discussed in more detail in chapter 9 and the mail carriers' in chapter 10. For references, see Jason Ditton, "Perks, Pilferage, and the Fiddle: The Historical Structure of Invisible Wages," *Theory and Society* 4, no. 1 (1977); and John Allen Bradford, "A General Perspective on Job Satisfaction: The Relation between Job Satisfaction, and Sociological and Psychological Variables," Doctoral Dissertation in Sociology, University of California, San Diego: 1976.

10. Gray zones are collective endeavors by nature, and therefore do not include individual, one-shot deals struck between a given employee and her employer. For examples of these deals, see Denise M. Rousseau, "Under the Table Deals: Idiosyncratic, Preferential or Unauthorized?" in *Dark Side of Organizational Behavior*, ed. R. Griffin and A. O'Leary-Kelly (San Francisco: Jossey-Bass, 2004).

11. Bradford, "A General Perspective on Job Satisfaction," 72.

12. Donald Roy, "Banana Time: Job Satisfaction and Informal Interaction," *Human Organization* 18 (1959); William F. Whyte, *Street Corner Society: The Social Structure of an Italian Slum* (Chicago: University of Chicago Press, 1943).

13. All organization, plant, and informant names have been changed to preserve confidentiality.

14. Theodor W. Adorno, *Prisms* (Cambridge, MA: MIT Press, 1967), 240.

15. French organizations employing more than a certain number of individuals are required by law to have an employee-elected Labor Council (often housed in or near the organization's main facility).

16. Most retirees registered since the free membership offered many benefits, such as discounted travel and entertainment.

17. The term "moral" is used throughout this book in its Durkheimian sense: that is what a society or a group defines as good, not as a universal ethical standard. For a discussion of this usage, see Marion Fourcade-Gourinchas and Kieran Healy, "Moral Views of Market Society," *Annual Review of Sociology* 33 (2007). Robert Bellah's introduction to Emile Durkheim's selected texts also details this usage; see Emile Durkheim, *Emile Durkheim on Morality and Society*, ed. Robert N. Bellah (Chicago: University of Chicago Press, 1973).

18. This assumes organizational goals are perceived by management as moral ones.

19. This validation mobilizes the "community of practice" around craftsmen. For a discussion of communities of practice, see Jean Lave and Etienne Wenger, *Situated Learning: Legitimate Peripheral Participation* (Cambridge: Cambridge University Press, 1991); Etienne Wenger, *Communities of Practice: Learning, Meaning and Identity* (Cambridge: Cambridge University Press, 1998).

20. Peter Blau, *The Dynamics of Bureaucracy* (Chicago: University of Chicago Press, 1955); Michael Burawoy, *Manufacturing Consent: Changes in the Labor Process under Monopoly Capitalism* (Chicago: University of Chicago Press, 1979); Alvin Gouldner, *Patterns of Industrial Bureaucracy* (New York: Free Press, 1954); Roy, "Banana Time: Job Satisfaction and Informal Interaction."

21. Gouldner, *Patterns of Industrial Bureaucracy*, 56.

22. Burawoy, *Manufacturing Consent*.

23. Certeau, *The Practice of Everyday Life*, 26.

24. For a discussion of other potentially valuable identities aside from occupational ones, see Michael J. Piore and Sean Safford, "Changing Regimes of Workplace Governance, Shifting Axes of Social Mobilization, and the Challenge to Industrial Relations Theory," *Industrial Relations* 45, no. 3 (2006).

Chapter One
Revisiting Social Systems in Organizations

1. George C. Homans, *The Human Group* (New Brunswick, NJ: Transaction Publishers, 1993), 87.

2. Talcott Parsons and Edward Albert Shils, *Toward a General Theory of Action* (Cambridge, MA: Harvard University Press, 1951), 107.

3. Melville Dalton, *Men Who Manage: Fusions of Feeling and Theory in Administration* (New York: Wiley, 1959); Gouldner, *Patterns of Industrial Bureaucracy*; Philip Selznick, *TVA and the Grass Roots: A Study in the Sociology of Formal Organization* (Berkeley: University of California Press, 1949).

4. Norbert Elias, *La Société de Cour* (Paris: Flammarion, 1985), 232 (author's translation).

5. Fritz J. Roethlisberger and William. J. Dickson, *Management and the Worker: An Account of a Research Program Conducted by the Western Electric Company* (Cambridge, MA: Harvard University Press, 1939).

6. For a review of these studies see Henry Landsberger, *Hawthorne Revisited* (Ithaca, NY: Cornell University Press, 1958).

7. These researchers even noted the "mental peculiarities" of each informant to understand the sentiments generated by belonging to this social system. See Fritz J. Roethlisberger and William J. Dickson, "Relay Assembly Test Room Case Histories 1927–1929" (Box 18, Hawthorne Studies Collection, Western Electric Company, Historical Collections. Boston: Baker Library, Harvard Business School, 1939).

8. Randy Hodson and Teresa A. Sullivan, *The Social Organization of Work* (Belmont, CA: Wadsworth, 2002); Charles Perrow, *Organizing America: Wealth, Power, and the Origins of Corporate Capitalism* (Princeton, NJ: Princeton University Press, 2002).

9. Peter Blau, *Exchange and Power in Social Life* (New York: Wiley, 1964), 12.

10. Roethlisberger and Dickson, *Management and the Worker*.

11. Steven P. Vallas, "Why Teamwork Fails: Obstacles to Workplace Change in Four Manufacturing Plants," *American Sociological Review* 68, no. 2 (2003).

12. Thomas J. Allen, *Managing the Flow of Technology: Technology Transfer and the Dissemination of Technological Information within the R&D Organization* (Cambridge, MA: MIT Press, 1977); Dalton, *Men Who Manage*; John P. Kotter, *The General Managers* (New York: Free Press, 1986); Henry Mintzberg, *The Nature of Managerial Work* (New York: Harper & Row, 1973).

13. Chester Barnard, *The Functions of the Executive* (Cambridge, MA: Harvard University Press, 1968); Michel Crozier, *Le Phénomène Bureaucratique* (Paris: Éditions du Seuil, 1963); Nicolas Hatzfeld, "La Pause Casse-Croûte: Quand les Chaînes s'Arrêtent à Peugeot-Sochaux," *Terrain* 39 (2002); Roy, "Banana Time: Job Satisfaction and Informal Interaction."

14. Anne-Laure Fayard and John Weeks, "Photocopiers and Water-Coolers: The Affordances of Informal Interaction," *Organization Studies* 28, no. 5 (2007).

15. Burawoy, *Manufacturing Consent*, 51–73.

16. Joanne Martin, *Cultures in Organizations: Three Perspectives* (New York: Oxford University Press, 1992); Ann Swidler, "Culture in Action: Symbols and Strategies," *American Sociological Review* 51, no. 2 (1986). For a recent review of organizational cultures, see chap. 3 in John Weeks, *Unpopular Culture: The Ritual of Complaint in a British Bank* (Chicago: University of Chicago Press, 2004).

17. *Oxford English Dictionary*, 2nd edition, 1989.

18. Whyte, *Street Corner Society*.

19. Pino Arlacchi, *Mafia, Peasants, and Great Estates: Society in Traditional Calabria* (Cambridge: Cambridge University Press, 1983); Albert K. Cohen, *Delinquent Boys: The Culture of the Gang* (London: Routledge and Kegan Paul, 1956); Nisha Menon, "Membership Has Its Rewards: The Nature of Female Gang and Clique Involvement in Boston" (A.B. Honors Thesis in Sociology, Harvard University, 1999); James F. Short, *Group Process and Gang Delinquency* (Chicago: University of Chicago Press, 1965).

20. Mark Mizruchi, "What Do Interlocks Do? An Analysis, Critique and Assessment of Research on Interlocking Directorates," *Annual Review of Sociology* (1996): 293.

21. Dawn Iacobucci and Amy Ostrom, "Commercial and Interpersonal Relationships: Using the Structure of Interpersonal Relationships to Understand Individual-to-Individual, Individual-to-Firm, and Firm-to-Firm Relationships in Commerce," *International Journal of Research in Marketing* 13 (1996).

22. Wayne Baker and Robert R. Faulkner, "The Social Organization of Conspiracy: Illegal Networks in the Heavy Electrical Equipment Industry," *American Sociological Review* 58, no. 6 (1993).

23. Marshall B. Clinard and Peter Yeager, *Corporate Crime* (New York: Free Press, 1980); Susan Shapiro, *Wayward Capitalists: Target of the Securities and Exchange Commissions* (New Haven, CT: Yale University Press, 1984).

24. Mark Granovetter and Richard Swedberg, *The Sociology of Economic Life* (Boulder, CO: Westview Press, 1992), 321.

25. Elton Mayo's work formed the basis of the Human Relations movement. Elton Mayo, *The Social Problems of an Industrial Civilization* (Cambridge, MA: Harvard University Press, 1945).

26. Charles Perrow, *Complex Organizations: A Critical Essay* (New York: McGraw-Hill, 1986), 60.

27. Rakesh Khurana, *From Higher Aims to Hired Hands: The Social Transformation of American Business Schools and the Unfulfilled Promise of Management as a Profession* (Princeton, NJ: Princeton University Press, 2007).

28. Marion Fourcade-Gourinchas, *Economists and Societies: Discipline and Profession in the United States, Great Britain and France* (Princeton, NJ: Princeton University Press, Forthcoming).

29. For an illustration of the impact of information technology, see JoAnne Yates and John Van Maanen, eds., *Information Technology and Organizational Transformation: History, Rhetoric, and Practice* (Thousand Oaks, CA: Sage Publications, 2001).

30. William J. Dickson and Fritz J. Roethlisberger, *Counseling in an Organization: A Sequel to the Hawthorne Researches* (Boston: Division of Research, Harvard Business School, 1966).

31. Richard L. Daft, "The Evolution of Organization Analysis in ASQ, 1959–1979," *Administrative Science Quarterly* 25, no. 4 (1980): 631.

32. Heather Haveman and Mukti Khaire, "Organizational Sociology and the Analysis of Work," in *Social Theory and Work*, ed. Marek Korczynski, Randy Hodson, and Paul Edwards (Oxford, UK: Oxford University Press, 2006).

33. Glenn R. Carroll and Michael T. Hannan, *The Demography of Corporations and Industries* (Princeton, NJ: Princeton University Press, 2000).

34. Michael T. Hannan and John Freeman, *Organizational Ecology* (Cambridge, MA: Harvard University Press, 1989).

35. Randy Hodson, "The Workplace Ethnography Project" (Ohio State University, 2002).

36. The "Chicago school" of sociology, based out of the University of Chicago, has maintained a strong tradition of participant observations. For an introduction to symbolic interactionism, see Erving Goffman, *The Presentation of Self in Everyday Life* (New York: Doubleday, 1959).

37. Gary A. Fine, "The Culture of Production: Aesthetic Choices and Constraints in Culinary Work," *American Journal of Sociology* 97, no. 5 (1992); Diego Gambetta and Heather Hamill, *Streetwise: How Taxi Drivers Establish Their Customers' Trustworthiness* (New York: Russell Sage Foundation, 2005); Robert Jackall, *Moral Mazes: The World of Corporate Managers* (New York: Oxford University Press, 1988); Calvin Morrill, *The Executive Way: Conflict Management in Corporations* (Chicago: University of Chicago Press, 1995); Diane Vaughan, *The Challenger Launch Decision: Risky Technology, Culture, and Deviance at NASA* (Chicago: University of Chicago Press, 1996).

38. Recent illustrations include Stéphane Beaud and Michel Pialoux, *Retour sur la Condition Ouvrière: Enquête Aux Usines Peugeot de Sochaux-Montbéliard* (Paris: Fayard, 1999); Gwenaële Rot, *Sociologie de l'Atelier: Renault, le Travail Ouvrier et le Sociologue* (Toulouse: Octarès Éditions, 2006).

39. Barley, "Technology as an Occasion for Structuring"; Gideon Kunda, *Engineering Culture: Control and Commitment in a High-Tech Corporation* (Philadelphia: Temple University Press, 1992); Leslie A. Perlow, "Boundary Control: The Social Ordering of Work and Family Time in a High-Tech Corporation," *Administrative Science Quarterly* 43, no. 2 (1998); John Van Maanen, "Identity Work: Notes on the Personal Identity of Police Officers," paper presented at the Annual Meeting of the Academy of Management (San Diego: 1998); Weeks, *Unpopular Culture.*

40. Aihwa Ong, *Spirits of Resistance and Capitalist Discipline: Factory Women in Malaysia* (Albany, NY: State University of New York Press, 1987); Florence Weber, *Le Travail À-Côté. Étude d'Ethnographie Ouvrière* (Paris: INRA—Éditions de l'EHESS, 1989). For other examples, see the society for the anthropology of work at the American Anthropological Association and Susan Wright, *Anthropology of Organizations* (London and New York: Routledge, 1994).

41. Stephen R. Barley and Gideon Kunda, "Bringing Work Back In," *Organization Science* 12, no. 1 (2001).

42. Florence Weber, "Formes de l'Échange, Circulation des Objets et Relations entre les Personnes," in *Hypothèses 2001* (Paris: Publications de la Sorbonne, 2002).

43. Paul DiMaggio and Hugh Louch, "Socially Embedded Consumer Transactions: For What Kinds of Purchases Do People Most Often Use Networks?" *American Sociological Review* 63, no. 5 (1998): 620.

44. Marion Fourcade-Gourinchas, "La Sociologie Économique: État des Lieux" (paper presented at the Économie et Sciences Sociales Conference, Paris: École Normale Supérieure, June 13–14, 2002); Mark Granovetter, "Economic Action and Social Structure: The Problem of Embeddedness," *American Journal of Sociology* 91, no. 3 (1985); David Stark, *For a Sociology of Worth*. Working Paper, Center on Organizational Innovation (Santa Fe Institute and Columbia University, 2000).

45. Beth Mintz and Michael Schwartz, *The Power Structure of American Business* (Chicago: University of Chicago Press, 1985); Mark S. Mizruchi and Linda Brewster Stearns "A Longitudinal Study of the Formation of Interlocking Directorates," *Administrative Science Quarterly* 33, no. 2 (1988); Brian Uzzi and Ryon Lancaster, "Embeddedness and Price Formation in the Corporate Law Market," *American Sociological Review* 69, no. 3 (2004); Brian Uzzi and Jarrett Spiro, "Collaboration and Creativity: The Small World Problem," *American Journal of Sociology* 111 (2005).

46. James S. Coleman, "Social Capital in the Creation of Human Capital," *American Journal of Sociology* 94 (supp.) (1988); Amitai Etzioni, *The Spirit of Community: Rights, Responsibilities, and the Communitarian Agenda* (New York: Crown Publishers, 1993); Robert Putnam, *Making Democracy Work: Civic Traditions in Modern Italy* (Princeton, NJ: Princeton University Press, 1993).

47. Coleman, "Social Capital in the Creation of Human Capital," S118.

48. Ibid., S98.

49. Ronald Burt, *Toward a Structural Theory of Action: Network Models of Social Structure, Perception and Action* (New York: Academic Press, 1982).

50. Lois M. Verbrugge, "Multiplexity in Adult Friendships," *Social Forces* 57, no. 4 (1979).

51. Joel M. Podolny and James N. Baron, "Resources and Relationships: Social Networks and Mobility in the Workplace," *American Sociological Review* 62, no. 5 (1997): 674.

52. Charles H. Cooley, *Human Nature and the Social Order* (New York: C. Scribner's Sons, 1902); Kenneth J. Gergen and Mary M. Gergen, "Narrative and the Self as Relationship," in *Advances in Experimental Social Psychology, 21*, ed. Leonard Berkowitz (San Diego: Academic Press, 1988); George H. Mead, *Mind, Self and Society from the Standpoint of a Social Behaviorist* (Chicago: University of Chicago Press, 1934).

53. Jan E. Stets and Peter J. Burke, "Identity Theory and Social Identity Theory," *Social Psychology Quarterly* 63, no. 3 (2000).

54. Eric M. Leifer, "Interaction Preludes to Role Setting: Exploratory Local Action," *American Sociological Review* 53, no. 6 (1988).

55. Everett C. Hughes, "Work and Self," in *The Sociological Eye: Selected Papers* (Chicago, IL and New York: Aldine-Atherton, 1971); Renaud Sainsaulieu, *L'Identité au Travail* (Paris: Presses de la Fondation Nationale des Sciences Politiques, 1977); John Van Maanen and Stephen R. Barley, "Occupational Commu-

nities: Culture and Control in Organizations," in *Research in Organizational Behavior*, ed. Barry Staw and Larry Cummings (Greenwich, CT: JAI Press, 1984).

56. Podolny and Baron, "Resources and Relationships."

57. Ibid.: 675.

58. Noel M. Tichy, Michael L. Tushman, and Charles Fombrun, "Social Network Analysis for Organizations," *Academy of Management Review* 4, no. 4 (1979).

59. Mihnea C. Moldoveanu and Nitin Nohria, *Master Passions: Emotion, Narrative, and the Development of Culture* (Cambridge, MA: MIT Press, 2002), 82–3.

60. Harrison C. White, *Identity and Control: A Structural Theory of Social Action* (Princeton, NJ: Princeton University Press, 1992).

61. Charles Perrow uses this expression of "finding oneself," though with heavy reservations about the possibility of it happening. See Perrow, *Complex Organizations: A Critical Essay*, 60.

62. Tiziana Casciaro's work provides a counterillustration of this trend. See Casciaro, "Seeing Things Clearly: Social Structure, Personality, and Accuracy in Social Network Perception," *Social Networks* 20, no. 4 (1998).

63. Arthur Stinchcombe, "Weak Structural Data," *Contemporary Sociology* 19 (1990): 381.

64. Gerald R. Salancik, "Wanted: A Good Network Theory of Organization," *Administrative Science Quarterly* 40, no. 2 (1995): 346.

65. Tim Hallett and Marc J. Ventresca, "Inhabited Institutions: Social Interactions and Organizational Forms in Gouldner's Patterns of Industrial Bureaucracy," *Theory and Society* 35, no. 2 (2006).

Chapter Two
The Side Production of Homers in Factories

1. All quotes from my fieldwork were translated from French to English.

2. *Larousse Universel* dictionary, 1874.

3. Denis Poulot, *Question Sociale: le Sublime ou le Travailleur Comme Il Est en 1870 et Ce Qu'il Peut Être* (Paris: Maspéro, 1980), 343–4.

4. Etienne de Banville, *L'Usine en Douce. Le Travail en "Perruque"* (Paris: L'Harmattan, 2001), 5.

5. Hachette multimedia dictionary, 1999.

6. Banville, *L'Usine en Douce. Le Travail en "Perruque"*; Marie de Banville and Bruno Dumont, *Perruque, Bricole et Compagnie . . . (Videotape)* (Paris: Solimane Production, 1988); Marie-José Hissard and Jean-René Hissard, "Interview d'Henri H. . . . Perruquiste," *Autrement* 16, November (1978).

7. Noëlle Gérôme, *Les Productions Symboliques des Travailleurs dans l'Entreprise: Action Syndicale et Rituelles* (Paris: Ministère de la Culture, Direction du Patrimoine, Mission du Patrimoine Ethnologique, 1983); Noëlle Gérôme, "Les Rituels Contemporains des Travailleurs de l'Aéronautique," *Ethnologie Française* 14, no. 2 (1984); Noëlle Gérôme, "Récompense et Hommages dans l'Usine," *Ethnologie Française* 28, no. 4 (1998).

8. Gérard Noiriel, *Longwy: Immigrés et Prolétaires, 1880–1980* (Paris: Presses Universitaires de France, 1984), 205.

9. Robert Kosmann, "La Perruque ou le Travail Masqué," *Renault Histoire* 11 (1999).

10. Hissard and Hissard, "Interview d'Henri H. . . . Perruquiste"; Gérôme, *Les Productions Symboliques des Travailleurs dans l'Entreprise*, 136.

11. For the usage of the term "homer," see Haraszti, *A Worker in a Worker's State*, 9.

12. Personal communication, Stoch W., October 2004.

13. For the usage of the term "government jobs," see Gouldner, *Patterns of Industrial Bureaucracy*, 51; Dalton, *Men Who Manage*, 205.

14. Bruce E. Nickerson, "Is There Folk in the Factory?" *Journal of American Folklore* 87, no. 344 (1974).

15. Personal communication, Alan F. (former GE employee), October 2005.

16. I thank Herb Saunders (personal communication) for pointing out the term "cumshaw."

17. For the usage of "pilfering," see Ditton, "Perks, Pilferage, and the Fiddle," 51; Gerald Mars, *Cheats at Work: An Anthropology of Workplace Crime* (Hants, UK; Brookfield, VT: Dartmouth Publishing, 1994), 1; Stephen Ackroyd and Paul Thompson, *Organizational Misbehaviour* (London: Sage Publications, 1999), 24–7.

18. California Court of Appeals, *Nattie Thunderburk v. United Food and Commercial Workers' Union, Local 324* (92 Cal. App. 4th 1332, 2001 Cal. App. Lexis 820, 2001).

19. Ontario Arbitration, "Abitibi-Consolidated Inc. and International Association of Machinist and Aerospace Workers, Lodge 771, Arbitration" (Arbitration 2000 CLASJ Lexis 7898, 2000 CLASJ 516728, 59 CLAS 360, 2000); Manitoba Arbitration, "Border Chemical Co. and Border Chemical Employees Association, Arbitration" (1997 CLASJ Lexis 16604, 1997 CLASJ 425510, 47 CLAS 455, 1997).

20. Manitoba Arbitration.

21. Ontario Arbitration.

22. Texas Court of Appeals, *Larry Stephens, Appellant v. Delhi Gas Pipeline Corporation* (Appellee. No. 06–95–00101–CV, Sixth District, Texarkana, 1996).

23. For the testimony, see Banville and Dumont, *Perruque, Bricole et Compagnie*. The case of the 1969 firing was narrated to me in a personal communication, Danièle L., 2002.

24. Cited in Lamy Prud-Hommes, *Jugements Prud'homaux Commentés* (Rueil Malmaison, France: Lamy, 2002), 104–5.

25. The search was conducted using the French terms "détournement de materiel," meaning theft of materials (more results were produced than by using theft of time) and "employeur" in www.legifrance.gouv.fr and in a database of first-level jurisdictions and appeals.

26. Chambre Sociale Cour de Cassation, Audience Publique du 18 Octobre 1995. Numéro de Pourvoi: 94–40735 (1995).

27. Chambre Sociale Cour de Cassation, Audience Publique du 18 Mai 1977. Numéro de Pourvoi: 76–40582 (1977).

28. François-Xavier Trivière, "Objets de Bricole, de l'Usine à l'Univers Domestique," in *Carriéres d'Objets: Innovations et Relances, Mission du Patrimoine*

Ethnologique, ed. C. Bromberger and D. Chevallier (Paris: Maison des Sciences de l'Homme, 1999).

29. Weber, *Le Travail À-Côté. Étude d'Ethnographie Ouvrière.*

30. Michel Prigent, "Pincemain Chez Tarasiève," *La République* (2001); Jean-Pierre Pincemain, "Individual Exhibit" (Barbizon, France: Suzanne Tarasiève Gallery, 2001).

31. Certeau, *The Practice of Everyday Life*, 25.

32. Jean-Luc Moulène, *Jean-Luc Moulène* (Paris: Hazan, 2002).

33. One cannot assume, however, that the monetarization of homers destroys the sentiments attached to the artifacts. As Viviana Zelizer has shown in multiple settings, money and socioemotional fibers can coexist. See Viviana A. Zelizer, "Circuits within Capitalism," in *The Economic Sociology of Capitalism*, ed. Victor Nee and Richard Swedberg (Princeton, NJ: Princeton University Press, 2005).

34. For a discussion of the distinction between arts and crafts, see Howard S. Becker, "Arts and Crafts," *American Journal of Sociology* 83, no. 4 (1978).

35. Nadia Simony and Michel Marcon, *Les Transformations du Comité d'Entreprise: Snecma Évry-Corbeil* (Paris: L'Harmattan, 1995).

36. Poulot, *Question Sociale.*

37. Dalton, *Men Who Manage.*

38. Haraszti, *A Worker in a Worker's State.*

39. Hissard and Hissard, "Interview d'Henri H. . . . Perruquiste."

40. Kosmann, "La Perruque ou le Travail Masqué."

41. Pierre Contesenne, "De la Perruque comme Prétexte" (Paris: manuscript, 1984).

42. Nickerson, "Is There Folk in the Factory?" 138.

43. Jolle Deniot, *Ethnologie du Décor en Milieu Ouvrier* (Paris: L'Harmattan, 1995), 269–97.

44. Véronique Moulinié, "Des 'Oeuvriers' Ordinaires, Lorsque L'Ouvrier Fait le/du Beau . . . ," *Terrain* 32 (1999).

45. Banville, *L'Usine en Douce. Le Travail en "Perruque."*

46. Thierry Bonnot, *La Vie des Objets* (Paris: Éditions de la Maison des Sciences de l'Homme, 2002), 41.

47. Gérôme, *Les Productions Symboliques des Travailleurs dans l'Entreprise*, 120.

48. Comité d'Établissement Snecma Évry-Corbeil, *Les Ouvriers de l'Imaginaire* (Évry, France: Presses de la STEP, 1984).

49. Gouldner, *Patterns of Industrial Bureaucracy*, 51.

50. Beaud and Pialoux, *Retour sur la Condition Ouvrière.*

51. Robert Kosmann, "Les Forgerons de la RATP: La Forge de l'Atelier Central de Championnet," in *La Région Parisienne Industrielle et Ouvrière*, 6 (Paris: Éditions RATP, Unité Mémoire de l'Entreprise, 2000).

52. Yves Lescot, Georges Menahem, and Patrick Pharo, *Savoirs Ouvriers, Normes de Production et Représentations. Rapport du Contrat Cordes 12–78* (Boulogne, France: ACT, 1980), 74.

53. Aurélie Messika, "L'Étude Socio-Organizationelle d'une Direction de la Recherche Chez un Constructeur Automobile Européen" (Master's Thesis in Sociology, IEP Paris, 2002).

54. There seem to be fewer traces of homers in industries employing younger individuals, a higher proportion of female employees, or more recently arrived immigrant labor. For a mapping of these industries, see Gérard Noiriel, *Les Ouvriers dans la Société Française: XIXᵉ–XXᵉ Siècle* (Paris: Éditions du Seuil, 2002), 249.

55. Anne Biroleau, *Les Règlements d'Ateliers: 1798–1936* (Paris: Bibliothèque Nationale, 1984).

56. This interpretation is suggested by Alain Cottereau in the prologue to Anne Biroleau's work.

57. Cited by Michel Bozon and Yannick Lemel, "Les Petits Profits du Travail Salarié. Moments, Produits et Plaisirs Dérobés," *Revue Française de Sociologie* 31, no. 1 (1990).

58. The notion of a decrease is relative since, in 1999, factory workers still represented 25.6% of the active French population, or close to 6 million individuals. (See Noiriel, *Les Ouvriers dans la Société Française*, xiii.)

59. Nicholas Lampert, *Whistleblowing in the Soviet Union: Complaints and Abuse under State Socialism* (London: MacMillan Press, 1985), 110.

60. Geert H. Hofstede, *Culture's Consequences: International Differences in Work-Related Values* (Beverly Hills: Sage, 1980).

61. Charles Tilly, *The Contentious French* (Cambridge, MA: Harvard University Press, 1986).

62. John P. Clark and Richard C. Hollinger, "Theft by Employees in Work Organizations" (Washington, DC: U.S. Department of Justice—National Institute of Justice, 1983), 13.

63. Nickerson, "Is There Folk in the Factory?" 138.

64. See Ackroyd and Thompson, *Organizational Misbehaviour*; Philippe Bernoux, *Un Travail à Soi* (Toulouse: Privat, 1981); Jason Ditton, "Baking Time," *Sociological Review* 27, no. 1 (1979); Jason Ditton, "Moral Horror versus Folk Terror—Output Restriction, Class, and Social-Organization of Exploitation," *Sociological Review* 24, no. 3 (1976); Ditton, "Perks, Pilferage, and the Fiddle"; Mars, *Cheats at Work*; Calvin Morrill, Mayer N. Zald, and Hayagreeva Rao, "Covert Political Conflict in Organizations: Challenges from Below," *Annual Review of Sociology* 29 (2003).

65. Isaac Joseph, "La Perruque," *Urbi* III (1980): 119. (author's translation).

66. Banville, *L'Usine en Douce. Le Travail en "Perruque,"* 83.

67. Several elements initially worked in my favor: first, an unspecified though fairly widely known family connection to the plant; second, my affiliation with respected external research institutions; and third, my presence at the plant's Labor Council over extended periods of time. Moreover, a rather unexpected endorsement by the Labor Council proved invaluable. (See appendixes A and B for more details.)

Chapter Three
The Pierreville Plant: Setting and Status Divides

1. For a classification (factorial mapping) of French industries, see Noiriel, *Les Ouvriers dans la Société Française*, 249.

2. All statistics were gathered from public sources: Pierreville's annual "social reports" (*bilans sociaux*). These plant-level reports are annual legal obligations for plants above a certain workforce size in France. France has legal employment categories that allow for the broad distinction of employed populations.

3. Pierreville Archives (PA). Human Resource Policies File.

4. Catherine Paradeise, "Sociabilité et Culture de Classe," *Revue Française de Sociologie* 21, no. 4 (1980); Olivier Schwartz, *Le Monde Privé des Ouvriers: Hommes et Femmes du Nord* (Paris: Presses Universitaires de France, 1990).

5. Craftsmen were part of the "workers" legal employment category, but some were promoted to the "technician" category toward the end of their careers, which allowed them to earn more income. Most newly hired technicians (post–1980s), however, held distinct degrees that combined practical and theoretical training ("Brevet de Technicien Supérieur"); not a CAP, and therefore were not considered craftsmen.

6. Weber, *Le Travail À-Coté. Étude d'Ethnographie Ouvrière.*

Chapter Four
Retirement Homers: An Entry into the Community

1. The relative occupational status of Pierreville members vis-à-vis craftsmen was mapped essentially on employment category levels, with two notable exceptions. First, the population of technicians was a hybrid, combining younger new recruits (who held *Brevet de Technicien Supérieur* or BTS degrees) and older craftsmen (who held CAP degrees). Younger technicians were not in my sample since they had not yet retired, and older technicians with CAP degrees were considered craftsmen (i.e., peers). Second, the population of workers was also a hybrid, combining unskilled workers and craftsmen. Unskilled workers without CAP degrees were considered lower status than craftsmen.

2. The discrepancy between the numbers of respondents on the generic gift question (124) versus the homer gift question (184) is explained by the fact that the gift question was only introduced after a first survey wave was conducted. See appendix A for details on the survey method.

3. More broadly, given that gift giving and receiving maintain alliances and have been shown to be scaled (in amount) to the emotional value of the relationship, these patterns are not surpising. See Marcel Mauss, *The Gift: Forms and Functions of Exchange in Archaic Societies* (New York: Norton, 1967), 71; Theodore Caplow, "Rule Enforcement without Visible Means: Christmas Gift Giving in Middletown," *American Journal of Sociology* 89, no. 6 (1984).

4. These years were 1982, 1983, 1987, 1988, 1993, 1994, 1995, and 1996.

5. For all of the analyses in this book, craftsmen who advanced to the technician level were still considered part of the craftsmen group and were identified by their training (CAP).

6. Laughter at work has been shown to convey uneasiness in other instances, as well. See Philip Bradney, "The Joking Relationship in Industry," *Human Relations* 10, no. 2 (1957); Jacqueline Frisch-Gauthier, "Le Rire dans les Relations de Travail," *Revue Française de Sociologie* 2 (1961).

7. In the 2003 annual statement delivered by AeroDyn's president to share-holders, the terms "competition" or "competitive" appear five times in a statement of less than 500 words.

8. Only a limited number of craftsmen made it up the hierarchy to become executives or engineers. Those who did, however, were more likely to recognize the respect components of retirement homer practices.

9. Labor Council Executives, personal communication, February 2003.

10. As mentioned previously, from the craftsmen's perspective, newly hired younger technicians, who were trained differently than craftsmen, were also considered "lower status." For a similar divide between younger and older workers in an automotive factory, see Stéphane Beaud and Michel Pialoux, "Between 'Mate' and 'Scab': The Contradictory Inheritance of French Workers in the Postfordist Factory," *Ethnography* 2, no. 3 (2001).

Chapter Five
Homers Gone Wrong: Delimiting the Gray Zone

1. Howard Becker, *Tricks of the Trade: How to Think about Your Research While You're Doing It.* (Chicago: University of Chicago Press, 1994); Howard S. Becker, *Outsiders: Studies in the Sociology of Deviance* (London: Free Press of Glencoe, 1963); Harold Garfinkel, *Studies in Ethnomethodology* (Englewood Cliffs, NJ: Prentice Hall, 1967); John Heritage, *Garfinkel and Ethnomethodology* (Cambridge, MA: Polity, 1984).

2. The high costs whistle-blowers pay is also documented in the Soviet Union: Lampert, *Whistleblowing in the Soviet Union.*

3. A search through the Pierreville archives produced only a limited number of company reports dealing with homer activities and suspicions of theft.

4. Pierreville Archives (PA), Box 32H, folder 8.

5. PA, Box 32H, folder 230.

6. PA, Box 32H, folder 131.

7. Case of Paul X. *Tribunal de Grande Instance* of the district where Pierreville is located. March 4, 1977.

8. PA, Box 32H, folder 230.

9. The disconnect between official rules and their local applications is referred to here as a flexibility and will later be shown to contribute to the regulation of group behaviors. Scott Snook provides a more critical read of such flexibilities in his work on incidents involving fellow military combatants. See Scott Snook, *Friendly Fire: The Accidental Shootdown of U.S. Black Hawks over Northern Iraq* (Princeton, NJ: Princeton University Press, 2000).

10. PA, Box 32H, folder 185.

11. PA, Box 32H, folder 230.

12. PA, Box 32H, folder 146.

13. PA, Box 32H, folder 105.

14. An alternate reading could be that theft involving lower-level employees is particularly likely to be disciplined and white-collar theft less so. See Edwin H. Sutherland, *White Collar Crime* (New York: Dryden, 1949). Thus, lower-level

plant members, as opposed to supervisors, executives, and engineers, are usually more severely disciplined. Because comparative data on levels of discipline were not collected at Pierreville, issues of social fairness with regard to discipline inside the plant are not addressed.

Chapter Six
Shades of Homer Meanings: Occupational Variations

1. When narrating homer events, references to hours spent on a job (such as "It only took me two hours") were usually evoked to highlight the relatively few hours spent making the homer. In instances of jobs or regular work homer narratives, the amount of time spent on the work (e.g., two or three hundred hours) instead of the ease with which the artifact had been made was sometimes stressed.

Chapter Seven
The Rise and Fall of Craftsmanship

1. Thierry Vivier, *La Politique Aéronautique Militaire de la France: Janvier 1933–Septembre 1939* (Paris: Éditions L'Harmattan, 1997).

2. Patrick Fridenson and Jean Lecuir, "L'Organisation de la Coopération Aérienne Franco-Britannique (1935–Mai 1940)," *Revue d'Histoire de la Seconde Guerre Mondiale* 73, no. January (1969); John McVickar Haight, *American Aid to France* (New York: Antheneum, 1970).

3. Between 1993 and 1999, 658 technicians were hired and 1,322 technicians left. During this period, the total technician population decreased by 601. This leaves a net increase of 63 technicians not accounted for by departures and hiring (i.e., the difference between [658–1322] and [-601]). Assuming these 63 are the result of internal promotions, this means that between 1993 and 1999, only 8.8% of new technicians were internally promoted.

4. CGT union leaflet, October 11, 1978.

5. CFDT union leaflet, September 21, 1978.

6. CFDT policy paper, March 1984.

7. Ibid.

8. CFDT leaflet, February 27, 1984.

9. Moulinié, "Des 'Oeuvriers' Ordinaires, Lorsque l'Ouvrier Fait le/du Beau. . . ."; Weber, *Le Travail À-Côté. Étude d'Ethnographie Ouvrière.*

10. John M. Vlach, "The Fabrication of a Traditional Fire Tool," *Journal of American Folklore* 86, no. 339 (1973).

11. Hughes, "Work and Self," 338.

Chapter Eight
Trading in Identity Incentives

1. For a theoretical argument about the need to account for identity incentives in organizations, see George A. Akerlof and Rachel E. Kranton, "Identity

and the Economics of Organizations," *Journal of Economic Perspective* 19, no. 1 (2005).

2. Levi, *The Drowned and the Saved*, 42.

3. Haraszti, *A Worker in a Worker's State*; Certeau, *The Practice of Everyday Life*; Joseph, "La Perruque."

4. Bronislaw Malinowski, *Argonauts of the Western Pacific: An Account of the Native Enterprise and Adventure in the Archipelagoes of Melanesian New Guinea* (Long Grove, IL: Waveland Press, 1984).

5. Annette B. Weiner, *The Trobrianders of Papua New Guinea* (Orlando, FL: Harcourt Brace, 1988), 159.

6. Randy Hodson and Vincent J. Roscigno, "Organizational Success and Worker Dignity: Complementary or Contradictory?" *American Journal of Sociology* 110, no. 3 (2004): 680.

7. Richard Sennett argues that the quest for dignity is typical of many current work settings. Richard Sennett, *The Corrosion of Character. The Personal Consequences of Work in the New Capitalism* (New York: Norton, 1998).

8. Weiner, *The Trobrianders of Papua New Guinea*, 148–54.

9. For a discussion of how boundary objects can accommodate competing meanings, see Susan Leigh Star and James R. Griesemer, "Institutional Ecology, 'Translations' and Boundary Objects: Amateurs and Professionals in Berkeley's Museum of Vertebrate Zoology, 1907–39," *Social Studies of Science* 19 (1989).

10. Mary Douglas, *Purity and Danger: An Analysis of Concepts of Pollution and Taboo* (New York: Routledge Classics, 2002).

11. Multivocality is here attached to a practice, not to an individual. For an example of multivocality attached to an individual, see John Padgett and Ansell Christopher, "Robust Action and the Rise of the Medici, 1400–1434," *American Journal of Sociology* 98, no. 6 (1993).

12. Alan Fiske and Philip Tetlock discuss reactions to potentially taboo trades in "Taboo Trade-Offs: Reactions to Transactions That Transcend the Spheres of Justice," *Political Psychology* 18, no. 2 (1997).

13. Michel Crozier and Erhard Friedberg, *L'Acteur et le Système* (Paris: Éditions du Seuil, 1977), 196.

14. Mauss, *The Gift: Forms and Functions of Exchange in Archaic Societies*.

15. Similar hidden incentive mechanisms operated in the industrial bakery setting described in the introduction. Management made sure enough extra bread was available on the stock shelves, where drivers were supposed to only take "their" extra bread to ensure a sufficient level of incentives. These incentives were monitored in the same manner as official wages, and like homers at Pierreville, were viewed by management as an effective way to control their workers. Bakery drivers then sold—with the tacit approval of supervisors— these "pilfered" loaves of bread to their customers. (Ditton, "Perks, Pilferage, and the Fiddle.")

16. Both positive and negative biases linked to recollection of past work memories have been documented, so the absence of references to internal politics should not be interpreted as a recollection bias. For examples of positive and negative biases in recollecting work memories, see, respectively, Philippe Hamman, "Quand le Souvenir Fait Lien . . . De la Délimitation des Domaines

de Validité des Énoncés Recueillis par le Sociologue en Situation d'Entretien," *Sociologie du Travail* 44, no. 2 (2002); Felicia Pratto and Oliver P. John, "Automatic Vigilance: The Attention-Grabbing Power of Negative Social Information," *Journal of Personality and Social Psychology* 61 (1991).

17. For an illustration of how informal rewards can be used in internal organizational politics, see chap. 4, "The Interlocking of Official and Unofficial Rewards," in Dalton, *Men Who Manage*, 194–217.

18. George Akerlof, "Labor Contracts as Partial Gift Exchange," *Quarterly Journal of Economics* 97, no. 4 (1982).

19. For a similar usage, see Jackall, *Moral Mazes*, 3.

20. Burawoy, *Manufacturing Consent*.

21. Martha Feldman evokes the social limits of these discretions in "Social Limits to Discretion: An Organizational Perspective," in *The Uses of Discretion*, ed. Keith Hawkins (Oxford: Clarendon Press, 1992).

22. Lawrence R. Zeitlin, "Stimulus/Response: A Little Larceny Can Do a Lot for Employee Morale," *Psychology Today* 5, no. 1 (1971).

23. For a similar usage of the term "situated" with respect to knowledge, see John Seely Brown and Paul Duguid, "Organizational Learning and Communities of Practice: Towards a Unified Way of Working, Learning, and Innovation," *Organization Science* 2, no. 1 (1991).

24. Certeau, *The Practice of Everyday Life*, 25.

25. For a discussion of normalizing, see John Van Maanen, "The Self, the Situation, and the Rules of Interpersonal Relations," in *Essays in Interpersonal Dynamics*, ed. Warren Bennis, et al. (Homewood, IL: The Dorsey Press, 1979), 89. For a full range of these normalizing narratives, see Blake E. Ashforth and Vikas Anand, "The Normalization of Corruption in Organizations," in *Research in Organizational Behavior*, ed. R. M. Kramer and B. M. Staw (Amsterdam: Elsevier, 2003).

26. See Johnny Cash's 1976 song titled "One Piece at a Time."

27. William Kornblum, *Blue Collar Community* (Chicago: University of Chicago Press, 1974); Mitchell Duneier, *Sidewalk* (New York: Farrar, Straus and Giroux, 1999).

28. See Adorno, *Prisms*, 240.

Chapter Nine
Organizational Gray Zones as Identity Distillers

1. Personal communication, Lucile M., September 2002.

2. Perrow, *Organizing America*, 36.

3. I thank a Princeton University Press anonymous reviewer for pointing out this example to me.

4. Georg Simmel, "The Sociology of Secrecy and of Secret Societies," *American Journal of Sociology* 11, no. 4 (1906).

5. Georg Simmel, *The Sociology of Georg Simmel*, ed. Kurt H. Wolff (New York: Free Press, 1950), 362.

6. Arlie Russell Hochschild, *The Managed Heart: Commercialization of Human Feeling* (Berkeley: University of California Press, 1983).

7. Bradford, "A General Perspective on Job Satisfaction."

8. Ibid., 71.

9. Bennie Graves, "Conflict and Work Force Stability in Pipeline Construction," *Urban Life and Culture* 2, no. 4 (1974).

10. C. Eddie Palmer and Sheryl M. Gonsoulin, "Paramedics, Protocols, and Procedures: 'Playing Doc' as Deviant Role Performance," *Deviant Behavior* 11, no. 3 (1990).

11. Dean A. Dabney, "Neutralization and Deviance in the Workplace—Theft of Supplies and Medicines by Hospital Nurses," *Deviant Behavior* 16, no. 4 (1995).

12. Gerald Mars, "Hotel Pilferage: A Case Study in Occupational Theft," in *The Sociology of the Workplace: An Interdisciplinary Approach*, ed. Malcolm Warner (London: George Allen and Unwin, 1973).

13. Mars, *Cheats at Work*, 100–107.

14. Ibid., 103.

15. Edward W. Sieh, "Garment Workers: Perceptions of Inequity and Employee Theft," *British Journal of Criminology* 27, no. 2 (1987).

16. Personal communication, YPC, May 2005.

17. Jonathan A. Knee, *The Accidental Investment Banker: Inside the Decade That Transformed Wall Street* (New York: Oxford University Press, 2006).

18. For an example of how artifacts can evoke key elements of an occupational identity, see Bechky, "Object Lessons."

19. Van Maanen and Barley, "Occupational Communities: Culture and Control in Organizations," 298.

20. This perspective traces its roots to social constructionism and symbolic interactionism. For illustrative works, see Cooley, *Human Nature and the Social Order*; Gergen and Gergen, "Narrative and the Self as Relationship"; Mead, *Mind, Self and Society*; Erving Goffman, *Interactions Rituals: Essays on Face-to-Face Behavior* (Chicago: Aldine, 1967).

21. Marilyn B. Brewer and Wendi L. Gardner, "Who Is This 'We'? Levels of Collective Identity and Self Representations," *Journal of Personality and Social Psychology* 71 (1996).

22. Gary A. Fine, "Justifying Work: Occupational Rhetorics as Resources in Restaurant Kitchens," *Administrative Science Quarterly* 41, no. 1 (1996).

23. Florence Weber, *L'Honneur des Jardiniers: Les Potagers dans la France du XXᵉ Siècle* (Paris: Belin, 1998).

24. Leifer, "Interaction Preludes to Role Setting: Exploratory Local Action."

25. White, *Identity and Control*.

26. Lave and Wenger, *Situated Learning*; Wenger, *Communities of Practice*.

27. White, *Identity and Control*, 313.

28. Ibid.

29. Weiner, *The Trobrianders of Papua New Guinea*, 161.

30. Morrill, *The Executive Way*; Steven Peter Vallas, "Workers, Firms, and the Dominant Ideology: Hegemony and Consciousness in the Monopoly Core," *Sociological Quarterly* 32 (1991).

Chapter Ten
Identities, Control, and Moralities

1. Burawoy, *Manufacturing Consent*, 199.
2. For an example of job crafting in a more open setting, see Amy Wrzes-niewski, Jane Dutton, and Gelaye Debebe, "Interpersonal Sensemaking and the Meaning of Work," in *Research in Organizational Behavior*, ed. B. Staw and R. M. Kramer (2003).
3. Gouldner, *Patterns of Industrial Bureaucracy*.
4. Ibid., 56.
5. Burawoy, *Manufacturing Consent*.
6. Gouldner, *Patterns of Industrial Bureaucracy*, 186–7.
7. Blau, *The Dynamics of Bureaucracy*.
8. Ibid., 192.
9. Roy, "Banana Time: Job Satisfaction and Informal Interaction."
10. This cooperative motive of humankind, implicit in the early social systems approaches and inspired by the Human Relations movement, led to sharp criticism of these approaches. See Perrow, *Complex Organizations*, 88–118.
11. As such, this study adds to the Human Relations model's historical deficiency in explaning workers' "rationality." For a discussion of this point, see Landsberger, *Hawthorne Revisited*, 31. The term judiciousness, suggesting less instrumentality, is here preferred to rationality.
12. Richard C. Edwards, "The Social Relations of Production at the Point of Production," in *Complex Organizations: Critical Perspectives*, ed. Mary Zey-Ferrell and Michael Aiken (Glenview, IL: Scott, Foresman, 1981); Perrow, *Complex Organizations*; Max Weber, *The Protestant Ethic and the Spirit of Capitalism* (San Francisco: Jossey-Bass, 1958).
13. Blau, *The Dynamics of Bureaucracy*; Randy Hodson, "Dignity in the Workplace under Participative Management: Alienation and Freedom Revisited," *American Sociological Review* 61, no. 5 (1996); Paul Osterman, *Securing Prosperity: The American Labor Market: How It Has Changed and What to Do About It.* (Princeton, NJ: Princeton University Press, 1999).
14. Hodson and Roscigno, "Organizational Success and Worker Dignity"; Morrill, Zald, and Rao, "Covert Political Conflict in Organizations."
15. Jean M. Bartunek and Michael K. Moch, "Multiple Constituencies and the Quality of Working Life Intervention at Foodcom," in *Reframing Organizational Culture*, ed. Peter J. Frost et al. (Newbury Park, CA: Sage, 1991); Robert G. Eccles and Nitin Nohria, *Beyond the Hype: Rediscovering the Essence of Management* (Cambridge, MA: Harvard Business School Press, 1992); Joseph L. Soeters, "Excellent Companies as Social Movements," *Journal of Management Science* 23 (1986).
16. Eugene F. Fama and Michael C. Jensen, "Separation of Ownership and Control," *Journal of Law & Economics* 26, no. 2 (1983); Richard J. Hackman and Greg R. Oldham, "Motivation through the Design of Work: Test of a Theory," *Organizational Behavior & Human Performance* 16, no. 2 (1976).

17. Mats Alvesson and Hugh Willmott, "Identity Regulation as Organizational Control: Producing the Appropriate Individual," *Journal of Management Studies* 39, no. 5 (2002); John Van Maanen and Edgar H. Schein, "Toward a Theory of Organizational Socialization," in *Research in Organizational Behavior*, ed. B. Staw and L. Cummings (Greenwich, CT: JAI Press, 1979).

18. Loïc Wacquant, *Body and Soul: Ethnographic Notebooks of an Apprentice Boxer* (New York: Oxford University Press, 2003).

19. White, *Identity and Control*, 236.

20. Akerlof and Kranton, "Identity and the Economics of Organizations," 11.

21. Debra Friedman and Doug McAdam, "Collective Identity and Activism: Networks, Choices and the Life of a Social Movement," in *Frontiers in Social Movement Theory*, ed. Carol Mueller and Aldon Morris (New Haven, CT: Yale University Press, 1992), 157.

22. Ralph Brower and Mitchell Abolafia, "Bureaucratic Politics: The View from Below," *Journal of Public Administration Research and Theory* 7, no. 2 (1997): 305.

23. Michael G. Pratt, "The Good, the Bad, and the Ambivalent: Managing Identification among Amway Distributors," *Administrative Science Quarterly* 45, no. 3 (2000).

24. Akerlof and Kranton, "Identity and the Economics of Organizations."

25. David Stark, "La Valeur du Travail et sa Redistribution en Hongrie," *Actes de la Recherche en Sciences Sociales* 85 (1990).

26. Banville, *L'Usine en Douce. Le Travail en "Perruque,"* 81.

27. Van Maanen and Barley, "Occupational Communities: Culture and Control in Organizations."

28. Kunda, *Engineering Culture*.

29. Perlow, "Boundary Control."

30. Philippe Bourgeois, *In Search of Respect: Selling Crack in El Barrio* (Cambridge: Cambridge University Press, 2003), 77–113.

31. Ditton, "Perks, Pilferage, and the Fiddle," 264.

32. Rosabeth Moss Kanter, *Commitment and Community: Communes and Utopias in Sociological Perspective* (Cambridge, MA: Harvard University Press, 1972), 234.

33. Edwards, "The Social Relations of Production at the Point of Production."

34. Van Maanen, "The Self, the Situation, and the Rules of Interpersonal Relations," 86.

35. Piore and Safford, "Changing Regimes of Workplace Governance, Shifting Axes of Social Mobilization, and the Challenge to Industrial Relations Theory."

36. Alvesson and Willmott, "Identity Regulation as Organizational Control."

37. Scott Stern, "Do Scientists Pay to Be Scientists?" *Management Science* 50, no. 6 (2004).

38. Ditton, "Perks, Pilferage, and the Fiddle."

39. Steven Peter Vallas, "The Concept of Skill—A Critical Review," *Work and Occupations* 17, no. 4 (1990).

40. Charles E. Bidwell, "The Young Professionals in the Army: A Study in Occupational Identity," *American Sociological Review* 26, no. 3 (1961).

41. Lotte Bailyn's research on engineers and the "plateau" they sometimes reach illustrates this possibility. See Lotte Bailyn, *Living with Technology: Issues at Mid-Career* (Cambridge, MA: MIT Press, 1980).

42. Burawoy, *Manufacturing Consent*, 28.

43. Van Maanen and Barley, "Occupational Communities: Culture and Control in Organizations," 331–3.

44. Van Maanen, "The Self, the Situation, and the Rules of Interpersonal Relations," 86.

45. For a more general discussion of boundaries in social sciences, see Michèle Lamont and Virág Molnár, "The Study of Boundaries across the Social Sciences," *Annual Review of Sociology* 28 (2002). For a discussion of moral order among working-class American and French men, see Michèle Lamont, *The Dignity of Working Men: Moralities and the Boundaries of Race, Class, and Immigration* (New York: Russel Sage Foundation, 2000).

46. Michèle Lamont, *Money, Morals, and Manners: The Culture of the French and American Upper-Middle Class* (Chicago: The University of Chicago Press, 1992).

47. Ibid., 4.

48. For other examples of artifacts being used to delimit an occupational boundary, see Barley, "Technology as an Occasion for Structuring"; and Bechky, "Object Lessons."

49. Jeffrey W. Riemer, "Becoming a Journeyman Electrician: Some Implicit Indicators in the Apprenticeship Process," *Sociology of Work and Occupations* 4, no. 1 (1977).

50. Stephen R. Barley, "Semiotics and the Study of Occupational and Organizational Cultures," *Administrative Science Quarterly* 28, no. 3 (1983).

51. Van Maanen and Barley, "Occupational Communities: Culture and Control in Organizations," 303.

52. Jackall, *Moral Mazes*.

53. Kornblum, *Blue Collar Community*, 210.

54. Duneier, *Sidewalk*, 316.

55. Ibid., 216–28.

56. Peter S. Bearman, *Doormen* (Chicago: University of Chicago Press, 2005), 102–38.

57. Calvin Morrill, "Conflict Management, Honor, and Organizational Change," *American Journal of Sociology* 97, no. 3 (1991).

58. Khurana, *From Higher Aims to Hired Hands*.

59. Eviatar Zerubavel, *The Fine Line: Making Distinctions in Everyday Life* (Chicago: University of Chicago Press, 1993).

60. Stark, "La Valeur du Travail et sa Redistribution en Hongrie."

61. Podolny and Baron, "Resources and Relationships," 675.

62. This awareness of inclusion and exclusion dynamics calls for clarifying my own position in relation to these boundary contests. (See appendix B, "Position in the Field.") Although my research design positioned me as an audience to these narratives, I also tried to maintain as much as I could my position as an outsider in these boundary-setting contests; volunteering, for instance,

little information as to what I might consider to be positive or negative moral qualities of the events narrated to me.

63. Bruce Fallick and Charles Fleischman, "The Importance of Employer-to-Employer Flows in the U.S. Labor Market," (Washington, DC: Federal Reserve Board, 2001), 3.

64. Emile Durkheim, *The Division of Labor in Society* (Glencoe, IL: Free Press, 1964), 28.

65. Mark A. Covaleski et al., "The Calculated and the Avowed: Techniques of Discipline and Struggles over Identity in Big Six Public Accounting Firms," *Administrative Science Quarterly* 43, no. 2 (1998).

66. Antoine de Saint-Exupéry, *The Little Prince* (New York: Harcourt Brace Jovanovich, 1971), 113.

67. A parallel reading also depends on our assumptions about the implications of the small. For instance, the intimacy associated with the small tends to be viewed fairly negatively in many organizations. See Viviana Zelizer, "Intimacy in Economic Organizations" (Paper presented at the MIT–Harvard Economic Sociology Seminar, Cambridge, MA, April 25, 2007).

68. George C. Homans, *The Human Group*, 468.

69. Levi, *The Drowned and the Saved*, 42.

70. For a discussion of the increased power of corporations, see Perrow, *Organizing America*.

71. Stephen R. Barley and Gideon Kunda, *Gurus, Hired Guns, and Warm Bodies: Itinerant Experts in a Knowledge Economy* (Princeton, NJ: Princeton University Press, 2006).

72. As an illustration, a physician working in a U.S. health maintenance organization can codify (with the hierarchy's tacit approval) regular patient visits as "counseling" (instead of "consultations") to spend more time with them (M.K., personal communication, August 2007).

73. Alain Renaut, *The Era of the Individual: A Contribution to a History of Subjectivity* (Princeton, NJ: Princeton University Press, 1999).

74. Kanter, *Commitment and Community*.

Appendix A
Data and Methods

1. Gouldner, *Patterns of Industrial Bureaucracy*; Dodee Fennell, "Beneath the Surface," *Radical America* 10 (1976); Bill Watson, "Counter-Planning on the Shop Floor," *Radical America* 5 (1971); Ditton, "Baking Time"; William E. Thompson, "Hanging Tongues: A Sociological Encounter with the Assembly Line," *Quantitative Sociology* 6 (1983); Tammy L. MacLean, "Thick as Thieves: A Social Embeddedness Model of Rule Breaking in Organizations," *Business and Society* 40, no. 2 (2001).

2. Robert Yin, *Case Study Research* (Thousand Oaks, CA: Sage Publications, 1994).

3. One noteworthy exception is the gradual construction of a fence around Pierreville, and the ensuing displacement of the employee parking lot outside

the fence, which made it more difficult to transfer homers from the shop floor to cars (usually car trunks).

4. Marcel Mauss, "Étude de Morphologie Sociale," in *Sociologie et Anthropologie* (Paris: Presses Universitaires de France, 1980) (author's translation).

5. Paul Lazarsfeld, "Reflections on Business," *American Journal of Sociology* 65 (1959); Paul Hirsch, "Organizational Analysis and Industrial Sociology: An Instance of Cultural Lag," *American Sociologist* 10 (1975).

6. Roethlisberger and Dickson, *Management and the Worker.*

7. Andrew Abbott, "From Causes to Events: Notes on Narrative Positivism," *Sociological Methods and Research* 20, no. 4 (1992).

8. White, *Identity and Control*, 67.

9. Examples of this method can be found in Gouldner, *Patterns of Industrial Bureaucracy*; Kunda, *Engineering Culture*; Morrill, "Conflict Management, Honor, and Organizational Change."

10. For examples, see Donald Roy, "Quota Restriction and Goldbricking in a Machine Shop," *American Journal of Sociology* 57, no. 5 (1952); Burawoy, *Manufacturing Consent.*

11. The methodology of using examples is a standard technique in the anthropology of law and was, for instance, used by Morrill (1991, 1995) in his analysis of executive conflict management.

12. Matthew B. Miles and A. Michael Huberman, *Qualitative Data Analysis* (Thousand Oaks, CA: Sage Publications, 1994), 277–80.

13. Michael Quinn Patton, *Qualitative Evaluation and Research Methods.* 2d ed. (London: Sage Publications, 1990), 184.

14. Wacquant, *Body and Soul.*

15. Brian Uzzi, "Social Structure and Competition in Interfirm Networks: The Paradox of Embeddedness," *Administrative Science Quarterly* 42, no. 1 (1997).

16. Morrill, "Conflict Management, Honor, and Organizational Change," 257; Morrill, *The Executive Way.*

17. Diane Vaughan, "Autonomy, Interdependence, and Social Control: NASA and the Space Shuttle Challenger," *Administrative Science Quarterly* 35, no. 2 (1990): 227; Vaughan, *The Challenger Launch Decision.*

18. The three main categories were craftsmen, individuals hierarchically above them (executives, engineers, and supervisors), and individuals "below" them (unskilled workers and office employees). An interviewee could discuss gray zone interactions not relating to his or her category (for instance, interactions between other coworkers he or she was familiar with). The relationship between the narrated interacting participants determined the relevant category of analysis.

19. Patton, *Qualitative Evaluation and Research Methods*, 174.

20. John Van Maanen, *Tales of the Field: On Writing Ethnography* (Chicago: University of Chicago Press, 1988), 45–72.

21. Ibid., 72–100.

22. Ibid., 101–24.

23. For a discussion of the relationships between researchers and their fields, see Tammy MacLean et al., "Talking Tainted Topics: Insights and Ideas

on Researching Socially Disapproved Organizational Behavior," *Journal of Management Inquiry* 15, no. 1 (2006).

24. Barney Glaser and Anselm L. Strauss, *The Discovery of Grounded Theory* (Chicago: Aldine, 1967); Miles and Huberman, *Qualitative Data Analysis*.

25. For a discussion of this, see Sam D. Sieber, "The Integration of Fieldwork and Survey Methods," *American Journal of Sociology* 78, no. 6 (1973).

26. Klaus-Friederich Koch, *War and Peace in Jalemo: The Management of Conflict in Highland New Guinea* (Cambridge, MA: Harvard University Press, 1974), 23–24; Mary P. Baumgartner, "Social Control in Suburbia," in *Towards a General Theory of Social Control Vol. 2, Selected Problems*, ed. Donald Black (Orlando, FL: Academic Press, 1984), 2; Morrill, "Conflict Management, Honor, and Organizational Change," 615.

Appendix B
Position in the Field

1. Pierre Bourdieu and Loïc J. D. Wacquant, *Réponses: Pour une Anthropologie Réflexive* (Paris: Seuil, 1992).

2. For details, see Michel Anteby, "The 'Moralities' of Poaching: Manufacturing Personal Artifacts on the Factory Floors," *Ethnography* 4, no. 2 (2003).

3. The nondisclosure of my precise link to the factory mirrored my relative's behavior in front of colleagues concerning his link to me. A same-sex relationship in this man's family links him to me.

4. This visit was an official tour of the factory that AeroDyn granted me when I requested to learn more about the plant.

5. Simony and Marcon, *Les Transformations du Comité d'Entreprise*.

6. Interestingly, the Labor Council did not ask for anonymity and was somewhat surprised (and perhaps even disappointed) when told that I would use pseudonyms for both the organization and the plant. The corporation, on the other hand, was generally reluctant to see its name associated with homer practices.

7. I thank Noëlle Gérôme for pointing this out to me. Pierre Fournier encountered similar resistance when conducting fieldwork in a French nuclear facility. Instead of relying, like I did, on the Labor Council, he relied on subcontractors to gain access to the facility. (See Pierre Fournier, "Des Observations Sous Surveillance," *Genèses* 24 (1996); Pierre Fournier, "Attention Dangers! Enquête Sur le Travail dans le Nucléaire," *Ethnologie Française* 31, no. 1 (2001).)

8. Pierre Bourdieu, *Méditations Pascaliennes* (Paris: Édition du Seuil, 1997).

References

Abbott, Andrew. "From Causes to Events: Notes on Narrative Positivism." *Sociological Methods and Research* 20, no. 4 (1992): 428–55.

Ackroyd, Stephen, and Paul Thompson. *Organizational Misbehaviour*. London: Sage Publications, 1999.

Adorno, Theodor W. *Prisms*. Cambridge, MA: MIT Press, 1967.

Akerlof, George. "Labor Contracts as Partial Gift Exchange." *Quarterly Journal of Economics* 97, no. 4 (1982): 543–69.

Akerlof, George A., and Rachel E. Kranton. "Identity and the Economics of Organizations." *Journal of Economic Perspective* 19, no. 1 (2005): 9–32.

Allen, Thomas J. *Managing the Flow of Technology: Technology Transfer and the Dissemination of Technological Information within the R&D Organization*. Cambridge, MA: MIT Press, 1977.

Alvesson, Mats, and Hugh Willmott. "Identity Regulation as Organizational Control: Producing the Appropriate Individual." *Journal of Management Studies* 39, no. 5 (2002): 619–44.

Anteby, Michel. "The 'Moralities' of Poaching: Manufacturing Personal Artifacts on the Factory Floors." *Ethnography* 4, no. 2 (2003): 217–39.

Appadurai, Arjun (ed.). *The Social Life of Things: Commodities in Cultural Perspective*. Cambridge: Cambridge University Press, 1986.

Arlacchi, Pino. *Mafia, Peasants, and Great Estates: Society in Traditional Calabria*. Cambridge: Cambridge University Press, 1983.

Ashforth, Blake E., and Vikas Anand. "The Normalization of Corruption in Organizations." In *Research in Organizational Behavior*, edited by R. M. Kramer and B. M. Staw, 1–52. Amsterdam: Elsevier, 2003.

Bailyn, Lotte. *Living with Technology: Issues at Mid-Career*. Cambridge, MA: MIT Press, 1980.

Baker, Wayne, and Robert R. Faulkner. "The Social Organization of Conspiracy: Illegal Networks in the Heavy Electrical Equipment Industry." *American Sociological Review* 58, no. 6 (1993): 837–60.

Banville, Etienne de. *L'Usine en Douce. Le Travail en "Perruque."* Paris: L'Harmattan, 2001.

Banville, Marie de, and Bruno Dumont. *Perruque, Bricole et Compagnie . . . (Videotape)*. Paris: Solimane Production, 1988.

Barley, Stephen R. "Semiotics and the Study of Occupational and Organizational Cultures." *Administrative Science Quarterly* 28, no. 3 (1983): 393–413.

———. "Technology as an Occasion for Structuring: Evidence from Observation of CT Scanners and the Social Order of Radiology Departments." *Administrative Science Quarterly* 31, no. 1 (1986): 78–108.

Barley, Stephen R., and Gideon Kunda. "Bringing Work Back In." *Organization Science* 12, no. 1 (2001): 76–95.

———. *Gurus, Hired Guns, and Warm Bodies: Itinerant Experts in a Knowledge Economy.* Princeton, NJ: Princeton University Press, 2006.

Barnard, Chester. *The Functions of the Executive.* Cambridge, MA: Harvard University Press, 1968.

Bartunek, Jean M., and Michael K. Moch. "Multiple Constituencies and the Quality of Working Life Intervention at Foodcom." In *Reframing Organizational Culture,* edited by Peter J. Frost, Larry F. Moore, Meryl R. Luis, Craig C. Lundberg, and Joanne Martin, 104–14. Newbury Park, CA: Sage, 1991.

Baumgartner, Mary P. "Social Control in Suburbia." In *Towards a General Theory of Social Control Vol. 2, Selected Problems,* edited by Donald Black, 79–103. Orlando, FL: Academic Press, 1984.

Bearman, Peter S. *Doormen.* Chicago: University of Chicago Press, 2005.

Beaud, Stéphane, and Michel Pialoux. "Between 'Mate' and 'Scab': The Contradictory Inheritance of French Workers in the Postfordist Factory." *Ethnography* 2, no. 3 (2001): 323–55.

———. *Retour sur la Condition Ouvrière: Enquête Aux Usines Peugeot de Sochaux-Montbéliard.* Paris: Fayard, 1999.

Bechky, Beth. "Object Lessons: Workplace Artifacts as Representations of Occupational Jurisdiction." *American Journal of Sociology* 109, no. 3 (2003): 720–52.

Becker, Howard. *Tricks of the Trade: How to Think About Your Research While You're Doing It.* Chicago: University of Chicago Press, 1994.

———. "Arts and Crafts." *American Journal of Sociology* 83, no. 4 (1978): 862–89.

———. *Outsiders: Studies in the Sociology of Deviance.* London: Free Press of Glencoe, 1963.

Bernoux, Philippe. *Un Travail à Soi.* Toulouse: Privat, 1981.

Bidwell, Charles E. "The Young Professionals in the Army: A Study in Occupational Identity." *American Sociological Review* 26, no. 3 (1961): 360–72.

Biroleau, Anne. *Les Règlements d'Ateliers: 1798–1936.* Paris: Bibliothéque Nationale, 1984.

Blau, Peter. *The Dynamics of Bureaucracy.* Chicago: University of Chicago Press, 1955.

———. *Exchange and Power in Social Life.* New York: Wiley, 1964.

Bonnot, Thierry. *La Vie des Objets.* Paris: Éditions de la Maison des Sciences de l'Homme, 2002.

Bourdieu, Pierre. *Méditations Pascaliennes.* Paris: Édition du Seuil, 1997.

Bourdieu, Pierre, and Loïc J.D. Wacquant, *Réponses: Pour une Anthropologie Réflexive.* Paris: Seuil, 1992.

Bourgeois, Philippe. *In Search of Respect: Selling Crack in El Barrio.* Cambridge: Cambridge University Press, 2003.

Bozon, Michel, and Yannick Lemel. "Les Petits Profits du Travail Salarié. Moments, Produits et Plaisirs Dérobés." *Revue Française de Sociologie* 31, no. 1 (1990): 101–27.

Bradford, John Allen. "A General Perspective on Job Satisfaction: The Relation between Job Satisfaction, and Sociological and Psychological Variables." Doctoral Dissertation in Sociology, University of California, San Diego, 1976.

Bradney, Philip. "The Joking Relationship in Industry." *Human Relations* 10, no. 2 (1957): 179–87.

Braudel, Fernand. *Civilisation Matérielle, Économie et Capitalisme: XVe–XVIIIe Siècle*. Vol. 1. Paris: A. Colin, 1979.

Brewer, Marilyn B., and Wendi L. Gardner. "Who Is This 'We'? Levels of Collective Identity and Self Representations." *Journal of Personality and Social Psychology* 71 (1996): 83–93.

Brower, Ralph, and Mitchell Abolafia. "Bureaucratic Politics: The View from Below." *Journal of Public Administration Research and Theory* 7, no. 2 (1997): 305–31.

Brown, John Seely, and Paul Duguid. "Organizational Learning and Communities of Practice: Towards a Unified Way of Working, Learning, and Innovation." *Organization Science* 2, no. 1 (1991): 40–57.

Burawoy, Michael. *Manufacturing Consent: Changes in the Labor Process under Monopoly Capitalism*. Chicago: University of Chicago Press, 1979.

Burt, Ronald. *Toward a Structural Theory of Action: Network Models of Social Structure, Perception and Action*. New York: Academic Press, 1982.

Byington, Robert H., ed. "Working Americans: Contemporary Approaches to Occupational Folklife." *Western Folklore* 37, no. 3 (1978).

California Court of Appeals. *Nattie Thunderburk v. United Food and Commercial Workers' Union, Local 324*. 92 Cal. App. 4th 1332, 2001 Cal. App. Lexis 820, 2001.

Callon, Michel. "Some Elements of a Sociology of Translation: Domestication of the Scallops and Fishermen of St. Brieuc Bay." In *Power in Action and Belief: A New Sociology of Knowledge*, edited by John Law, 196–233. London: Routledge, 1986.

Caplow, Theodore. "Rule Enforcement without Visible Means: Christmas Gift Giving in Middletown." *American Journal of Sociology* 89, no. 6 (1984): 1306–23.

Carroll, Glenn R., and Michael T. Hannan. *The Demography of Corporations and Industries*. Princeton, NJ: Princeton University Press, 2000.

Casciaro, Tiziana. "Seeing Things Clearly: Social Structure, Personality, and Accuracy in Social Network Perception." *Social Networks* 20, no. 4 (1998): 331–51.

Certeau, Michel de. *The Practice of Everyday Life*. Berkeley: University of California Press, 1988.

Clark, John P., and Richard C. Hollinger. "Theft by Employees in Work Organizations." Washington, DC: U.S. Department of Justice—National Institute of Justice, 1983.

Clinard, Marshall B., and Peter Yeager. *Corporate Crime*. New York: Free Press, 1980.

Cohen, Albert K. *Delinquent Boys: The Culture of the Gang*. London: Routledge and Kegan Paul, 1956.

Coleman, James S. "Social Capital in the Creation of Human Capital." *American Journal of Sociology* 94 (supp.) (1988): S95—S120.

Comité d'Établissement Snecma Évry-Corbeil. *Les Ouvriers de l'Imaginaire.* Évry, France: Presses de la STEP, 1984.

Contesenne, Pierre. "De la Perruque comme Pretexte." Paris (manuscript), 1984.

Cooley, Charles H. *Human Nature and the Social Order.* New York: C. Scribner's Sons, 1902.

Cour de Cassation, Chambre Sociale. Audience Publique du 18 Mai 1977. Numéro de Pourvoi: 76–40582. 1977.

———. Audience Publique du 18 Octobre 1995. Numéro de Pourvoi: 94–40735. 1995.

Covaleski, Mark A., Mark W. Dirsmith, James B. Heian, and Sajay Samuel. "The Calculated and the Avowed: Techniques of Discipline and Struggles over Identity in Big Six Public Accounting Firms." *Administrative Science Quarterly* 43, no. 2 (1998): 293–327.

Crozier, Michel. *Le Phénomène Bureaucratique.* Paris: Éditions du Seuil, 1963.

Crozier, Michel, and Erhard Friedberg. *L'Acteur et le Système.* Paris: Éditions du Seuil, 1977.

Dabney, Dean A. "Neutralization and Deviance in the Workplace—Theft of Supplies and Medicines by Hospital Nurses." *Deviant Behavior* 16, no. 4 (1995): 313–31.

Daft, Richard L. "The Evolution of Organization Analysis in ASQ, 1959–1979." *Administrative Science Quarterly* 25, no. 4 (1980): 623–36.

Dalton, Melville. *Men Who Manage: Fusions of Feeling and Theory in Administration.* New York: Wiley, 1959.

Deniot, Joëlle. *Ethnologie du Décor en Milieu Ouvrier.* Paris: L'Harmattan, 1995.

Dickson, William J., and Fritz J. Roethlisberger. *Counseling in an Organization: A Sequel to the Hawthorne Researches.* Boston: Division of Research, Harvard Business School, 1966.

DiMaggio, Paul, and Hugh Louch. "Socially Embedded Consumer Transactions: For What Kinds of Purchases Do People Most Often Use Networks?" *American Sociological Review* 63, no. 5 (1998): 619–37.

Ditton, Jason. "Baking Time." *Sociological Review* 27, no. 1 (1979): 157–67.

———. "Moral Horror Versus Folk Terror—Output Restriction, Class, and Social-Organization of Exploitation." *Sociological Review* 24, no. 3 (1976): 519–44.

———. "Perks, Pilferage, and the Fiddle: The Historical Structure of Invisible Wages." *Theory and Society* 4, no. 1 (1977): 39–71.

Douglas, Mary. *Purity and Danger: An Analysis of Concepts of Pollution and Taboo.* New York: Routledge Classics, 2002.

Duneier, Mitchell. *Sidewalk.* New York: Farrar, Straus and Giroux, 1999.

Durkheim, Emile. *The Division of Labor in Society.* Glencoe, IL: Free Press, 1964.

———. *Emile Durkheim on Morality and Society.* Edited by Robert N. Bellah. Chicago: University of Chicago Press, 1973.

Eccles, Robert G., and Nitin Nohria. *Beyond the Hype: Rediscovering the Essence of Management.* Cambridge, MA: Harvard Business School Press, 1992.

Edwards, Richard C. "The Social Relations of Production at the Point of Production." In *Complex Organizations: Critical Perspectives*, edited by Mary Zey-Ferrell and Michael Aiken, 156–82. Glenview, IL: Scott, Foresman, 1981.

Elias, Norbert. *La Société de Cour*. Paris: Flammarion, 1985.

Etzioni, Amitai. *The Spirit of Community: Rights, Responsibilities, and the Communitarian Agenda*. New York: Crown Publishers, 1993.

Fallick, Bruce and Charles Fleischman. "The Importance of Employer-to-Employer Flows in the U.S. Labor Market." Washington, DC: Federal Reserve Board, 2001.

Fama, Eugene F., and Michael C. Jensen. "Separation of Ownership and Control." *Journal of Law & Economics* 26, no. 2 (1983): 301–25.

Fayard, Anne-Laure, and John Weeks. "Photocopiers and Water-Coolers: The Affordances of Informal Interaction." *Organization Studies* 28, no. 5 (2007): 605–34.

Feldman, Martha. "Social Limits to Discretion: An Organizational Perspective." In *The Uses of Discretion*, edited by Keith Hawkins, 163–83. Oxford: Clarendon Press, 1992.

Fennell, Dodee. "Beneath the Surface." *Radical America* 10 (1976): 15–29.

Fine, Gary A. "The Culture of Production: Aesthetic Choices and Constraints in Culinary Work." *American Journal of Sociology* 97, no. 5 (1992): 1268–94.

———. "Justifying Work: Occupational Rhetorics as Resources in Restaurant Kitchens." *Administrative Science Quarterly* 41, no. 1 (1996): 90–115.

Fiske, Alan P., and Philip E. Tetlock. "Taboo Trade-Offs: Reactions to Transactions That Transcend the Spheres of Justice." *Political Psychology* 18, no. 2 (1977): 255–97.

Fourcade-Gourinchas, Marion. *Economists and Societies: Discipline and Profession in the United States, Great Britain and France*. Princeton, NJ: Princeton University Press, Forthcoming.

———. "La Sociologie Économique: État des Lieux." Paper presented at the Économie et Sciences Sociales Conference, Paris: École Normale Supérieure, June 13–14, 2002.

Fourcade-Gourinchas, Marion, and Kieran Healy. "Moral Views of Market Society." *Annual Review of Sociology* 33 (2007): 285–311.

Fournier, Pierre. "Attention Dangers! Enquête Sur le Travail dans le Nucléaire." *Ethnologie Française* 31, no. 1 (2001): 69–80.

———. "Des Observations Sous Surveillance." *Genèses* 24 (1996): 103–19.

Fridenson, Patrick, and Jean Lecuir. "L'Organisation de la Coopération Aérienne Franco-Britannique (1935–Mai 1940)." *Revue d'Histoire de la Seconde Guerre Mondiale* 73, January (1969): 43–74.

Friedman, Debra, and Doug McAdam. "Collective Identity and Activism: Networks, Choices and the Life of a Social Movement." In *Frontiers in Social Movement Theory*, edited by Carol Mueller and Aldon Morris, 156–73. New Haven, CT: Yale University Press, 1992.

Frisch-Gauthier, Jacqueline. "Le Rire dans les Relations de Travail." *Revue Française de Sociologie* 2 (1961): 292–303.

Gambetta, Diego, and Heather Hamill. *Streetwise: How Taxi Drivers Establish Their Customers' Trustworthiness.* New York: Russell Sage Foundation, 2005.

Garfinkel, Harold. *Studies in Ethnomethodology.* Englewood Cliffs, NJ: Prentice Hall, 1967.

Gergen, Kenneth J., and Mary M. Gergen. "Narrative and the Self as Relationship." In *Advances in Experimental Social Psychology, 21*, edited by Leonard Berkowitz, 17–56. San Diego: Academic Press, 1988.

Gérôme, Noëlle. *Les Productions Symboliques des Travailleurs dans l'Entreprise: Action Syndicale et Rituelles.* Paris: Ministére de la Culture, Direction du Patrimoine, Mission du Patrimoine Ethnologique, 1983.

———. "Les Rituels Contemporains des Travailleurs de l'Aéronautique." *Ethnologie Française* 14, no. 2 (1984): 177–96.

———. "Récompense et Hommages dans l'Usine." *Ethnologie Française* 28, no. 4 (1998): 551–62.

Glaser, Barney, and Anselm L. Strauss. *The Discovery of Grounded Theory.* Chicago: Aldine, 1967.

Goffman, Erving. *Interactions Rituals: Essays on Face-to-Face Behavior.* Chicago: Aldine, 1967.

———. *The Presentation of Self in Everyday Life.* New York: Doubleday, 1959.

Gouldner, Alvin. *Patterns of Industrial Bureaucracy.* New York: Free Press, 1954.

Granovetter, Mark. "Economic Action and Social Structure: The Problem of Embeddedness." *American Journal of Sociology* 91, no. 3 (1985): 481–510.

Granovetter, Mark, and Richard Swedberg. *The Sociology of Economic Life.* Boulder, CO: Westview Press, 1992.

Graves, Bennie. "Conflict and Work Force Stability in Pipeline Construction." *Urban Life and Culture* 2, no. 4 (1974): 415–31.

Hackman, Richard J., and Greg R. Oldham. "Motivation through the Design of Work: Test of a Theory." *Organizational Behavior & Human Performance* 16, no. 2 (1976): 250–79.

Hallett, Tim, and Marc J. Ventresca. "Inhabited Institutions: Social Interactions and Organizational Forms in Gouldner's Patterns of Industrial Bureaucracy." *Theory and Society* 35, no. 2 (2006): 213–36.

Hamman, Philippe. "Quand le Souvenir Fait Lien . . . De la Délimitation des Domaines de Validité des Énoncés Recueillis par le Sociologue en Situation d'Entretien." *Sociologie du Travail* 44, no. 2 (2002): 175–91.

Hannan, Michael T., and John Freeman. *Organizational Ecology.* Cambridge, MA: Harvard University Press, 1989.

Haraszti, Miklos. *A Worker in a Worker's State: Piece-Rates in Hungary.* New York: Universe Books, 1978.

Hatzfeld, Nicolas. "La Pause Casse-Croûte: Quand les Chaînes s'Arrêtent à Peugeot-Sochaux." *Terrain* 39 (2002): 33–48.

Haveman, Heather, and Mukti Khaire. "Organizational Sociology and the Analysis of Work." In *Social Theory and Work*, edited by Marek Korczynski, Randy Hodson, and Paul Edwards, 272–98. Oxford: Oxford University Press, 2006.

Heritage, John. *Garfinkel and Ethnomethodology.* Cambridge, MA: Polity, 1984.

Hirsch, Paul. "Organizational Analysis and Industrial Sociology: An Instance of Cultural Lag." *American Sociologist* 10 (1975): 3–12.

Hissard, Marie-José, and Jean-René Hissard. "Interview d'Henri H. . . . Perruquiste." *Autrement* 16, November (1978): 75–83.

Hochschild, Arlie Russell. *The Managed Heart: Commercialization of Human Feeling*. Berkeley: University of California Press, 1983.

Hodson, Randy. "Dignity in the Workplace under Participative Management: Alienation and Freedom Revisited." *American Sociological Review* 61, no. 5 (1996): 719–38.

———. "The Workplace Ethnography Project." Ohio State University, 2002.

Hodson, Randy, and Vincent J. Roscigno. "Organizational Success and Worker Dignity: Complementary or Contradictory?" *American Journal of Sociology* 110, no. 3 (2004): 672–708.

Hodson, Randy, and Teresa A. Sullivan. *The Social Organization of Work*. Belmont, CA: Wadsworth, 2002.

Hofstede, Geert H. *Culture's Consequences: International Differences in Work-Related Values*. Beverly Hills: Sage, 1980.

Homans, George C. *The Human Group*. New Brunswick, NJ: Transaction Publishers, 1993.

Hughes, Everett C. "Work and Self." In *The Sociological Eye: Selected Papers*, 338–47. Chicago, IL and New York: Aldine-Atherton, 1971.

Iacobucci, Dawn, and Amy Ostrom. "Commercial and Interpersonal Relationships: Using the Structure of Interpersonal Relationships to Understand Individual-to-Individual, Individual-to-Firm, and Firm-to-Firm Relationships in Commerce." *International Journal of Research in Marketing* 13 (1996): 53–72.

Jackall, Robert. *Moral Mazes: The World of Corporate Managers*. New York: Oxford University Press, 1988.

Joseph, Isaac. "La Perruque." *Urbi* III (1980): 115–19.

Kanter, Rosabeth Moss. *Commitment and Community: Communes and Utopias in Sociological Perspective*. Cambridge, MA: Harvard University Press, 1972.

Khurana, Rakesh. *From Higher Aims to Hired Hands: The Social Transformation of American Business Schools and the Unfulfilled Promise of Management as a Profession*. Princeton, NJ: Princeton University Press, 2007.

Knee, Jonathan A. *The Accidental Investment Banker: Inside the Decade That Transformed Wall Street*. New York: Oxford University Press, 2006.

Koch, Klaus-Friederich. *War and Peace in Jalemo: The Management of Conflict in Highland New Guinea*. Cambridge, MA: Harvard University Press, 1974.

Kopytoff, Igor. "The Cultural Biography of Things: Commoditization as Process." In *The Social Life of Things: Commodities in Cultural Perspective*, edited by Arjun Appadurai, 64–91. Cambridge: Cambridge University Press, 1986.

Kornblum, William. *Blue Collar Community*. Chicago: University of Chicago Press, 1974.

Kosmann, Robert. "La Perruque ou le Travail Masqué." *Renault Histoire* 11 (1999): 20–27.

Kosmann, Robert. "Les Forgerons de la RATP: La Forge de l'Atelier Central de Championnet." In *La Région Parisienne Industrielle et Ouvrière*, 6, 145–55. Paris: Éditions RATP, Unité Mémoire de l'Entreprise, 2000.

Kotter, John P. *The General Managers*. New York: Free Press, 1986.

Kunda, Gideon. *Engineering Culture: Control and Commitment in a High-Tech Corporation*. Philadelphia: Temple University Press, 1992.

Lamont, Michèle. *The Dignity of Working Men: Moralities and the Boundaries of Race, Class, and Immigration*. New York: Russel Sage Foundation, 2000.

———. *Money, Morals, and Manners: The Culture of the French and American Upper-Middle Class*. Chicago: University of Chicago Press, 1992.

Lamont, Michèle, and Virág Molnár. "The Study of Boundaries across the Social Sciences." *Annual Review of Sociology* 28 (2002): 167–95.

Lampert, Nicholas. *Whistleblowing in the Soviet Union: Complaints and Abuse under State Socialism*. London: MacMillan Press, 1985.

Lamy Prud-Hommes. *Jugements Prud'homaux Commentés*. Rueil Malmaison, France: Lamy, 2002.

Landsberger, Henry. *Hawthorne Revisited*. Ithaca, NY: Cornell University Press, 1958.

Lave, Jean, and Etienne Wenger. *Situated Learning: Legitimate Peripheral Participation*. Cambridge: Cambridge University Press, 1991.

Lazarsfeld, Paul. "Reflections on Business." *American Journal of Sociology* 65 (1959): 1–31.

Leifer, Eric M. "Interaction Preludes to Role Setting: Exploratory Local Action." *American Sociological Review* 53, no. 6 (1988): 865–78.

Lescot, Yves, Georges Menahem, and Patrick Pharo. *Savoirs Ouvriers, Normes de Production et Représentations. Rapport du Contrat Cordes 12–78*. Boulogne, France: ACT, 1980.

Levi, Primo. *The Drowned and the Saved*. New York: Vintage International, 1989.

MacLean, Tammy L. "Thick as Thieves: A Social Embeddedness Model of Rule Breaking in Organizations." *Business and Society* 40, no. 2 (2001): 167–96.

MacLean, Tammy, Michel Anteby, Bryant Hudson, and Jenny Rudolph. "Talking Tainted Topics: Insights and Ideas on Researching Socially Disapproved Organizational Behavior." *Journal of Management Inquiry* 15, no. 1 (2006): 59–68.

Malinowski, Bronislaw. *Argonauts of the Western Pacific: An Account of the Native Enterprise and Adventure in the Archipelagoes of Melanesian New Guinea*. Long Grove, IL: Waveland Press, 1984.

Manitoba Arbitration. "Border Chemical Co. and Border Chemical Employees Association, Arbitration." 1997 CLASJ Lexis 16604, 1997 CLASJ 425510, 47 CLAS 455, 1997.

Mars, Gerald. *Cheats at Work: An Anthropology of Workplace Crime*. Hants, UK; Brookfield, VT: Dartmouth Publishing, 1994.

———. "Hotel Pilferage: A Case Study in Occupational Theft." In *The Sociology of the Workplace: An Interdisciplinary Approach*, edited by Malcolm Warner, 200–210. London: George Allen and Unwin, 1973.

Martin, Joanne. *Cultures in Organizations: Three Perspectives*. New York: Oxford University Press, 1992.

Mauss, Marcel. "Étude de Morphologie Sociale." In *Sociologie et Anthropologie*, 391. Paris: Presses Universitaires de France, 1980.

———. *The Gift: Forms and Functions of Exchange in Archaic Societies*. New York: Norton, 1967.

Mayo, Elton. *The Social Problems of an Industrial Civilization*. Cambridge, MA: Harvard University Press, 1945.

McVickar Haight, John. *American Aid to France*. New York: Antheneum, 1970.

Mead, George H. *Mind, Self and Society from the Standpoint of a Social Behaviorist*. Chicago: University of Chicago Press, 1934.

Menon, Nisha. "Membership Has Its Rewards: The Nature of Female Gang and Clique Involvement in Boston." A.B. Honors Thesis in Sociology, Harvard University, 1999.

Messika, Aurélie. "L'Étude Socio-Organizationelle d'une Direction de la Recherche Chez un Constructeur Automobile Européen," 47–50. Master's Thesis in Sociology, IEP Paris, 2002.

Miles, Matthew B., and A. Michael Huberman. *Qualitative Data Analysis*. Thousand Oaks, CA: Sage Publications, 1994.

Mintz, Beth, and Michael Schwartz. *The Power Structure of American Business*. Chicago: University of Chicago Press, 1985.

Mintzberg, Henry. *The Nature of Managerial Work*. New York: Harper & Row, 1973.

Mizruchi, Mark. "What Do Interlocks Do? An Analysis, Critique and Assessment of Research on Interlocking Directorates." *Annual Review of Sociology* (1996): 22, 271–98.

Mizruchi, Mark S., and Linda Brewster Stearns. "A Longitudinal Study of the Formation of Interlocking Directorates." *Administrative Science Quarterly* 33, no. 2 (1988): 194–210.

Moldoveanu, Mihnea C., and Nitin Nohria. *Master Passions: Emotion, Narrative, and the Development of Culture*. Cambridge, MA: MIT Press, 2002.

Morrill, Calvin. "Conflict Management, Honor, and Organizational Change." *American Journal of Sociology* 97, no. 3 (1991): 585–621.

———. *The Executive Way: Conflict Management in Corporations*. Chicago: University of Chicago Press, 1995.

Morrill, Calvin, Mayer N. Zald, and Hayagreeva Rao. "Covert Political Conflict in Organizations: Challenges from Below." *Annual Review of Sociology* 29 (2003): 391–415.

Moulène, Jean-Luc. *Jean-Luc Moulène*. Paris: Hazan, 2002.

Moulinié, Véronique. "Des 'Oeuvriers' Ordinaires, Lorsque l'Ouvrier Fait le/du Beau. . . . " *Terrain* 32 (1999): 37–54.

Mukerji, Chandra. *Territorial Ambitions and the Gardens of Versailles*. Cambridge: Cambridge University Press, 1997.

Myers, Fred R.V., ed. *The Empire of Things: Regimes of Value and Material Culture*. Santa Fe, NM: School of American Research Press, 2001.

Nickerson, Bruce E. "Is There Folk in the Factory?" *Journal of American Folklore* 87, no. 344 (1974): 133–9.

Noiriel, Gérard. *Les Ouvriers dans la Société Française: XIXe–XXe Siécle*. Paris: Éditions du Seuil, 2002.

Noiriel, Gérard. *Longwy: Immigrés et Prolétaires, 1880–1980*. Paris: Presses Universitaires de France, 1984.

Ong, Aihwa. *Spirits of Resistance and Capitalist Discipline: Factory Women in Malaysia*. Albany: State University of New York Press, 1987.

Ontario Arbitration. "Abitibi-Consolidated Inc. and International Association of Machinist and Aerospace Workers, Lodge 771, Arbitration." Arbitration 2000 CLASJ Lexis 7898, 2000 CLASJ 516728, 59 CLAS 360, 2000.

Osterman, Paul. *Securing Prosperity: The American Labor Market: How It Has Changed and What to Do About It*. Princeton, NJ: Princeton University Press, 1999.

Padgett, John, and Ansell Christopher. "Robust Action and the Rise of the Medici, 1400–1434." *American Journal of Sociology* 98, no. 6 (1993): 1259–1319.

Palmer, C. Eddie, and Sheryl M. Gonsoulin. "Paramedics, Protocols, and Procedures: 'Playing Doc' as Deviant Role Performance." *Deviant Behavior* 11, no. 3 (1990): 207–19.

Paradeise, Catherine. "Sociabilité et Culture de Classe." *Revue Française de Sociologie* 21, no. 4 (1980): 571–97.

Parsons, Talcott, and Edward Albert Shils. *Toward a General Theory of Action*. Cambridge, MA: Harvard University Press, 1951.

Patton, Michael Quinn. *Qualitative Evaluation and Research Methods*. Second Edition. London: Sage Publications, 1990.

Perlow, Leslie A. "Boundary Control: The Social Ordering of Work and Family Time in a High-Tech Corporation." *Administrative Science Quarterly* 43, no. 2 (1998): 328–57.

Perrow, Charles. *Complex Organizations: A Critical Essay*. New York: McGraw-Hill, 1986.

———. *Organizing America: Wealth, Power, and the Origins of Corporate Capitalism*. Princeton, NJ: Princeton University Press, 2002.

Pincemain, Jean-Pierre. "Individual Exhibit." Barbizon, France: Suzanne Tarasiève Gallery, 2001.

Piore, Michael J., and Sean Safford. "Changing Regimes of Workplace Governance, Shifting Axes of Social Mobilization, and the Challenge to Industrial Relations Theory." *Industrial Relations* 45, no. 3 (2006): 299–325.

Podolny, Joel M., and James N. Baron. "Resources and Relationships: Social Networks and Mobility in the Workplace." *American Sociological Review* 62, no. 5 (1997): 673–93.

Poulot, Denis. *Question Sociale: le Sublime ou le Travailleur Comme Il Est en 1870 et Ce Qu'il Peut Étre*. Paris: Maspéro, 1980.

Pratt, Michael G. "The Good, the Bad, and the Ambivalent: Managing Identification among Amway Distributors." *Administrative Science Quarterly* 45, no. 3 (2000): 456–93.

Pratto, Felicia, and Oliver P. John. "Automatic Vigilance: The Attention-Grabbing Power of Negative Social Information." *Journal of Personality and Social Psychology* 61 (1991): 380–91.

Prigent, Michel. "Pincemain Chez Tarasiève." *La République* (2001): Melun, France.

Putnam, Robert. *Making Democracy Work: Civic Traditions in Modern Italy.* Princeton, NJ: Princeton University Press, 1993.

Renaut, Alain. *The Era of the Individual: A Contribution to a History of Subjectivity.* Princeton, NJ: Princeton University Press, 1999.

Riemer, Jeffrey W. "Becoming a Journeyman Electrician: Some Implicit Indicators in the Apprenticeship Process." *Sociology of Work and Occupations* 4, no. 1 (1977): 87–98.

Roethlisberger, Fritz J., and William J. Dickson. "Relay Assembly Test Room Case Histories 1927–1929." Box 18, Hawthorne Studies Collection, Western Electric Company, Historical Collections. Boston: Baker Library, Harvard Business School, 1939.

———. *Management and the Worker: An Account of a Research Program Conducted by the Western Electric Company.* Cambridge, MA: Harvard University Press, 1939.

Rot, Gwenaële. *Sociologie de l'Atelier: Renault, le Travail Ouvrier et le Sociologue.* Toulouse: Octarès Éditions, 2006.

Rousseau, Denise M. "Under the Table Deals: Idiosyncratic, Preferential or Unauthorized?" In *Dark Side of Organizational Behavior*, edited by R. Griffin and A. O'Leary-Kelly, 262–90. San Francisco: Jossey-Bass, 2004.

Roy, Donald. "Banana Time: Job Satisfaction and Informal Interaction." *Human Organization* 18 (1959): 158–68.

———. "Quota Restriction and Goldbricking in a Machine Shop." *American Journal of Sociology* 57, no. 5 (1952): 427–42.

Sainsaulieu, Renaud. *L'Identité au Travail.* Paris: Presses de la Fondation Nationale des Sciences Politiques, 1977.

Saint-Exupéry, Antoine de. *The Little Prince.* New York: Harcourt Brace Jovanovich, 1971.

Salancik, Gerald R. "Wanted: A Good Network Theory of Organization." *Administrative Science Quarterly* 40, no. 2 (1995): 345–9.

Schwartz, Olivier. *Le Monde Privé des Ouvriers: Hommes et Femmes du Nord.* Paris: Presses Universitaires de France, 1990.

Selznick, Philip. *TVA and the Grass Roots: A Study in the Sociology of Formal Organization.* Berkeley: University of California Press, 1949.

Sennett, Richard. *The Corrosion of Character. The Personal Consequences of Work in the New Capitalism.* New York: Norton, 1998.

Shapiro, Susan. *Wayward Capitalists: Target of the Securities and Exchange Commissions.* New Haven, CT: Yale University Press, 1984.

Short, James F. *Group Process and Gang Delinquency.* Chicago: University of Chicago Press, 1965.

Sieber, Sam D. "The Integration of Fieldwork and Survey Methods." *American Journal of Sociology* 78, no. 6 (1973): 1335–59.

Sieh, Edward W. "Garment Workers: Perceptions of Inequity and Employee Theft." *British Journal of Criminology* 27, no. 2 (1987): 174–90.

Simmel, Georg. *The Sociology of Georg Simmel.* Edited by Kurt H. Wolff. New York: Free Press, 1950.

———. "The Sociology of Secrecy and of Secret Societies." *American Journal of Sociology* 11, no. 4 (1906): 441–98.

Simony, Nadia, and Michel Marcon. *Les Transformations du Comité d'Entreprise: Snecma Évry-Corbeil.* Paris: L'Harmattan, 1995.

Snook, Scott. *Friendly Fire: The Accidental Shootdown of U.S. Black Hawks over Northern Iraq.* Princeton, NJ: Princeton University Press, 2000.

Soeters, Joseph L. "Excellent Companies as Social Movements." *Journal of Management Science* 23 (1986): 299–312.

Star, Susan Leigh, and James R. Griesemer. "Institutional Ecology, 'Translations' and Boundary Objects: Amateurs and Professionals in Berkeley's Museum of Vertebrate Zoology, 1907–39." *Social Studies of Science* 19 (1989): 387–420.

Stark, David. *For a Sociology of Worth.* Working Paper, Center on Organizational Innovation, Santa Fe Institute and Columbia University, 2000.

———. "La Valeur du Travail et sa Redistribution en Hongrie." *Actes de la Recherche en Sciences Sociales* 85 (1990): 3–19.

Stern, Scott. "Do Scientists Pay to Be Scientists?" *Management Science* 50, no. 6 (2004): 835–53.

Stets, Jan E., and Peter J. Burke. "Identity Theory and Social Identity Theory." *Social Psychology Quarterly* 63, no. 3 (2000): 224–37.

Stinchcombe, Arthur L. "Weak Structural Data." *Contemporary Sociology* 19 (1990): 380–82.

Sutherland, Edwin H. *White Collar Crime.* New York: Dryden, 1949.

Swidler, Ann. "Culture in Action: Symbols and Strategies." *American Sociological Review* 51, no. 2 (1986): 273–86.

Texas Court of Appeals. *Larry Stephens, Appellant v. Delhi Gas Pipeline Corporation.* Appellee. No. 06–95–00101-CV, Sixth District, Texarkana, 1996.

Thompson, William E. "Hanging Tongues: A Sociological Encounter with the Assembly Line." *Quantitative Sociology* 6 (1983): 215–37.

Tichy, Noel M., Michael L. Tushman, and Charles Fombrun. "Social Network Analysis for Organizations." *Academy of Management Review* 4, no. 4 (1979): 507–19.

Tilly, Charles. *The Contentious French.* Cambridge, MA: Harvard University Press, 1986.

Trivière, François-Xavier. "Objets de Bricole, de l'Usine à l'Univers Domestique." In *Carrières D'objets: Innovations et Relances, Mission du Patrimoine Ethnologique,* edited by C. Bromberger and D. Chevallier, 83–97. Paris: Maison des Sciences de l'Homme, 1999.

Uzzi, Brian. "Social Structure and Competition in Interfirm Networks: The Paradox of Embeddedness." *Administrative Science Quarterly* 42, no. 1 (1997): 35–67.

Uzzi, Brian, and Ryon Lancaster. "Embeddedness and Price Formation in the Corporate Law Market." *American Sociological Review* 69, no. 3 (2004): 319–44.

Uzzi, Brian, and Jarrett Spiro. "Collaboration and Creativity: The Small World Problem." *American Journal of Sociology* 111 (2005): 447–504.

Vallas, Steven P. "Why Teamwork Fails: Obstacles to Workplace Change in Four Manufacturing Plants." *American Sociological Review* 68, no. 2 (2003): 223–50.

———. "The Concept of Skill—A Critical Review." *Work and Occupations* 17, no. 4 (1990): 379–98.

———. "Workers, Firms, and the Dominant Ideology: Hegemony and Consciousness in the Monopoly Core." *Sociological Quarterly* 32 (1991): 61–83.

Van Maanen, John. "Identity Work: Notes on the Personal Identity of Police Officers." Paper presented at the Annual Meeting of the Academy of Management. San Diego, 1998.

———. "The Self, the Situation, and the Rules of Interpersonal Relations." In *Essays in Interpersonal Dynamics*, edited by Warren Bennis, John Van Maanen, Edgar H. Schein, and Fred I. Steele, 43–101. Homewood, IL: Dorsey Press, 1979.

———. *Tales of the Field: On Writing Ethnography.* Chicago: University of Chicago Press, 1988.

Van Maanen, John, and Stephen R. Barley. "Occupational Communities: Culture and Control in Organizations." In *Research in Organizational Behavior*, edited by Barry Staw and Larry Cummings, 287–366. Greenwich, CT: JAI Press, 1984.

Van Maanen, John, and Edgar H. Schein. "Toward a Theory of Organizational Socialization." In *Research in Organizational Behavior*, edited by B. Staw and L. Cummings, 209–64. Greenwich, CT: JAI Press, 1979.

Vaughan, Diane. "Autonomy, Interdependence, and Social Control: NASA and the Space Shuttle Challenger." *Administrative Science Quarterly* 35, no. 2 (1990): 225–57.

———. *The Challenger Launch Decision: Risky Technology, Culture, and Deviance at NASA.* Chicago: University of Chicago Press, 1996.

Verbrugge, Lois M. "Multiplexity in Adult Friendships." *Social Forces* 57, no. 4 (1979): 1286–1309.

Vivier, Thierry. *La Politique Aéronautique Militaire de la France: Janvier 1933–Septembre 1939.* Paris: Éditions L'Harmattan, 1997.

Vlach, John M. "The Fabrication of a Traditional Fire Tool." *Journal of American Folklore* 86, no. 339 (1973): 54–7.

Wacquant, Loïc. *Body and Soul: Ethnographic Notebooks of an Apprentice Boxer.* New York: Oxford University Press, 2003.

Watson, Bill. "Counter-Planning on the Shop Floor." *Radical America* 5 (1971): 77–85.

Weber, Florence. "Formes de l'Échange, Circulation des Objets et Relations entre les Personnes." In *Hypothèses 2001*, 287–98. Paris: Publications de la Sorbonne, 2002.

———. *L'Honneur des Jardiniers: Les Potagers dans la France du XXe Siècle.* Paris: Belin, 1998.

———. *Le Travail À-Côté. Étude d'Ethnographie Ouvrière.* Paris: INRA—Éditions de l'EHESS, 1989.

Weber, Max. *The Protestant Ethic and the Spirit of Capitalism.* San Francisco: Jossey-Bass, 1958.

Weeks, John. *Unpopular Culture: The Ritual of Complaint in a British Bank.* Chicago: University of Chicago Press, 2004.

Weiner, Annette B. *The Trobrianders of Papua New Guinea*. Orlando, FL: Harcourt Brace, 1988.

Wenger, Etienne. *Communities of Practice: Learning, Meaning and Identity*. Cambridge: Cambridge University Press, 1998.

White, Harrison C. *Identity and Control: A Structural Theory of Social Action*. Princeton, NJ: Princeton University Press, 1992.

Whyte, William F. *Street Corner Society: The Social Structure of an Italian Slum*. Chicago: University of Chicago Press, 1943.

Wright, Susan. *Anthropology of Organizations*. London and New York: Routledge, 1994.

Wrzesniewski, Amy, Jane Dutton, and Gelaye Debebe. "Interpersonal Sensemaking and the Meaning of Work." In *Research in Organizational Behavior*, edited by B. Staw and R. M. Kramer, 93–135, 2003.

Yates, JoAnne, and John Van Maanen, eds. *Information Technology and Organizational Transformation: History, Rhetoric, and Practice*. Thousand Oaks, CA: Sage Publications, 2001.

Yin, Robert. *Case Study Research*. Thousand Oaks, CA: Sage Publications, 1994.

Zeitlin, Lawrence R. "Stimulus/Response: A Little Larceny Can Do a Lot for Employee Morale." *Psychology Today* 5, no. 1 (1971): 22.

Zelizer, Viviana. "Intimacy in Economic Organizations." Paper presented at the MIT-Harvard Economic Sociology Seminar, Cambridge, MA, April 25, 2007.

Zelizer, Viviana A. "Circuits within Capitalism." In *The Economic Sociology of Capitalism*, edited by Victor Nee and Richard Swedberg, 289–322. Princeton, NJ: Princeton University Press, 2005.

Zerubavel, Eviatar. *The Fine Line: Making Distinctions in Everyday Life*. Chicago: University of Chicago Press, 1993.

Ford Foundation, 22
friction moments, 10, 149–52
Fuchs-Epstein, Cynthia, 166
funeral home directors, 164–65

games, 19, 162
gangs, 19
gardeners, French community, 148
garment workers, 145–46
Georges (former craftsman), 70–72
glassblowers, 158
Gouldner, Alvin, 31, 36, 155
government jobs, 30–31. *See also* homers
Granovetter, Mark, 21, 24
gray zones, 10–12; audiences and, 10,
147–49; definition of, 2, 139–40; identity
and, 139–47, 153–56, 168; inclusion/ex-
clusion dynamics of, 163, 167; organizational conditions favoring, 161–63, 169–
70; persistance/sustainability of, 12,
140–41, 170

Haraszti, Miklos, 1–2, 30, 34
Hawthorne Plant (Western Electric Company), 17, 21–22
hiding during work, 2–3, 142
high-tech workers, 159
Homans, George, 17, 21, 169
homers and homer-making: artistic traces
of, 33–34; autobiographical/ethno-
graphic traces of, 34–37; definition of,
1, 29–31; denunciations of, 81–83, 89;
disciplinary actions for, 85, 129; disclosure of, 80–81; elusiveness/attrac-
tiveness of, 40–42; as a French phenomenon, 39–40; frequency of, 37–39; legal
traces of, 31–33; meanings of, 8–9, 90–
105, 123–27; missteps of meaning and,
103–5; normalizing strategies and, 89,
134–36; occupational identity and, 99–
103; refusals to engage in, 78–81, 89;
settings for making of, 37; situated moralities and, 132–36; theft and, 7–8, 39,
83–90, 123, 133–35. *See also* retirement
homers
Hughes, Everett, 121
Human Relations movement, 21,
207nn10–11
Hungary, 39

identity, 3; audiences and, 10, 147–49; dynamics of, in social systems, 26–27; friction moments and, 10, 149–52; gray
zones and, 139–47, 153–56, 168; patterns of meaning and, 99–105, 122–27;
relevance through work and, 118–21
identity incentives control, 9–11, 127–32,
156–63
illegal activities, 19–20. *See also* theft
inconsequentiality arguments, 135
independence, as status enhancer, 58–59,
89, 111
indulgency patterns, 155
investment bankers/analysts, 2, 146, 147

Jackall, Robert, 165
Jacqueline (executive), 73
Jacques (craftsman), 58–59, 67, 111
Joseph, Isaac, 41

Khurana, Rakesh, 166
Kornblum, William, 165
Kosmann, Robert, 30
Kranton, Rachel, 157

labor unions, 40–41, 47, 112–15, 186–87
Lamont, Michèle, 163, 167
Laurent (worker), 57–58, 75
Levi, Primo, 2, 123, 169
longshoremen, 145, 146, 149, 150
Luc (former craftsman), 70

MacLean, Tammy, 173
mail carriers, 2–3, 142–43, 147, 150
making out, 19, 155
management: identity incentives control
and, 9–11, 127–32, 156–63; patterns of
meaning and, 100–102; requests for
homers by, 80, 96, 132; retirement homers for, 72–74, 76; tolerance/complicity
of, 40–41, 83, 85, 123, 140, 154–56; as
workforce component, 108
manual skills, as status enhancer, 56–58,
89, 111
Manuel (craftsman), 55–56, 58
Marc (executive), 73
Mars, Gerald, 31
Mauss, Marcel, 127, 174
military personnel, 158, 162